Professional and Practice-based Learning

Volume 6

For further volumes:
http://www.springer.com/series/8383

Series Editors:

Professional and practice-based learning brings together international research on the individual development of professionals and the organisation of professional life and educational experiences. It complements the Springer journal *Vocations and Learning: Studies in vocational and professional education.*

Professional learning, and the practice-based processes that often support it, are the subject of increased interest and attention in the fields of educational, psychological, sociological, and business management research, and also by governments, employer organisations and unions. This professional learning goes beyond, what is often termed professional education, as it includes learning processes and experiences outside of educational institutions in both the initial and ongoing learning for the professional practice. Changes in these workplaces requirements usually manifest themselves in the everyday work tasks, professional development provisions in educational institution decrease in their salience, and learning and development during professional activities increase in their salience.

There are a range of scientific challenges and important focuses within the field of professional learning. These include:

- understanding and making explicit the complex and massive knowledge that is required for professional practice and identifying ways in which this knowledge can best be initially learnt and developed further throughout professional life.
- analytical explications of those processes that support learning at an individual and an organisational level.
- understanding how learning experiences and educational processes might best be aligned or integrated to support professional learning.

The series integrates research from different disciplines: education, sociology, psychology, amongst others. The series is comprehensive in scope as it not only focusses on professional learning of teachers and those in schools, colleges and universities, but all professional development within organisations.

Johannes Bauer • Christian Harteis
Editors

Human Fallibility

The Ambiguity of Errors for Work and Learning

Springer

Editors
Johannes Bauer
TUM School of Education
Technische Universität München
Schellingstraße 33
80799 Munich
Germany

Christian Harteis
Fakultät für Kulturwissenschaften
Universität Paderborn
Warburger Straße 100
33098 Paderborn
Germany

ISSN 2210-5549 ISSN 2210-5557 (electronic)
ISBN 978-90-481-3940-8 ISBN 978-90-481-3941-5 (eBook)
DOI 10.1007/978-90-481-3941-5
Springer Dordrecht Heidelberg New York London

Library of Congress Control Number: 2012934818

Printed on acid-free paper

Springer is part of Springer Science+Business Media (www.springer.com)

Series Editors' Foreword

Human fallibility is a particular source for practice-based learning. Specifically, learning from errors has become an issue of increased and widespread interest and recognition, as complexity becomes a crucial feature of various domains of daily life: Business, society, education, biography. Two insights are now accepted as features of these domains. Firstly, complex problems and fuzzy rules shape an environment of human behaviour which makes errors unavoidable; and, secondly, errors can be fruitful incidents for further development. Hence, contemporary life on the one hand offers the increased prospect of human fallibility, but, on the other hand, provides a rich source for (lifelong) learning. However, scientific analyses of errors have a long tradition. For example, errors shape the crucial moment of Darwin's evolutionary theory of variation and selection. Frederick Taylor established his approach of scientific management amongst others on the idea of avoiding errors by precise regulation of work division. These examples indicate the role that errors have already played during the nineteenth century. Yet, research on learning from errors is still quite young in its development, and it is quite scattered across academic disciplines. Up to now, many of the published accounts focus on learning from errors in school or university contexts. However, some work has also been conducted in the area of working life contexts, and this body of work stands to directly contribute to developing a coherent pattern for learning from errors. Insight is necessary into how best to describe errors, the processes of learning through them and their outcomes.

This volume seeks to make these contributions explicit, including methodological issues associated with understanding errors and their relationships to learning. It comprises four parts. The contributions to Part I and Part II address general issues of researching learning from errors. Parts III and IV comprise contributions that focus on specific work contexts and on the challenge of how to support learning from errors in daily working life. In this way, the purpose of the volume is to integrate international research conducted more or less independently at different locations and under different theoretical or methodological paradigms within one book. In an overview, this volume describes theoretical approaches of identifying errors, tracing processes of learning from errors, supporting learning from errors and identifying outcomes of learning from errors – especially in professional contexts of daily life. Hence, it provides theoretical concepts and empirical evidence for understanding under what conditions professionals or teams of professionals are able to learn from their errors at work. In this context, 'errors' are conceptualised as actions or decisions that result in a deficient deviation from a desired goal and endanger the attainment of higher order goals. The interest in the topic emerged for the editors from observations that professionals and the organisations they are working for often act under particular error avoidance strategies. This error aversion probably results from concerns about costs and risks at various levels of impact. On the individual level, one reason individuals dislike errors is that they cause distress. They indicate deficiencies in performance, for instance, where we did not pay enough attention, or misjudged a situation, thus questioning our standing and our pride as proficient workers. Furthermore, errors may be dangerous and can cause undesirable events to occur. On the level of an organisation, they can endanger the creation of economic value, but can also be hazardous to employees, clients, or customers. Certainly, the research on safety and accidents is full of examples of minor errors leading to disastrous outcomes. As a consequence, there is a long tradition of research on human factors and safety management, aiming to provide approaches for estimating a system's reliability, evaluating the potential damage from specific errors, analysing error causes, and preventing errors. Unfortunately, in contrast to the existing lines of inquiry on error prevention, less empirical evidence underpins views about potential benefits of errors at work. In particular, the issue of experiential individual or team learning from errors in the process of daily work has received little attention in research. Evidence for the ways in which the potential of errors can contribute to individuals' and teams' learning in terms of the improvement of their knowledge and performance is presented here from studies on learning environments in school as well as in work contexts. Moreover, research on the development of expertise, experiential learning, case-based reasoning, and learning through work has indicated that errors can be significant sources for professional learning. In all, the contributors to this volume elaborate in different approaches professional and practice-based learning from errors.

Stephen Billett, Hans Gruber and Christian Harteis

Contents

Contributors

Philipp Aerni, Ph.D., graduated in Geography and Economics at the University of Zurich in 1996 and received his Ph.D. from the Institute of Agricultural Economics at the Swiss Federal Institute of Technology (ETH) in Zurich in 1999. He is lecturer and senior research fellow at the ETH Zurich and the World Trade Institute in Bern. He is also co-founder and member of the management steering team of the Geneva-based NGO '*Africa Technology Development Forum*' (ATDF). The main objective of ATDF is to promote science, technology and entrepreneurship in Africa. (aernip@ethz.ch)

Johannes Bauer, Ph.D., is postdoctoral research fellow at TUM School of Education, Technische Universität München (TUM), Germany. He received his Ph.D. in Educational Science at the University of Regensburg. Prior to his appointment in Munich, he was postdoc at the Educational Science/Research Methodology department of the Leibniz Institute for Science and Mathematics Education (IPN) in Kiel. In his research, he focuses on professional and workplace learning, expertise, teachers' professional development, and learning from errors. (jbauer@tum.de)

Stephen Billett, Ph.D., is Professor of Adult and Vocational Education, Griffith University, Brisbane, Australia. He researches principally in learning through work and working life and in the origins and manifestations of working knowledge. He is Editor-in-chief of the Journal *Vocations and Learning – Studies in Vocational and Professional Education*. (s.billett@griffith.edu.au)

Inger Marie Dalehefte, Ph.D., is a researcher at the Leibniz Institute for Science and Mathematics Education (IPN) at the Christian Albrechts University (Christian-Albrechts-Universität), Kiel, Germany. Her research focuses on teaching and learning processes in instruction. (dalehefte@ipn.uni-kiel.de)

Shmuel Ellis, Ph.D., is Professor of Organisational Behaviour at the Faculty of Management, Tel Aviv University, Israel. He is currently the chairperson of the department of undergraduate management. His main areas of interest are learning from experience, organizational learning, knowledge management, organizational genealogy and social networks. (sellis@post.tau.ac.il)

Franziska Frost is Ph.D. student at the TUM School of Education, Technische Universität München, Germany. She received her diploma degree in educational sciences at the University of Regensburg (Germany). Her research topics include assessment and admission procedures for teacher trainees. (franziska.frost@tum.de)

Martin Gartmeier, Ph.D., is postdoctoral research fellow at TUM School of Education, Technische Universität München, Germany. He earned his PhD at the University of Regensburg, focusing on the investigation of employees' negative knowledge in different professional contexts. His other research interests focus upon personal initiative, change at the workplace and communicative competence. (martin.gartmeier@tum.de)

Hans Gruber, Ph.D., is Professor of Educational Science and currently Vice-Rector for Study Affairs of the University of Regensburg (Germany). Main research interests: professional learning, expertise, workplace learning, social network analysis, higher education. He is member of the Review Board "Education Sciences" of the German Research Foundation and of the Executive Committee of the EARLI. (hans.gruber@paedagogik.uni-regensburg.de)

Christian Harteis, Dr. phil., is Professor of Educational Science, Educational Management and Research on Further Education at the University of Paderborn (Germany). His research interests comprise workplace and professional learning, intuition, and learning from errors. He is Associate Editor of the Journal *Vocations and Learning – Studies in Vocational and Professional Education*. (Christian.harteis@upb.de)

Helmut Heid, Dr. rer. pol., is Professor Emeritus at the Institute for Educational Science, University of Regensburg, Germany. He studies conditions of responsibility, learning supportive work conditions, and the convergence of economic and educational rationality in human resource development. General topics of his research are the philosophy of science of educational research and the ideologically critical analysis of educational policy principles, such as educational equality and the merit principle. (helmut.heid@paedagogik.uni-regensburg.de)

Christine Hofer, M.Sc., studied Educational Sciences in Fribourg (Switzerland). She currently works as a technical college teacher. She is interested in learning from errors, negative knowledge, and error culture. (christine.e.hofer@bluewin.ch)

Nina Keith, Ph.D., is Professor of Organizational and Business Psychology at the Technical University of Darmstadt (Technische Universität Darmstadt), Germany. She received her diploma degree in psychology (M.S. in Psychology) from the University of Frankfurt (Germany) and her Ph.D. in Industrial/Organizational Psychology in 2005 from the University of Giessen (Germany). For her dissertation, she has received the George E. Briggs Dissertation Award of Division 21 (Applied Experimental and Engineering Psychology) of the American Psychological Association. Nina Keith worked as Post-doctoral fellow at Florida State University in Tallahassee, Florida (USA). Her research focuses on formal and informal learning in organizations and deals with topics such as learning from errors, training effectiveness, and the role of self-regulated practice activities in the workplace. (keith@psychologie.tu-darmstadt.de)

Annette Kluge, Dr. rer. pol., is Professor for Economic and Organizational Psychology at the Faculty of Engineering Sciences, University of Duisburg-Essen, Germany, and visiting professor for Organizational Psychology at the Research Institute for Organizational Psychology, University of St. Gallen, Switzerland. Her research covers cognitive requirement analysis to derive training models for controlling complex systems, organizational learning from errors, as well as service quality and customer satisfaction. (annette.kluge@uni-due.de)

Klaus Mehl, Ph.D., is research psychologist at the Department of Education, Carl von Ossietzky University Oldenburg, Germany. Research interests are human error, the function of errors in learning processes and simulator based training. (klaus.mehl@uni-oldenburg.de)

Michael Mohe, Dr. rer. pol., is Professor for Business Administration at the Campus Minden of the University of Applied Science Bielefeld. His research interest focuses on consulting research, professional service firms, and organizational and personnel development. (michael.mohe@fh-bielefeld.de)

Catherine Näpflin, M.Sc., is a doctoral student and working as project leader at University of Fribourg. Her research topics focus on moral education related with interdisciplinary in Swiss gymnasiums and conceptual change. Since 2010, she has been working in the project "Entrepreneurship-Program in vocational education" together with the University St.Gallen. (Catherine.Naepflin@unifr.ch)

Fritz K. Oser, Dr. Dr. h.c. mult., is Professor Emeritus at the Department of Educational Science, University of Fribourg, Switzerland. Among his research topics are moral development and teacher education as well as learning from errors, negative knowledge, and error culture. (Fritz.Oser@unifr.ch)

Yvonne Pfeiffer, Ph.D., received a M. Sc. in Psychology from the Albert-Ludwigs-University of Freiburg im Breisgau, Germany, and a Ph.D. in Work and Organizational Psychology from ETH Zurich, Switzerland. She currently works as a postdoctoral research fellow at the MIT Sloan School of Management in Cambridge, USA, together with Prof. John Carroll on the role of mental models in organizational learning from safety-relevant events and is funded by a fellowship of the Swiss National Science Foundation. In her prior research, Dr. Pfeiffer has focused on motivational reasons for underreporting of incidents in healthcare and on the assessment of safety climate in hospitals. (ypfeiffer@ethz.ch)

Manfred Prenzel, Ph.D., is Dean of the TUM *School of School of Education* and holds the Susanne Klatten Endowed Chair of Educational Research at the Technische Universitaet Muenchen (TUM). From 1993 he was Professor of Educational Psychology at the University of Regensburg, before he changed (in 1997) to the

Leibniz-Institute for Science Education (IPN) in Kiel. From 2000 until summer 2009, he was the Managing Director of IPN. The main topics of his research relate to issues of learning and teaching in different domains (science, mathematics, medicine, economics), especially on motivation/interest, conceptual change, and patterns of teaching and learning. He was/is the National Project Manager for OECD-PISA 2003, 2006 and 2012 in Germany. (manfred.prenzel@tum.de)

Daniel Putz, Ph.D., works as a specialist of personnel and organisational development at AachenMünchener, one of Germany's largest insurance companies. His main responsibilities cover the identification and development of high potentials, the moderation of change processes and the participation in strategic projects. Daniel studied psychology at Oldenburg and Aachen in Germany. Between 2006 and 2010 he worked as research assistant and lecturer at the Department of Industrial and Organizational Psychology at RWTH Aachen University, where he also received his Ph.D. His main research interests involve issues of personnel assessment and development as well as organizational analysis and change. (daniel.putz@amv.de)

Jan Schilling, Ph.D., is Professor of Work and Organizational Psychology at the University of Applied Administrative Sciences in Hannover. He studied psychology at the University of Bielefeld and RWTH Aachen University in Germany, where he also received his doctoral degree in 2001. His thesis is titled "What do leaders talk about when they are talking about leadership – An analysis of implicit leadership theories". Between 2001 and 2002, he worked as a process mediator at the HR-department of Ford in Cologne, Germany. His areas of research involve organizational learning, leadership, and organizational cynicism. (Jan.Schilling@nds-sti.de)

Elke M. Schüttelkopf, Mag. M.Sc. MBA, works as a business consultant in Austria and Germany. As a trainer, she aims at improving employees' attitudes towards errors, establishing effective strategies to handle errors and improving organizational error culture. To accomplish this, she builds upon her experience gathered while researching organisational error cultures. For more information, see http://www.fehlerkultur.com. (elke.m.schuettelkopf@fehlerkultur.at)

Tina Seidel, Ph.D., is Professor of Education and holds the Friedl Schöller Endowed Chair for Teaching and Learning Research at TUM School of Education, Munich, Germany. Prior to her appointment in Munich she was Professor of Educational Psychology at University of Jena, as well as Assistant Professor of Education and Vice Head of the Educational Department at the Leibniz-Institute for Science Education at the University of Kiel, Germany. She was Visiting Professor at the School of Education at Stanford University. Her current work includes (video-based) analysis of teaching and learning processes in classrooms and professional learning of teachers. (tina.seidel@tum.de)

Theo Wehner, Ph.D., is Professor at the Swiss Federal Institute of Technology (ETH) Zurich (Switzerland) and holds the Chair of Work and Organizational Psychology. He specializes in human error, technological innovation, knowledge management, and corporate volunteering. He has conducted research in various industries. (twehner@ethz.ch)

Marianne van Woerkom, Ph.D., lectures in learning and development at Tilburg University, department of Human Resource Studies. Her research interests are in the area of strengths and positive psychology, workplace learning, organizational learning, team learning, critical reflection and coaching. (M.vanWoerkom@uvt.nl)

Chapter 1
The Ambiguity of Errors for Work and Learning: Introduction to the Volume

Johannes Bauer and Christian Harteis

"By mistakes we learn" is a commonly used truism. However, from the perspective of research, the questions on how and under what conditions we learn from mistakes are hard to answer. One reason for this is that there is a huge variety of errors (e.g., lapses of memory versus using a wrong cognitive strategy for solving a problem; Norman, 1981; Rasmussen, 1987a; Reason, 1990). In addition, errors occur in various contexts (e.g., school, work, sports, everyday life), which may involve multiple causes and may lead to different learning potentials. Therefore, investigating under what conditions individuals, teams, or organisations can learn from errors is a demanding issue for research, which poses theoretical and methodological challenges (Billett, 2012; Mehl, 2010; Mehl & Wehner, 2012).

The present volume comprises analyses on these questions in the context of professional work. In this context, we understand 'errors' to be actions or decisions that could result in a deviation from a desired goal and endanger the attainment of higher order goals (Frese & Zapf, 1994; Hacker, 1998; Lipshitz, 1997; Rasmussen, 1987b; Senders & Moray, 1991; Zhao & Olivera, 2006). In professional contexts, we require more elaborate theoretical frameworks, which explain learning from errors, methods and research instruments that allow its measurement, as well as systematic research that investigates relevant determinants of learning from errors in different professions. Knowing what conditions may enhance or constrain learning from errors at work is relevant for explaining individual or collective differences in it as well as

J. Bauer, Ph.D. (✉)
TUM School of Education, Technische Universität München (TUM),
Munich, Germany
e-mail: jbauer@tum.de

C. Harteis, Ph.D.
University of Paderborn, Paderborn, Germany
e-mail: Christian.harteis@upb.de

J. Bauer and C. Harteis (eds.), *Human Fallibility: The Ambiguity of Errors for Work and Learning*, Professional and Practice-based Learning 6,
DOI 10.1007/978-90-481-3941-5_1,

for the practical goal of creating work environments that support learning from errors (Bauer, Mehl, & Wehner, 2010; Bauer & Mulder, 2011; Harteis, Bauer, & Gruber, 2008).

The main idea of this book dates back to the year 2002 when we started a project, together with Hans Gruber and Helmut Heid at the University of Regensburg, aimed at investigating and describing work conditions that are supportive for employees' workplace learning and professional development. One of our major interests was how errors – that are inevitably made in all work contexts – may serve as learning opportunities for individuals, teams, and organisations (Bauer, Gartmeier, & Harteis, 2012; Harteis et al., 2008). This question resulted from the observation that professionals and their organisations often seem to act according to particular error avoidance strategies (Tjosvold, Yu, & Hui, 2004; Van Dyck, Frese, Baer, & Sonnentag, 2005; Wehner & Mehl, 2003; Zapf, Frese, & Brodbeck, 1999). On the individual level, one reason for our dislike of errors is that they cause us distress (Zapf, 1991). Errors show our deficiencies, including where we did not pay enough attention, or when we misjudged a situation, thus questioning our reputation and our pride as proficient workers. Besides, errors may be dangerous and can cause adverse things to happen (Glendon, Clarke, & McKenna, 2006; Perrow, 1984; Reason, 1990). On the organisational level, errors can endanger the creation of economic value and may also put employees, clients, or customers at risk. The research on safety and accidents has endless examples of minor errors leading to disastrous outcomes (Perrow, 1984; Reason, 1990). As a consequence, there is a long tradition of research on human factors and safety management with the aim of providing approaches for estimating a system's reliability, evaluating the potential damage from specific errors, analysing error causes, and preventing errors (Flanagan, 1954; Glendon et al., 2006; Rasmussen, 1987a; Senders & Moray, 1991; Strauch, 2002; Woods, Dekker, Cook, Johannesen, & Starter, 2010; Zimolong, 1990).

The error-avoidance approach described creates a dialectical tension: on the one hand, professionals as well as companies are keen to avoid errors; on the other hand, scholars have indicated that errors cannot be completely prevented and that a heavy reliance on error prevention can have detrimental effects (Kohn, Corrigan, & Donaldson, 1999; Perrow, 1984; Rybowiak, Garst, Frese, & Batinic, 1999; Senders & Moray, 1991; Van Dyck et al., 2005; Volpert, 1992; Wehner, 1992; Wehner & Mehl, 2003; Wehner, Mehl, & Dieckmann, 2010; Zapf et al., 1999). Instances of such detrimental effects are: the potential occurrence of errors may be insufficiently anticipated; employees lose their skills in dealing with them; and learning opportunities are missed.

For these reasons, a shift from an exclusive error prevention approach to an error management strategy has been proposed (e.g., Zapf et al., 1999). Error management concepts suggest, in addition to prevention, an efficient way of dealing with errors and learning from them. The error management approach is based on the assumption that a systematic analysis of occurring errors can provide organisations with information about necessary adjustments of knowledge, strategies, and behaviour. Moreover, errors may evoke new insights that lead to learning beyond the mere prevention of similar errors (Ellström, 2001; Peters & Peters, 1987; Wehner, 1992). Consequently, learning from errors is an important technique of organisational learning (Argote & Todocara, 2007; Argyris, 1982; Cannon & Edmondson, 2005; Ellström, 2001; Kriegesmann, Kley, & Schwering, 2005; Peters & Peters, 1987; Senge, 1990; Sitkin, 1992).

Hence, although it seems obvious that errors should be avoided in professional work because they endanger the attainment of desired goals, a prerequisite for avoiding errors as well as for capturing the potential benefits that arise through errors is to be open to their occurrence and to learn from them (Harteis et al., 2008; Van Dyck et al., 2005; Wehner, 1992). This seeming dilemma shapes the ambiguity of errors for work and for learning.

In the following section, we briefly sketch the current state of research on errors at work and learning from them as an introduction to the present volume. Next, we provide an overview of the articles in this book and how they contribute to the existing lines of inquiry.

Perspectives on Errors at Work and Learning from Them

Several areas of research on errors and learning from errors already exist (cf. Bauer et al., 2010; Bauer & Mulder, 2008). First, there is a large body of research on *human error and safety management* that focuses on the conditions, classification, and prevention of human error. There are several classical discourses on this topic (Frese & Zapf, 1991; Perrow, 1984; Rasmussen, 1987c; Reason, 1990; Senders & Moray, 1991) as well as a vast literature on safety management in general and on issues in specific domains such as health care (Aspden, Corrigan, Wolcott, & Erickson, 2004; Bogner, 1994; Glazinski & Wiedensohler, 2004; Glendon et al., 2006; Holzer, Thomeczek, Hauke, Cohnen, & Hochreutener, 2005; Kohn et al., 1999; Strauch, 2002). A special topic is the discussion on critical incident reporting systems (IRS), that is, knowledge management databases – which are used, for example, in aviation and health care – serving for the collection and analysis of occurring critical incidents (Barach & Small, 2000; Dovey & Phillips, 2004; Hofinger, 2010; Holzer et al., 2005; Kaufmann et al., 2002; Uribe, Schweikhart, Pathak, & Marsh, 2002; Zhao & Olivera, 2006). The actual contribution of IRS to learning from errors is, however, still a subject of debate among experts in the field (Hofinger, 2010; Pfeiffer & Wehner, 2012).

Second, in contrast to error prevention, there is a smaller but more diverse body of literature focusing on potential positive effects of errors for developmental processes and on detrimental effects of a very strict emphasis given to error prevention. This literature on *error friendliness* employs arguments from evolutionary biology (von Weizsäcker & von Weizsäcker, 1998), the irony of automation (Bainbridge, 1987), or work psychology (Mehl, 1993; Volpert, 1992; Wehner, 1992). Recently, Gartmeier (2009) advanced the notion of error friendliness in his work on the acquisition of error-related knowledge (cf. Gartmeier & Schüttelkopf, 2012).

Third, *organisational learning and human resource management* research has focused on optimising inner-firm processes and firm performance by applying strategies of quality management and organisational learning. Next to the classical works on organisational learning (Argyris & Schön, 1996; Senge, 1990), a number of journal articles and book chapters have stressed the importance of learning from errors for organisational learning (e.g., Argote & Todocara, 2007; Kriegesmann et al., 2005; Sitkin, 1992).

Fourth, there is a line of inquiry focusing on enabling learning from errors in the context of *education and professional training*. In education, learning from errors has been an issue in research on learning and instruction (Große & Renkl, 2007; Mathan & Koedinger, 2005; Van Lehn, 1988). Starting with some seminal studies in Switzerland, an intensive discussion about the prevalence and creation of a constructive error culture in the classroom has begun (Althof, 1999; Oser & Spychiger, 2005; see also Dalehefte, Prenzel, & Seidel, 2012; Heinze & Reiss, 2007; Klockmann, 2005; Meyer, Seidel, & Prenzel, 2006; Seifried & Wuttke, 2010; Weingardt, 2004). A related field investigates training that aims at the development of strategies to deal with errors in an efficient and learning-oriented way (Frese, 1995; Heimbeck, Frese, Sonnentag, & Keith, 2003; Keith, 2005, 2012; Keith & Frese, 2005, 2008).

Finally, studies on individual and team learning from errors in professional contexts arose from various lines of research on *professional learning and development, expertise, and workplace learning*. Some classic analyses from work and organisational psychology have explained processes of learning from errors in the context of action–regulation theories (Frese & Zapf, 1994; Hacker, 1998; Volpert, 1992). Recent studies have focused on the organisational climate for learning from errors (Kluge, Schilling, & Putz, 2010; Putz, Schilling, & Kluge, 2012) or on the role of negative emotions (Zhao, 2011). Moreover, research on the development of expertise, experiential learning, case-based reasoning, and learning through work has indicated that errors can be significant sources for professional learning (Ellström, 2001; Eraut, 1994; Ericsson, 2006; Gruber, 1999; Klein, 1997; Kolodner, 1983; Ohlsson, 1996). Hence, learning from errors has already been addressed in studies on expertise, the development of professional competence, and learning in the process of work (Arndt, 1996; Bauer & Gruber, 2007; Bauer et al., 2010; Bauer & Mulder, 2007, 2008, 2010, 2011; Cannon & Edmondson, 2001; Cseh, Watkins, & Marsick, 2000; Edmondson, 1996; Ellis, 2012; Ellis & Davidi, 2005; Eraut et al., 1998; Harteis et al., 2008; Harteis & Frost, 2012; Meurier, Vincent, & Parmar, 1997; Tjosvold et al., 2004; Tucker & Edmondson, 2003; Van Woerkom, 2003, 2012). A particular challenge in this context is modelling and measuring outcomes of learning from errors, and from errors that almost occurred, in terms of knowledge (Gartmeier, Bauer, Gruber, & Heid, 2008, 2010; Gartmeier, Gruber, & Heid, 2010; Gartmeier, Lehtinen, Gruber, & Heid, 2010; Gartmeier & Schüttelkopf, 2012; Gruber & Mohe, 2012; Järvinen & Poikela, 2001; Oser, Näpflin, Hofer, & Aerni, 2012).

Overview of the Book

Scope and Audience

As discussed in the previous section, there is a huge body of research on errors and learning from errors at work from various disciplines and fields of inquiry. However, there is currently no coherent book which systematically presents these different perspectives in order to explain the processes and determinants of learning from errors in professional contexts. The primary objective of this volume is to integrate theoretical and empirical studies on learning from errors at work written by researchers of various backgrounds. This book contributes towards a deeper understanding of the conditions in which professionals are able to deal with errors productively and to learn from them by bringing together theoretical models and useful research strategies as well as empirical evidence on processes and outcomes of learning from errors from diverse perspectives. Together, the chapters in this volume draw a quite comprehensive picture of the current state of the art in research on human fallibility and learning from errors at work. Moreover, the reader will also be impressed by the wealth of different approaches.

The intended audience of this volume are researchers who are interested in human fallibility and learning from errors, for example those in the fields of education, cognitive and educational psychology, psychology and sociology of organisations and work, management, human resource development and workplace learning. Likewise, evidence-oriented practitioners in the said fields and in workplaces that demand high levels of safety will find new significant perspectives. We hope that the contributions in this volume will inspire theory, research, and evidence-based practice in these fields.

Organisation and Content

This volume is organised in four major parts. *Part A* contains theoretical contributions on errors, their learning potential, and the processes of learning from errors. A particular theme is modelling the outcomes of learning from errors in terms of knowledge. *Part B* presents chapters which address the question on what methodological procedures and instruments are appropriate for investigating errors and learning from errors. *Part C* presents results from empirical studies on learning from errors, its determinants, and outcomes in selected professions. Finally, *Part D* includes research on interventions and training studies, which aim to utilise errors for learning and the creation of conditions that enable learning from errors. Readers can find an overview of the chapters in their respective parts below.

Part A: Errors, Their Learning Potential, and the Processes of Learning from Errors

Billett (2012) opens the discussion on errors and learning from errors at work from a socio-cultural perspective. His contribution in this chapter anchors the issues of errors and learning from them in a deep theoretical understanding of the processes and conditions of workplace learning. Referring to recent studies and theorising about the subjective or personal and social bases of learning through work, Billett discusses what constitutes an error and how learning can arise from errors depending relationally on personal and social (i.e., cultural and situational) factors. That is, errors and learning from errors happen through and are dependent on the interaction of individual workers – considering their personal background – with the socially and culturally shaped affordances that workplaces provide.

Gartmeier and *Schüttelkopf* (2012) emphasise the importance of investigating the outcomes of learning from errors. Similar to Oser et al. (2012), they advance the concept of *negative knowledge* as a conceptual framework, that is, knowledge about potential errors in a given situation and conditions for their occurrence. After sketching the advantages of a perspective on the outcomes of learning from errors and elaborating on the concept of negative knowledge, the authors provide a discussion of conceptual and methodological conclusions for the investigation of negative knowledge. Particularly, they argue that error-related knowledge should be seen as dually embedded in an individual's experience and in a particular social context.

Oser et al. (2012) continue the discussion of negative knowledge and address the question on how mistakes that were prevented just in time (i.e., near misses) may foster the development of such knowledge. Their chapter aims to show that near misses can bear an equal – if not superior – learning potential as compared to errors that actually happened. From their qualitative research, the authors present compelling examples of near miss situations in everyday and professional domains. Moreover, in a further quantitative study with apprentices, they show that there is a positive correlation between the apprentices' perception of a positive culture of learning from mistakes within companies and achievement-related variables, such as the apprentices' self-efficacy and performance motivation. The positive correlation of the above mentioned variables is moderated by gender differences, that is, males seem to depend on a supportive error culture more strongly than females.

Gruber and *Mohe* (2012) review and integrate theory and research on knowledge about errors from various disciplines, such as educational science, business management, work psychology, and computer science. Based on a classification model from the psychology of knowledge, the authors distinguish the acquisition, representation, and application of knowledge about errors. The authors exemplify the results of their analysis in relation to the professional domain of business consulting.

Part B: Methodological Strategies

Mehl and *Wehner* (2012) raise critical questions concerning methodological problems in research on errors and learning from them. Referring to the examples of classic studies, they demonstrate that the search for potential causes – a hallmark of models of learning from errors – quickly becomes a matter of attribution from hindsight that may be biased and rests upon untestable assumptions. Also, the authors show that the classification of error types is not such a clear-cut matter as existing taxonomies of error types may suggest. They conclude the chapter by arguing convincingly that training simulators provide an appropriate setting for the investigation of learning from errors and probably help to overcome many of the methodological problems.

Putz et al. (2012) present a study on the development of a questionnaire, which measures the organisational climate for learning from errors. They developed this instrument according to a theoretical model that systematically combines "process-stages" of learning from errors with relevant influences on the individual level (i.e., employees' and supervisors' behaviour) and on the level of the workplace affordances (i.e., operating procedures and task structures, organisational principles and values) (cf. Billett, 2012). In their study, the authors evaluated the psychometric properties of the instrument and found evidence that supports the assumed theoretical structure. In addition, correlations of the newly developed instrument with external criteria, such as group cohesion and customer satisfaction, provide first evidence of criterion-related validity.

Part C: Learning from Errors in the Professions

Van Workom (2012) investigates the error orientation of teams and how this orientation mediates the relationship between other team characteristics and the innovative potential of teams. Her findings from a large study involving teams from several organisations indicate that team autonomy is an important predictor for problem solving orientation toward errors within a team. Moreover, teams with such a problem solving orientation also tend to feel they are in a more innovative team climate. In contrast, teams with a blaming approach to errors are rated as being significantly less innovative by their managers. These findings illustrate the importance of creating a social climate and culture in organisations that allows dealing with errors openly and in a reflective manner (cf. Putz et al., 2012).

Harteis and *Frost* (2012) investigate error orientation in emergency medicine, a domain that requires rapid and intuitive decision making. In their laboratory study, the authors test the hypothesis that physicians' error orientation influences their intuitive behaviour as well as the quality of their casework on simulated emergency situations. The most important finding from this study is that physicians with a less anxious orientation towards errors make better intuitive decisions in the medication of emergency cases. As expected, the physicians' work experience had an impact on their decision making, with this impact being moderated by the emotional handling of errors.

Bauer et al. (2012) summarise findings from a research program involving multiple studies on the processes, outcomes, and conditions of learning from errors in various professions. A major finding is that socially shared reflection with colleagues about potential causes of an error as well as joint development of strategies for improved performance are important activities for learning from errors. Engagement in such learning activities seems to depend on the subjective estimation of errors as relevant for learning as opposed to motivational tendencies to conceal errors. Concerning the outcomes of learning from errors, negative knowledge about relevant errors and conditions for their occurrence could be elicited in studies with geriatric nurses.

Part D: Enabling Learning from Errors

Keith (2012) reviews research on how errors can be used in training for supporting competence development. She presents a theoretical model along with supportive evidence showing that encouraging participants to make and explore errors during training (i.e., error management training) leads to better performance in tasks that require adaptive transfer. This effect is mediated by emotional control and metacognitive activity. These variables are also fostered by error management training. In sum, the presented findings are an impressive demonstration of the potential of learning from errors.

Dalehefte et al. (2012) present a study on errors in the context of the teaching profession. In shaping learning environments that are conducive to students' learning, teachers have the task to foster a learning-oriented approach towards errors and to create a supportive social climate. In their study, the authors analysed classroom conditions for making errors and the social climate for dealing with them by comparing classrooms in Germany and the German-speaking parts of Switzerland. Based on videos of physics lessons and data from student questionnaires, the authors found differences between these countries indicating that Swiss teachers are better at creating a supportive climate for learning from errors.

Ellis (2012) discusses the role of after-event reviews, that is, an experiential learning procedure for learning from errors. After-event reviews involve structured reflection processes after completing a task in order to analyse and understand potential reasons for their performance. This process is guided by a facilitator. In this chapter, Ellis reviews findings from several of his studies that provide explanations how after-event reviews promote learning from experience. Most importantly, after-event reviews enhance the quality of self-explanation, data verification and interpretation processes, provide process feedback, enhance self-efficacy, and have beneficial effects on motivation.

Pfeiffer and *Wehner* (2012) provide a critical discussion on how IRS in hospitals can contribute to individual and organisational learning from errors. Based on learning theories, the authors analyse questions about the subjects of IRS, the motivation of clinicians for using them, modes of learning, and potential learning outcomes. As a result of their analysis, Pfeiffer and Wehner conclude that current forms of the implementation of IRS remain within a single-loop learning scenario and largely fail to stimulate a deeper, more critical reflection of organisational routines, premises and values. Based on their analysis, the authors draw conclusions for the future improvement of IRS.

References

Althof, W. (Ed.). (1999). *Fehlerwelten – vom Fehlermachen und Lernen aus Fehlern* [Error worlds: On making errors and learning from them]. Leverkusen, Germany: Leske+Budrich.

Argote, L., & Todocara, G. (2007). Organizational learning. In G. P. Hodgkinson & J. K. Ford (Eds.), *International review of industrial and organizational psychology* (Vol. 22, pp. 193–234). Chichester, UK: Wiley.

Argyris, C. (1982). *Reasoning, learning, and action. Individual and organizational*. San Francisco: Jossey-Bass.

Argyris, C., & Schön, D. (1996). *Organizational learning II: Theory, method, and practice*. Reading, MA: Addison-Wesley.

Arndt, M. (1996). Aus Fehlern lernen [Learning from errors]. *Pflege, 9*, 12–18.

Aspden, P., Corrigan, J. M., Wolcott, J., & Erickson, S. M. (2004). *Patient safety*. Washington, DC: National Academies Press.

Bainbridge, L. (1987). Ironies of automation. In J. Rasmussen, K. Duncan, & J. Leplat (Eds.), *New technology and human error* (pp. 276–283). Chichester, UK: Wiley.

Barach, P., & Small, S. D. (2000). Reporting and preventing medical mishaps: Lessons from non-medical near miss reporting systems. *British Medical Journal, 320*, 759–765.

Bauer, J., Gartmeier, M., & Harteis, C. (2012). Learning from errors in the professions: Empirical findings on processes, outcomes, and supportive conditions. In J. Bauer & C. Harteis (Eds.), *Human fallibility. The ambiguity of errors for work and learning*. Dordrecht, the Netherlands: Springer.

Bauer, J., & Gruber, H. (2007). Workplace changes and workplace learning: Advantages of an educational micro perspective. *International Journal of Lifelong Education, 26*, 675–688.

Bauer, J., Mehl, K., & Wehner, T. (2010). Aus Fehlern lernen [Learning from errors]. *Wirtschaftspsychologie, 12*, 3–6.

Bauer, J., & Mulder, R. H. (2007). Modelling learning from errors in daily work. *Learning in Health and Social Care, 6*, 121–133.

Bauer, J., & Mulder, R. H. (2008). Conceptualisation of learning through errors at work – A literature review. In S. Billett, C. Harteis, & A. Eteläpelto (Eds.), *Emerging perspectives on learning through work* (pp. 115–128). Rotterdam, the Netherlands: Sense.

Bauer, J., & Mulder, R. H. (2010). In search of a good method for measuring learning from errors at work. In M. van Woerkom & R. Poell (Eds.), *Workplace learning: Concepts, measurement and application* (pp. 111–127). London: Routledge.

Bauer, J., & Mulder, R. H. (2011). Engagement in learning after errors at work. Enabling conditions and types of engagement. *Journal of Education and Work*. doi:10.1080/13639080.2011.573776. Advance online publication.

Billett, S. (2012). Errors and learning from errors at work. In J. Bauer & C. Harteis (Eds.), *Human fallibility. The ambiguity of errors for work and learning*. Dordrecht, the Netherlands: Springer.

Bogner, M. S. (Ed.). (1994). *Human error in medicine*. Hillsdale, NJ: LEA.

Cannon, M. D., & Edmondson, A. C. (2001). Confronting failure: Antecedents and consequences of shared beliefs about failure in organizational work groups. *Journal of Organizational Behavior, 22*, 161–177.

Cannon, M. D., & Edmondson, A. C. (2005). Failing to learn and learning to fail (intelligently): How great organisations put failure to work to innovate and improve. *Long Range Planning: International Journal of Strategic Management, 38*, 299–319.

Cseh, M., Watkins, K. E., & Marsick, V. J. (2000). Informal and incidental learning in the workplace. In G. Straka (Ed.), *Conceptions of self-directed learning: Theoretical and conceptional considerations* (pp. 59–74). Münster, Germany: Waxmann.

Dalehefte, I. M., Prenzel, M., & Seidel, T. (2012). Reflecting on learning from errors in school instruction. Findings and suggestions from a Swiss-German video study. In J. Bauer & C. Harteis (Eds.), *Human fallibility. The ambiguity of errors for work and learning*. Dordrecht, the Netherlands: Springer.

Dovey, S. M., & Phillips, R. L. (2004). What should we report to medical error reporting systems? *Quality & Safety in Health Care, 13*, 322–323.

Edmondson, A. C. (1996). Learning from mistakes is easier said than done: Group and organisational influences on the detection and correction of human error. *The Journal of Applied Behavioral Science, 32*, 5–28.

Ellis, S. (2012). Learning from errors: The role of after-event reviews. In J. Bauer & C. Harteis (Eds.), *Human fallibility. The ambiguity of errors for work and learning*. Dordrecht, the Netherlands: Springer.

Ellis, S., & Davidi, I. (2005). After-event reviews: Drawing lessons from successful and failed experience. *Journal of Applied Psychology, 90*, 857–871.

Ellström, P.-E. (2001). Integrating learning and work: Problems and prospects. *Human Resource Development Quarterly, 12*, 421–435.

Eraut, M. (1994). *Developing professional knowledge and competence*. London: RoutledgeFalmer.

Eraut, M., Alderton, J., Cole, G., & Senker, P. (1998). *Development of knowledge and skills in employment* (Research Rep. No. 5). Sussex, UK: University of Sussex, Institute of Education.

Ericsson, K. A. (2006). The influence of experience and deliberate practice on the development of superior expert performance. In K. A. Ericsson, N. Charness, P. J. Feltovich, & R. R. Hoffman (Eds.), *The Cambridge handbook of expertise and expert performance* (pp. 683–703). Cambridge, UK: Cambridge University Press.

Flanagan, J. C. (1954). The critical incident technique. *Psychological Bulletin, 51*, 327–358.

Frese, M. (1995). Error management in training: Conceptual and empirical results. In C. Zucchermaglio, S. Bagnara, & S. U. Stucky (Eds.), *Organizational learning and technological change* (pp. 112–124). Berlin, Germany: Springer.

Frese, M., & Zapf, D. (Eds.). (1991). *Fehler bei der Arbeit mit dem Computer* [Errors in working with computers]. Bern, Switzerland: Huber.

Frese, M., & Zapf, D. (1994). Action as the core of work psychology: A German approach. In H. C. Triandis, M. D. Dunette, & L. M. Hough (Eds.), *Handbook of industrial and organizational psychology* (2nd ed., Vol. 4, pp. 271–340). Palo Alto, CA: Consulting Psychologists Press.

Gartmeier, M. (2009). *Fehlerfreundlichkeit im Arbeitskontext: Positive Einstellungen gegenüber Fehlern und negatives Wissen als Ressourcen professionellen Handelns* [Error friendliness in work contexts: On positive attitudes towards errors and negative knowledge as resources for professional action]. Dissertation, Universität Regensburg, Regensburg. Retrieved June 30, 2011, from http://epub.uni-regensburg.de/9275/1/GARTMEIER.pdf

Gartmeier, M., Bauer, J., Gruber, H., & Heid, H. (2008). Negative knowledge: Understanding professional learning and expertise. *Vocations and Learning: Studies in Vocational and Professional Education, 1*, 87–103.

Gartmeier, M., Bauer, J., Gruber, H., & Heid, H. (2010). Workplace errors and negative knowledge in elder care nursing. *Human Resource Development International, 13*, 5–25.

Gartmeier, M., Gruber, H., & Heid, H. (2010). Tracing error-related knowledge in interview data: Negative knowledge in elder care nursing. *Educational Gerontology, 36*, 733–752.

Gartmeier, M., Lehtinen, E., Gruber, H., & Heid, H. (2010). Negative expertise: Comparing differently experienced elder care nurses' negative knowledge. *European Journal of Psychology of Education, 26*, 273–300.

Gartmeier, M., & Schüttelkopf, E. (2012). Tracing outcomes of learning form errors on the level of knowledge. In J. Bauer & C. Harteis (Eds.), *Human fallibility. The ambiguity of errors for work and learning*. Dordrecht, the Netherlands: Springer.

Glazinski, R., & Wiedensohler, R. (2004). *Patientensicherheit und Fehlerkultur im Gesundheitswesen* [Patient safety and error culture in health care]. Eschborn, Germany: Brainwave.

Glendon, I., Clarke, S. G., & McKenna, E. F. (2006). *Human safety and risk management*. Boca Raton, FL: Taylor & Francis.

Große, C. S., & Renkl, A. (2007). Finding and fixing errors in worked examples: Can this foster learning outcomes? *Learning and Instruction, 17*, 612–634.

Gruber, H. (1999). *Erfahrung als Grundlage kompetenten Handelns* [Experience as basis for competent action]. Bern, Switzerland: Huber.

Gruber, H., & Mohe, M. (2012). Professional knowledge is (also) knowledge about errors. In J. Bauer & C. Harteis (Eds.), *Human fallibility. The ambiguity of errors for work and learning*. Dordrecht, the Netherlands: Springer.

Hacker, W. (1998). *Allgemeine Arbeitspsychologie. Psychische Regulation von Arbeitstätigkeiten* [General work psychology. Psychological regulation of action at work]. Bern, Switzerland: Huber.

Harteis, C., Bauer, J., & Gruber, H. (2008). The culture of learning from mistakes: How employees handle mistakes in everyday work. *International Journal of Educational Research, 47*, 223–231.

Harteis, C., & Frost, F. (2012). Error orientation and intuitive decision making: Results of an exploratory study in the domain of emergency medicine. In J. Bauer & C. Harteis (Eds.), *Human fallibility. The ambiguity of errors for work and learning*. Dordrecht, the Netherlands: Springer.

Heimbeck, D., Frese, M., Sonnentag, S., & Keith, N. (2003). Integrating errors in the training process: The function of error management instructions and the role of goal orientation. *Personnel Psychology, 56*, 333–361.

Heinze, A., & Reiss, K. (2007). Mistake-handling activities in the mathematics classroom: Effects of an in-service teacher training on students' performance in geometry. In J. H. Woo, H. C. Lew, K. S. Park, & D. Y. Seo (Eds.), *Proceedings of the 31st Conference of the International Group for the Psychology of Mathematics Education* (Vol. III, pp. 9–16). Seoul, South Korea: The Korea Society of Educational Studies in Mathematics.

Hofinger, G. (2010). Zwischenfallberichtssysteme als Instrument organisationalen Lernens aus Fehlern in Krankenhäusern [Incident reporting systems as a tool for organisational learning from errors in hospitals]. *Wirtschaftspsychologie, 12*, 87–96.

Holzer, E., Thomeczek, C., Hauke, E., Cohnen, D., & Hochreutener, A. -A. (Eds.). (2005). *Patientensicherheit. Leitfaden für den Umgang mit Risiken im Gesundheitswesen* [Patient safety: Guideline for dealing with risks in health care]. Wien, Austria: Facultas.

Järvinen, A., & Poikela, E. (2001). Modeling reflective and contextual learning at work. *Journal of Workplace Learning, 13*, 282–289.

Kaufmann, M., Staender, S., von Below, G., Brunner, H. H., Portenier, L., & Scheidegger, D. (2002). Computerbasiertes anonymes Critical Incident Reporting: Ein Beitrag zur Patientensicherheit [Computer based anonymous Critical Incident Reporting: A contribution to patient safety]. *Schweizerische Ärztezeitung, 83*, 2554–2558.

Keith, N. (2005). *Self-regulatory processes in error management training*. Giessen, Germany: Justus-Liebig-Universität.

Keith, N. (2012). Dealing effectively with errors during training. In J. Bauer & C. Harteis (Eds.), *Human fallibility. The ambiguity of errors for work and learning*. Dordrecht, the Netherlands: Springer.

Keith, N., & Frese, M. (2005). Self-regulation in error management training: Emotion control and metacognition as mediators of performance effects. *Journal of Applied Psychology, 90*, 677–691.

Keith, N., & Frese, M. (2008). Effectiveness of error management training: A meta analysis. *Journal of Applied Psychology, 93*, 59–69.
Klein, G. (1997). The recognition-primed decision (RPD) model: Looking back, looking forward. In C. E. Zsambok & G. Klein (Eds.), *Naturalistic decision making* (pp. 285–292). Mahwah, NJ: LEA.
Klockmann, D. (2005). Didaktische Modellierung und empirische Annäherung an das Lernen aus Fehlern [A didactic model and empirical investigation of learning from errors]. In P. Gonon, R. Huisinga, F. Klauser, & R. Nickolaus (Eds.), *Kompetenz, Kognition und neue Konzepte der beruflichen Bildung* (pp. 177–189). Wiesbaden, Germany: VS-Verlag.
Kluge, A., Schilling, J., & Putz, D. (2010). Organisationales Klima für ein Lernen aus Fehlern: Die Rolle von charismatisch-zielorientierter und aktivierender Führung [Organisational learning from errors: The impact of charismatic goal-orientation and activating leadership]. *Wirtschaftspsychologie, 12*, 29–40.
Kohn, L. T., Corrigan, J. M., & Donaldson, M. S. (Eds.). (1999). *To err is human. Building a safer health system*. Washington, DC: National Academy Press.
Kolodner, J. (1983). Towards an understanding of the role of experience in the evolution from novice to expert. *International Journal of Man-Machine Studies, 19*, 497–518.
Kriegesmann, B., Kley, T., & Schwering, M. G. (2005). Creative errors and heroic failures: Capturing their innovative potential. *Journal of Business Strategy, 26*, 57–64.
Lipshitz, R. (1997). Naturalistic decision making perspectives on decision errors. In C. E. Zsambok & G. Klein (Eds.), *Naturalistic decision making* (pp. 151–169). Mahwah, NJ: LEA.
Mathan, S. A., & Koedinger, K. R. (2005). Fostering the intelligent novice: Learning from errors with metacognitive tutoring. *Educational Psychologist, 40*, 257–265.
Mehl, K. (1993). *Über einen funktionalen Aspekt von Handlungsfehlern. Was lernt man wie aus Fehlern?* [On the functional aspect of errors. What can be learnt how from errors?]. Münster, Germany: Lit.
Mehl, K. (2010). Von einem, der auszog aus Fehlern zu lernen: Anmerkungen zu analytisch-methodischen Fragen psychologischer Fehlerforschung [Learning by mistake: Notations on analytic-methodical questions in error research]. *Wirtschaftspsychologie, 12*, 78–86.
Mehl, K., & Wehner, T. (2012). Research on errors and learning form them: Methodological perspectives. In J. Bauer & C. Harteis (Eds.), *Human fallibility. The ambiguity of errors for work and learning*. Dordrecht, the Netherlands: Springer.
Meurier, C. E., Vincent, C. A., & Parmar, D. G. (1997). Learning from errors in nursing practice. *Journal of Advanced Nursing, 26*, 111–119.
Meyer, L., Seidel, T., & Prenzel, M. (2006). Wenn Lernsituationen zu Leistungssituationen werden: Untersuchungen zur Fehlerkultur in einer Videostudie [When learning situations become achievement situations: Investigation of error culture in a video study]. *Schweizerische Zeitschrift für Bildungswissenschaften, 28*, 21–41.
Norman, D. A. (1981). Categorization of action slips. *Psychological Review, 88*, 1–15.
Ohlsson, S. (1996). Learning from performance errors. *Psychological Review, 103*, 241–262.
Oser, F., Näpflin, C., Hofer, C., & Aerni, P. (2012). Towards a theory of Negative Knowledge (NK): Almost-mistakes as drivers of episodic memory amplification. In J. Bauer & C. Harteis (Eds.), *Human fallibility. The ambiguity of errors for work and learning*. Dordrecht, the Netherlands: Springer.
Oser, F., & Spychiger, M. (2005). *Lernen ist schmerzhaft* [Learning is painful]. Weinheim, Germany: Basel.
Perrow, C. (1984). *Normal accidents: Living with high risk technologies*. Princeton, NJ: Princeton University Press.
Peters, T. J., & Peters, T. (1987). *Thriving on Chaos: Handbook for a management revolution*. New York: Alfred Knopf.
Pfeiffer, Y., & Wehner, T. (2012). Incident reporting systems in hospitals: How does learning occur using this organisational instrument? In J. Bauer & C. Harteis (Eds.), *Human fallibility. The ambiguity of errors for work and learning*. Dordrecht, the Netherlands: Springer.

Putz, D., Schilling, J., & Kluge, A. (2012). Measuring organisational climate for learning from errors at work. In J. Bauer & C. Harteis (Eds.), *Human fallibility. The ambiguity of errors for work and learning*. Dordrecht, the Netherlands: Springer.

Rasmussen, J. (1987a). Reasons, causes, and human error. In J. Rasmussen, K. Duncan, & J. Leplat (Eds.), *New technology and human error* (pp. 293–301). Chichester, UK: Wiley.

Rasmussen, J. (1987b). Cognitive control and human error mechanisms. In J. Rasmussen, K. Duncan, & J. Leplat (Eds.), *New technology and human error* (pp. 53–60). Chichester, UK: Wiley.

Rasmussen, J. (1987c). The definition of human error and a taxonomy for technical system design. In J. Rasmussen, K. Duncan, & J. Leplat (Eds.), *New technology and human error* (pp. 23–30). Chichester, UK: Wiley.

Reason, J. T. (1990). *Human error*. Cambridge, UK: Cambridge University Press.

Rybowiak, V., Garst, H., Frese, M., & Batinic, B. (1999). Error orientation questionnaire (EOQ): Reliability, validity, and different language equivalence. *Journal of Organizational Behavior, 20*, 527–547.

Seifried, J., & Wuttke, E. (2010). "Professionelle Fehlerkompetenz" – Operationalisierung einer vernachlässigten Kompetenzfacette von Lehrkräften ["Professional error competence": How to operationalise a neglected competence of (future) teachers]. *Wirtschaftspsychologie, 12*, 17–28.

Senders, J. W., & Moray, N. P. (1991). *Human error. Cause, prediction, and reduction*. Hillsdale, NJ: LEA.

Senge, P. (1990). *The fifth discipline: The art and practice of the learning organization*. New York: Random House.

Sitkin, S. B. (1992). Learning through failure: The strategy of small losses. *Research in Organizational Behavior, 14*, 231–266.

Strauch, B. (2002). *Investigating human error: Incidents, accidents, and complex systems*. Aldershot, UK: Ashgate.

Tjosvold, D., Yu, Z.-Y., & Hui, C. (2004). Team learning from mistakes: The contribution of cooperative goals and problem solving. *Journal of Management Studies, 41*, 1223–1245.

Tucker, A. L., & Edmondson, A. C. (2003). Why hospitals don't learn from failures: Organizational and psychological dynamics that inhibit system change. *California Management Review, 45*, 55–72.

Uribe, C. L., Schweikhart, S. B., Pathak, D. S., & Marsh, G. B. (2002). Perceived barriers to medical-error reporting: An exploratory investigation. *Journal of Healthcare Management, 47*, 264–279.

Van Dyck, C., Frese, M., Baer, M., & Sonnentag, S. (2005). Organizational error management culture and its impact on performance: A two-study replication. *Journal of Applied Psychology, 90*, 1228–1240.

Van Lehn, K. (1988). Towards a theory of impasse-driven learning. In H. Mandl & A. Lesgold (Eds.), *Learning issues for intelligent tutoring systems* (pp. 19–41). New York: Springer.

Van Woerkom, M. (2003). *Critical reflection at work. Bridging individual and organisational learning*. Twente, the Netherlands: Twente University Press.

Van Woerkom, M. (2012). Innovation by learning from mistakes: The relationships between team characteristics, error orientation, and team innovation. In J. Bauer & C. Harteis (Eds.), *Human fallibility. The ambiguity of errors for work and learning*. Dordrecht, the Netherlands: Springer.

Volpert, W. (1992). *Wie wir handeln – was wir können* [How we act – What we can do]. Heidelberg, Germany: Asanger.

von Weizsäcker, E. U., & von Weizsäcker, C. (1998). Information, evolution, and "error friendliness". *Biological Cybernetics, 79*, 501–506.

Wehner, T. (Ed.). (1992). *Sicherheit als Fehlerfreundlichkeit* [Safety as error friendliness]. Leverkusen, Germany: Westdeutscher.

Wehner, T., & Mehl, K. (2003). Über die Vitalität fehlerhaften Handelns und den vermeintlichen Gegensatz zur Unfall- und Sicherheitsforschung [On the vitality of errors and the seeming contradiction with research on accidents and safety]. In B. Boothe & W. Marx (Eds.), *Panne, Irrtum, Missgeschick. Die Psychopathologie des Alltagslebens aus interdisziplinärer Perspektive* (pp. 107–126). Bern, Germany: Huber.

Wehner, T., Mehl, K., & Dieckmann, P. (2010). Handlungsfehler und Fehlerprävention [Errors and their prevention]. In U. Kleinbeck & K. -H. Schmidt (Hrsg.), *Arbeitspsychologie* [Enzyklopädie der Psychologie] (S. 785–820). Göttingen, Germany: Hogrefe.

Weingardt, M. (2004). *Fehler zeichnen uns aus* [Errors define us]. Bad Heilbrunn, Germany: Klinkhardt.

Woods, D. D., Dekker, S., Cook, R., Johannesen, L., & Starter, N. (2010). *Behind human error*. Farnham, UK: Ashgate.

Zapf, D. (1991). Fehler, Stress und organisationaler Kontext [Errors, stress, and organisational context]. In M. Frese & D. Zapf (Eds.), *Fehler bei der Arbeit mit dem Computer* (pp. 106–117). Bern, Germany: Huber.

Zapf, D., Frese, M., & Brodbeck, F. C. (1999). Fehler und Fehlermanagement [Errors and error management]. In C. G. Hoyos & D. Frey (Eds.), *Organisations psychologie* (pp. 398–411). Weinheim, Germany: Beltz PVU.

Zhao, B. (2011). Learning from errors: The role of context, emotion, and personality. *Journal of Organizational Behavior, 32*, 435–463.

Zhao, B., & Olivera, F. (2006). Error reporting in organisations. *Academy of Management Review, 31*, 1012–1030.

Zimolong, B. (1990). Fehler und Zuverlässigkeit [Errors and reliability]. In B. Zimolong & C. G. Hoyos (Eds.), *Enzyklopädie der Psychologie, Themenbereich D, Serie III, Band 2, Ingenieurspsychologie* (pp. 313–345). Göttingen, Germany: Hogrefe.

Part I
Errors, Their Learning Potential, and the Processes of Learning from Errors

Chapter 2
Errors and Learning from Errors at Work

Stephen Billett

Errors, Learning and Work

Coming to understand what constitutes errors at work and what learning can potentially arise from them are quite central to considerations of work and learning as arising through socially-shaped, but personally enacted practices. It is proposed here that, through engaging in activities and interactions, such as those at work, individuals come to both practice and learn, much of it through incomplete, partial or poorly performed actions and activity (i.e. in error, insofar as they fail to completely meet the needs of the goal-directed activity). So, from such a definition of errors, the very processes of undertaking work and learning through and for work and across working lives are inherently premised on making and resolving errors, and, moreover, these processes underpin both working and learning. If this was not the case, the process of learning new knowledge and its refinement and honing would be straightforward and our subsequent performance would be flawless. Instead, the very process of learning through or for work is mainly incremental and, sometimes, transformational. Incrementally, much of our learning of work activities is a process of improving on our previous performance, which had perhaps then wholly fulfilled work requirements. Technically, this process is referred to as engaging in increasingly mature approximations of the tasks to be achieved (Collins, Brown, & Newman, 1989). Yet, this process is un-ending across working lives as performance work requirements change and even those nominated as experts continue to make errors both in learning and work (Ericsson, 2006). Through our ongoing engagement in work tasks, we have the opportunity to undertake and repeat activities through

S. Billett, Ph.D. (✉)
School of Education and Professional Studies, Griffith University, Brisbane, Australia
e-mail: s.billett@griffith.edu.au

J. Bauer and C. Harteis (eds.), *Human Fallibility: The Ambiguity of Errors for Work and Learning*, Professional and Practice-based Learning 6,
DOI 10.1007/978-90-481-3941-5_2, © Springer Science+Business Media Dordrecht 2012

rehearsal and come to ultimately perform at a required level. In this way, our initial attempts are likely to fall short of the required performance (i.e. they are errors). Yet, progressively, the errors associated with new learning are eliminated through processes of refinement and honing, but this process is never complete because we are constantly engaged in new learning. Therefore, there are close associations among errors, learning and work. As a starting point, therefore, making errors when engaging in work activities should not be taken as being inherently wrong or undesirable. It is central to individuals' development of capacities and the inevitable process of engaging in work and other kinds of tasks.

Moreover, this error-making is usually anticipated in the places where work is enacted. It exists as a social fact used to shape the sequencing and access to activities and interactions in the workplace by workers. Indeed, often, workplace tasks are organised on this very premise: that is, the engagement in activities is ordered on a premise of managing errors. Lave (1990) identifies the management of errors and their consequences as a central principle of organising apprentices' work and learning experiences. She noted how apprentice tailors engaged in activities premised on the likelihood and consequence of errors, with only experienced workers engaging in tasks where the consequences of errors would be unredeemable. For example, when I first started working in the pattern-making department of a large clothing manufacturing company, my activities were restricted to cutting patterns for components that did not require the same level of precision as the lining and fabric patterns that I progressively went on to complete later. To avoid me making errors on patterns where the implications of those errors would be expensive and far reaching, my initial tasks were organised to restrict my errors to components that would tolerate my developing skills. Indeed, the most common form of learning people undertake, the honing and refinement of what we do, is directed towards progressively securing levels of adequate performance. That is, learning through a process that progressively reduces the elements of error in what we do.

Moreover, the learning of new knowledge quite often also arises through making errors with and discovering the inadequacy of our existing knowledge. That is, we are confronted with situations for which our existing knowledge is inadequate and we make errors, albeit in how we spell a word, cook a meal, interact with colleagues, and perform societal roles, such as being a parent to a growing child. It is in attempting to spell the word, cooking a particular kind of meal, misunderstanding the purpose and process of interaction with colleagues and how we engage with our children as we move through different levels of maturity in our activities through which we make mistakes. If errors comprise incompetent performance of an activity or an interaction, then these are central to both our learning new knowledge and engaging in tasks that are novel to us. In addition, it is through deliberate efforts to avoid errors that direct our intentional learning.

So, to reinforce this point, engaging in processes that involve making errors is central to how we learn, and come to perform in and through work and across working life. Of course, immature, incomplete or downright wrong performances can have a range of consequences and need to be managed for both the purposes of work and learning. Yet, these consequences also merely heighten the fundamental relations between errors and learning. Therefore, it is worthwhile considering the form and nature of errors of their relationship with both learning and work.

However, beyond emphasising this key relationship, the central claim made here is that errors are not wholly objective events. That is, a behaviour can always be taken as an unqualified error. Instead, what constitutes errors have both personal and social connotations. Indeed, they have dualistic qualities existing in the separate domains of the personal and social worlds, and are premised on relational bases between the two of them. In preview, individuals may or may not view a particular action as being an error, and that error may or may not be recognised as such in the setting in which it is enacted. Instead, what constitutes an error is often person and situation dependent. What for one individual is seen to be an inadequate performance, for another it might be seen as being quite an adequate or even excellent performance. The elite soccer player who kicks the ball right across the football field towards the goal, only to see the ball land close to and be caught by the goalkeeper, might view that performance as an error. Whereas, for others, myself for instance, even getting a football into the penalty area would be an excellent performance. Moreover, if the elite footballers' team has a six goal lead over the opposing side, it is unlikely the footballer will be chastised for this error by his team mates and managers. However, if the footballers' team is one goal down and in the final moments of the cup final and she had previously made this 'error' before, then she might be taken to be error prone and incompetent by the team supporters, spectators, team members and her coach alike. Of course, this relational account of errors can easily be applied to other forms of work. The hospital surgeon who fails to save the life of a road trauma victim by not recognising a specific life-threatening injury, when having been successful with previous patients, might be seen to have made an error. However, this would not be the case for the local general practice doctor who was first on the scene at a road crash, and whose skills and experiences were not helpful in assisting her in recognising and treating that injury. Yet, if this victim was only one of 50 elderly tourists who had been injured in a bus crash and the surgeon was simultaneously caring for many critically injured passengers, this oversight would be less likely to be seen as being a crucial error, except perhaps by the deceased's family. So, there are both relationally personal and situational factors that shape what constitutes errors, and what are taken as the consequences from that error making.

Moreover, both individual and situational factors will also shape how productive learning can arise from the error. For instance, depending whether those making errors are allowed to admit to them and gain support for learning from them, or need to hide their mistakes if at all possible, will likely shape the potential for learning (Bauer & Mulder, 2007). Hence, the degree by which the culture of the workplace is tolerant of errors, and the situations in which they occur are supportive or punishing of what is taken and constitutes mistakes, will both be central to the mediation of individuals' learning. Therefore, to conceptualise and understand further what constitutes errors and what learning arises from them requires considerations of personal and situational factors and relationships between these factors.

These propositions are now elaborated and discussed, drawing on recent studies and theorising about both the subjective and social bases of engaging in and learning through work. Work practices and workplaces are particularly helpful to understand what constitutes errors because the goal-directed activities in workplaces are focused on achieving specific ends, yet performed by individuals with different levels of capacities and interest in those activities. Yet, because much of work performance is shaped by goals that are situated in specific work settings, this performance and what constitutes errors needs to be understood both separately from, but alongside, the constructions of work tasks and errors by individual workers. Moreover, given the capacities of workplaces to sustain particular kinds and levels of performance, and workers' different levels of concerns for performing effectively, the negotiations between these personal and social worlds will be central to the kinds of learning that occur though work. So, more than being good or bad, or generative of rich or weak learning, a consideration of errors at work can richly inform about learning through work.

In advancing this case, the situational, cultural and personal bases for what constitutes errors and the relationships among them are discussed and elaborated in the next section. This is followed by a brief concluding section on considerations of how individuals learning through errors are shaped through these relational bases. However, before engaging in these discussions it is important to understand what constitutes human performance at work, as fallibility with and errors in work are commonly associated with failure to perform adequately (i.e. falling short of a required performance).

Performance and Errors at Work: The Social Dimension

To explain what constitutes errors and how individuals might learn through them at work, it is necessary to identify the benchmarks of what constitutes work performance. These benchmarks permit an informed account of what constitutes failures to perform adequately: errors and human fallibility. Yet, understanding what comprises competence at work needs to accommodate both socially-derived and personally-constituted perspectives of that competence. Here, the social perspective is advanced.

Much of the requirements for performance of occupational activities in workplaces are expressions of needs and requirements of the social world. Searle (1995) refers to these as institutional facts that require human needs and institutions for their existence. These facts include sets of human needs for survival, shelter, sustenance, good health, education, order and security that often find form as paid occupations. So, for instance, the performance of nurses, cooks and police officers are premised, respectively, upon societal needs when we seek to be taken care of, to produce food to eat, and law and order. Hence, most occupations arise from particular institutional needs and requirements and are shaped, and also transformed, by particular cultural requirements.

It follows, therefore, that there are expectations of occupational performance that arise from these defined cultural needs. Hence, errors are seen to occur when these requirements are not met. Consequently, when nurses are seen to be not caring for patients, food judged to be inedible, and police officers seemingly failing to secure law and order then they are seen to be in error. These expectations are often at the heart of what constitutes competence at work. For instance, beyond the technical requirements of being a competent nurse, there are expectations that they will be discreet and act personably, even under duress. So, there are a set of culturally prescribed performance expectations that constitute the adequate or inadequate (i.e. in error) forms of work, and, beyond that, occupational performance can be quite situational.

Rather than being uniform across occupations, however, the expectations of work performance are quite diverse across work situations. Although there are occupationally common concepts, values and practices – the canonical knowledge of the occupation, which if violated is seen to be in error – across workplaces, their application likely differs quite widely. This is because there are quite distinct performance requirements in specific work situations. As Darrah (1997, p. 249) claims "… jobs seem so diverse as to obviate the need for generalisations about how people perform work". Therefore, what constitutes the performance of these occupations is likely to differ across the situations in which they are applied.

Across countries and cultures, there are different requirements for occupational performance thereby making what constitute performance errors subject to these cultural requirements. Different cuisines requiring quite particular techniques, ingredients and expectations have particular geneses. Restaurant customers selecting particular cuisines do so on the basis of expectations about the kind of food they are ordering. Hence, work performance is likely premised on meeting those expectations, which may have to be modified in response to the available ingredients. Therefore, performance and performance errors are premised upon expectations about that cuisine. As with cuisine, differences in climate may also extend to performance. The requirements for occupations are often played out differently in countries that have hot summers and frigid winters. Some of the tasks undertaken and performance required of automotive engineers and construction workers in northern Europe, Canada, and northern American states are unlikely to be the same as their counterparts in most places in Australia, South American countries, or other warmer climates, and vice versa. One occupational requirement for the former is to ensure that vehicles and houses are protected against very cold weather. So, mechanic or construction workers from a warmer climate would be in error if they failed to account for these brute facts.

Other differences shape occupational requirements within similar kinds of work. For instance, some retail work is highly segmented and routinised, as is the case in grocery stores. Shoppers in large supermarkets would have little expectation that retail staff would be able to advise them about the attributes of particular products. Errors in performance here are more likely to be associated with directing a customer to the wrong aisle to find goods, which would be expected, than advice about particular items, which would not. Yet, in hardware stores, retail workers are expected to provide advice to customers about products and processes for applying products (Bernhardt, 1999). Consequently, in what constitutes work performance comprising the same occupation, there are variations in occupational practices that necessitate particular forms of workplace competence.

However, beyond performance requirements at the cultural level, there are also situational factors that shape these workplace competencies. For instance, it was found that performance for hairdressing had distinctive features across four salons (Billett, 2003), three of which were in the same Australian state. What comprises hairdressers' work, for instance, is likely shaped by a combination of factors comprising the location, clientele, staff and workplace arrangements. In a fashionable inner-city salon, the performance requirements were the ability to transform the clients' appearance through interesting haircuts and colouring. The hairdressers were also required to have appearance, interests and values aligned with its clientele. Here, not being fashionably dressed or 'cool' would be an error. Yet, in a salon in a low socio-economic suburb, an important work requirement was to manage a precarious business and a clientele that included demanding and difficult clients. A key performance requirement here was to manage these 'awkward' customers, particularly when they complained about their treatment. Hence, an error here would be to not remind these clients repeatedly that the treatments they demanded would require considerable care and maintenance and the use of particular kinds of conditioners. In another salon, the clientele comprised elderly women who came to the salon fortnightly, as much for companionship as to have their hair dressed. Here, the hairdressers' knowledge of clients' personal histories, knowing the names and circumstances of family and friends, was an important expectation of the clientele. Hence, confusing the name of one of the clients' brothers or sisters with a relative who had died recently could be taken as a significant error. In these ways, local factors shaped in quite distinct ways what constituted expectations of workplace performance in each of these salons. In each situation, failing to fulfil these expectations would be seen as an error within that particular salon. Such considerations are not restricted to this kind of occupation. For instance, the work of nurses, motor mechanics, teachers and doctors, to name a few, are shaped by the circumstances in which they practice. In a country like Australia with many small and remote communities, the requirements of those occupations are likely to be quite different in those communities, than in regional centres and cities. Hence, both performance requirements and the making of errors will be shaped by the expectations of those communities. Consequently, understanding what constitutes workplace performance and errors with that performance cannot wholly rely on occupational-level 'objective' analyses. Instead, national, cultural, local, and enterprise-level factors all shape workplace performance requirements: the 'objective' account of workplace requirements, and what are taken as errors.

Moreover, the requirements for performance also change over time, meaning that what is an acceptable performance at one point in time will be inadequate (i.e. an error) at another. The entrepreneurial banker, praised in times of strong growth and shareholder demand for high return, may well be later seen as erring in imprudence when bad debts mount, and, of course, vice versa. Work requirements are constantly being transformed by new products and technologies, short production cycles, changing production concepts, such as a high discretion workforce, and strategies of rationalisation (e.g. Darrah, 1996; Ellstrom, 1998). Hence, expectations of what constitute performance will change accordingly and constantly over time. These requirements for workplace competence can be found in the need to accommodate constant change, and the intellectual demands for work in terms of its conceptual (symbolic) requirements and procedural bases. Yet, it has been shown that workers with well-developed capacities with one form of technology may well be error prone in another, because their ways of knowing are not well aligned with that other form of knowing (Martin & Scribner, 1991). Indeed, the need to accommodate for constant change can render work practice to be inherently non-routine and demanding, making otherwise highly competent workers seemingly full of errors. Because of this constant transformation, changes to work include relinquishing past practices and the displacement of existing competence and confidence. In these ways, the requirements for competence and what constitutes errors are constantly changing. The scope and form of these changing requirements are not uniform; they are shaped by societal and situational factors.

The explanations provided above about the nature of work performance and, therefore, what might constitute errors (i.e. failures to perform adequately) has emphasised an objective socially derived view. That is, observable and quantifiable changes to work requirements and their diversity are proposed as a set of objective requirements for participation in paid work. In particular, it emphasises how the requirements for work performance and what constitute errors are shaped by socially and culturally derived expectations. These are the institutional facts (Searle, 1995) that comprise paid work. It has been proposed that the requirements for performance – expertise if you like – are likely to be highly situated both within the setting in which work occurs and also the time when it occurs (Billett, 2001). Yet, these are also often fleeting. This is because the circumstances that constitute the requirements for performance in particular workplace settings are subject to constant transformation, as are breaches of the required performance (i.e. errors). However, although there are many variations in work requirements, even in the same industry sector or occupational practice, there are also requirements that are more or less common.

There are also issues of the way in which performance requirements are articulated and able to be monitored and managed in workplaces. Quite personally specific accounts of what constitute performance may well arise, and clear and shared understandings about what constitutes performance may be taken for granted rather than being shared. Part of these quite personal accounts or conceptions of what constitutes work performance and what might be taken as transgressions is the difficulty to account for all the measures that constitute performance. Indeed, it is often the unforeseen problems or tasks which lead to changes to work requirements. Then, there are situational factors that determine whether the error is acceptable, accepted or seen as an opportunity to learn and develop, and for whom. In the hairdressing salons mentioned above, for instance, it was likely that mistakes by owners and managers would be treated differently than those of other staff. Across my long working life, I can recount numerous incidents in which the way a workplace mistake was treated was premised on who made it. Whether it was a member of the family that owned the business, the standing of the person in the workplace, their gender or class, or whether they were intimates of powerful people in the workplace, all shaped how an apparent misdemeanour was viewed and treated.

This variable treatment reflects both personal and social factors, and emphasises the need to account for the subjective and person-dependent basis upon judgements about what constitutes an error that warrants sanctions, how individuals engage in work, and what constitutes errors. Therefore, it is important to include the person-dependent and subjective process that shapes individuals' engagement in and performance at work.

Performance and Errors at Work: The Personal Dimension

The socially-derived accounts advanced above offer a perspective of workplace performance and bases for what constitutes errors at work: that of the social world beyond the individual. It is often this view that is accepted as being the most important, because of the observable bases of performance and errors at work. As noted above, it is on these bases that judgements of performance and failings are most based; individuals either perform or fail to perform the requirements of particular work at particular points in time. These judgements have consequences for individuals in terms of their employability, advancement, etc. As noted, depending on how these errors are treated (i.e. tolerated or otherwise), the potential for support for learning from these situations can be weaker or stronger (Gartmeier, Bauer, Gruber, & Heid, 2008). Yet, there is also a personal dimension for performance and what constitutes errors that it is important to consider, particularly because of its impact upon learning.

Ultimately, work is something exercised by individuals and is premised on their capacities, interests, perspectives and agency: that is, how individuals perform workplace activities and interactions. It is individuals who engage in work, make sense of what is required, and deploy their capacities in workplace participation and, in doing so, make either acceptable or incorrect judgements about how they go about their work (Billett, 2009). Individuals do not bring to or engage in work tasks with a uniform base of experience, knowledge, and ways of knowing or engaging in work. Instead, they have diverse and personally distinct bases for conceptualising and construing what they experience in the workplace (Billett, 2003; Valsiner, 2000), and in deciding what task and approach is the most appropriate. These personally distinct bases for engaging in work arise through individuals' development across the life history or ontogeny. That is, how they come to construal and construct what they experience and then act upon that product of their personal history. From engaging in particular sets of experiences in educational and workplace settings, they have learnt and continued to learn through the ongoing and everyday problem-solving processes that were outlined above.

As advanced above, the very process of human learning is a process of encountering experiences and requests that warrant a response (i.e. a problem solution). Through these, individuals develop a repertoire of knowledge which has at least conceptual, procedural and dispositional dimensions. Much of what this process of learning comprised is the making of mistakes (i.e. incomplete, partial or erroneous responses) and learning from them even incrementally or transformationally. Yet, the importance of the concept of ontogeny is that individuals have socially derived and personally unique sets of experiences from which they construal and construct their knowledge. However, while being shaped by the socially derived experience, the immediate social world does not determine what individuals' construal and construct, come to know or act (Valsiner, 2000). Instead, each of these experiences is comprised of negotiation between the cognitive experience of the individual and what they encounter in the social and brute world beyond them. These negotiations are those between personal and social factors, and ultimately shape individuals' learning and development. For instance, in the study of hairdressers mentioned above (Billett, 2003), in each of the hairdressing salons there was a particular approach which was adopted for these workplaces. These set of norms and practices might be described as the 'culture of practice' (Brown, Collins, & Duguid, 1989), the rules, norms and practices that are accepted in that workplace. These were important factors in how the apprentices and hairdressers went about their work. There were, for instance, preferred kinds of hairdressing styles and approaches in each of the salons. Nevertheless, as noted, within the scope of discretion which these hairdressers had, which was quite considerable in even the most controlled environments, these hairdressers were able to exercise their personal preferences in styling hair. At a range of points along the process of understanding their clients' needs, suggesting a particular style of haircut and enacting that haircut, they were a range of opportunities for the individual preferences of the hairdresser to be enacted.

Explanations provided from cognitive perspective account for these differences by elaborating the bases by which engagement in tasks shapes the cognitive process and outcomes (Anderson, 1982, 1993). There are also likely to be quite diverse conceptions by individuals of what constitutes work practice across different kinds and categories of workers. It is this very negotiation which constitutes decisions that individuals make when confronting a work task. That is, their engagement with that task is based upon how they conceptualise it, value it and think about it. These are intensely personal processes that arise through their ontogenetic development (i.e. learning across life history). Consequently, how individuals conceptualise a particular task is based upon their existing understandings (i.e. conceptual knowledge), and also their procedures capacities, which are both directed by their dispositions (i.e. values, interests). Most likely, matters that are central to an individual's interests will be those that they will engage most actively and potentially most fully. However, these very interests suggest that, when confronted with a series of options or alternatives, individuals may well take those which they believe to be the most effective, those they prefer or those with which they are most competent. In this way, the enactment of work tasks is very much subject to the personally-based decision making of those who enact those tasks. Hence, there may be conflict between the preferences of individuals and those of the workplace. For instance, Hodges (Hodges, 1998) reported that there was a conflict between how she felt children should be cared for in early childhood educational settings, and the requirements of those who organised and regulated those settings, and the educational programs that prepare people for early childhood work. This conflict led her to leave that workplace. Elsewhere, there are instances of differences of standards of performance between those who work and those who manage and own workplaces.

In this way, the personal preference of the individual can be highly influential of what constitutes an error and the consequences of it. For instance, if the individuals are in a position of power (i.e. supervisors, employers or owners) their view of what constitutes an error will often be privileged over those of the individual who is being supervised, an employee or someone contracted in some way to provide a service. This personally subjective account of what constitutes workplace performance, and, therefore, error, is central to not only judgement about what constitutes an error at work but also whether that error can be the basis for developmental opportunity or chastisement. Again, this subjective conception of errors likely plays out in personally relational ways. If, for instance, what is perceived by a more expert partner as being an error is also accepted by the individual who performed it as also being an error, then there may well be an easier process of acknowledging and responding to that error, than when the performer or the observer disagree on whether an error has occurred. There are quite likely to be distinct outcomes across these situations. When an individual concedes they have made a mistake and wishes to direct efforts to improve their performance, and then are assisted in such by somebody who they respect, then the opportunity for rich and collaborative development likely arises. However, if there is disagreement about whether it was an error that has actually occurred, the prospects for productive learning from that incident are likely to be more diminished. There is also the dispositional element which may drive an individual to seek to learn and improve their performance because they believe they have erred. Hence, taking the example of the footballer mentioned earlier, even if their performance is not taken by others to be an error, that individual might believe it to be the case because she did not achieve what was intended in kicking the football. Hence, she might seek to remedy or improve their performance through practice, seeking advice or coaching, all of which has occurred without there being an error, as a publicly defined failure in performance.

Therefore, it follows that what constitutes workplace performance and errors are likely to be person dependent. These considerations prompt caution in claims about being able to identify the objective qualities of workplace competence and what constitutes errors. Ultimately, individuals' subjective processes shape their participation in work activities and interactions. Moreover, so much of individuals' performance is premised on subjective measures, not measurable facts. Indeed, even the most seemingly objective instances of work performance are in part subjective.

For instance, in the clothing industry, a common task was 'rate setting' of clothing machinists performing specific operations. In many ways, this is emblematic of attempting to provide the objective account of what constitutes work. Methods personnel measure the time it takes a machinist to perform a sewing task, and this time is used to set a rate for the job, and possible bonuses for working more quickly. When being timed, machinists attempt to secure a generous time allowance for the operation, to secure a bonus. The standard approach is to work slowly when being timed, whilst giving the appearance of working at normal speed. The methods officer, of course, knows this and attempts to calculate at what level of potential performance the machinist is working. The machinist also knows how the methods officer operates and appears to be working very quickly, while foxing on the speed of task completion. The methods officer also knows that the machinist knows this to be case, and so it goes on. Ultimately, this 'objective' process of timing an operation is reduced to a judgement on the part of the rate setter. The point here is that the conduct of work is premised on work being enacted by individuals, and that conduct includes their experience, capabilities and intentions, and also the judgement of the observer. So, even in a situation when a deliberate process is being enacted in order to capture the objective character and qualities of work, it needs to be mediated between the observer and the actor. The actual performance of work is ultimately a subjective process. (Billett, 2009)

The point here is that much, perhaps most, work performance ultimately comprises a subjective judgement about performance, which may or may not be proven 'wrong', if in some way it was possible to prove it right or wrong. Yet, it would be wrong to views errors as wholly subjective events. Clearly, there are abrogations of the requirements of work activities and occupational performance that are wrong and potentially inexcusable. There are mistakes that have profound implications for those affected by them. And, of course, there are many ways of appraising work performance, and some are claimed to be measurable. So, there are both objective measures and subjective accounts of what constitutes errors, and rather than being wholly separable, the relationships between them.

Relational Basis for Understanding What Constitutes Errors at Work and Human Fallibility

What has been proposed above is that what constitutes workplace performance and, importantly, errors are often not objectively ascertainable. Mistakes and human fallibility are inevitable, yet what actually comprises a mistake and human fallibility is often constituted relationally between the circumstances and the action, and by decisions and judgments by actors not the least being those who perform those activities. Certainly, there are norms and practices that are known about and when violated an individual is deemed to be in error. But there will also be judgments about what is the source of that error. In all, it is suggested that consideration of what constitutes errors has situational, personal and cultural dimensions, and relationships among them.

Situational

There are clear situational requirements for performance, which means that what constitutes performance and errors will be premised upon the particular situation in which the response occurs. What will be seen as an elegant solution in one situation may be seen as being disastrous and inappropriate in another. Hence, what constitutes an error is subject to situational factors and judgments.

Cultural

There is also a cultural basis to what constitutes an error. Cultural practices, such as the occupations in which the majority of adults are engaged, have particular norms and practices. These are central to the performance of that practice and what constitutes an error. Hence, while sharing information with colleagues might be seen to be a good workplace practice, if you are working with patients, students, clients, etc. then there are clear limits about the information that you can be sure about and the way in which that information is shared. Moreover, there are culturally appropriate practices to do with language, etiquette and values that shape performance, and the shortfalls in performance (i.e. errors).

Personal

Then, there is a personal dimension to performance and errors: how individuals go about their work, make judgments about that performance, and seek to change or extend their approaches and capacities.

Consequently, many mistakes are made in work and in workplaces that expose human fallibility only too frequently and consistently. Yet, what constitutes that fallibility has premises in and judgments about it that exist not only at the level of observable performance but also from a personal perspective. The latter is particularly important when considering learning from errors because learning is a personal process. It is something that people do, albeit mediated by the social world. Therefore, if learning is to arise productively from errors, it is important that processes that support learning from errors need to account for both personal and social factors, and the relationships between them. In the brief concluding section, learning from and through errors is explained through the dualities of personal engagement and workplace affordances. Also, some suggestions for further inquiry are advanced.

Learning from and Through Errors at Work

To provide an explanation about the processes of and potential for learning from and through errors at work, the concept of relational interdependencies (Billett, 2003) is adopted to account for both personal and social (i.e. situational and cultural) factors.

In particular, this concept refers to the interdependence of both social and personal factors in learning, yet the relationship between these factors is not fixed, it is something negotiated between them. Here, the dualities of workplace affordances and individual engagement are used to consider these processes of learning from and through errors at work.

Workplaces Affordances

Workplace affordances refer to the degree to which workplaces invite individuals to engage in work activities, and learn from them. These invitational qualities include the kinds of activities individuals are able to engage in and the support they are provided in those activities and, therefore, the access to potentially rich learning experiences. Yet, the invitational qualities can be either high or low, depending on the activities and interactions afforded by the workplace. They can also be intentionally supportive of learning or can inhibit productive learning. For instance, Filliettaz, de Saint-Georges, and Duc (2010) indicate how apprentices' perceived errors (i.e. being unable to complete demonstrated tasks) in their workplaces are sometimes treated with ridicule and intolerance, and the support for productive learning is limited. Ultimately, these apprentices can become more confused and anxious, and seemingly error-prone. So, in this environment, errors are seen as a basis to stigmatise and humiliate, and it is not surprising that the apprentice attempts to conceal difficulties with his work and only seek advice from co-workers as a last resort. Alternatively, there are instances where workplaces are tolerant of mistakes and use these to support learning.

Indeed, Bauer and Drechsel (2010) note that such is the quality of workplace environment that some workers will try and cover up for their mistakes and not advise others that they have made an error. Moreover, these individuals have learnt that errors are not tolerated and drawing attention to them is not advisable. It follows that the degree to which workplaces afford opportunities for learning from mistakes will likely shape their potential as learning experiences. That is, at best, opportunities for reflection, discussion about errors and then, if required, support and guidance are likely to develop the capacities to avoid that error again and so provide rich learning outcomes. As noted, many and perhaps most workplaces offer another kind of affordance: that of only inviting those individuals to perform tasks of which they have the capacities to engage in reasonably mature approximations and not place them in a situation in which they may make catastrophic errors. For instance, in addition to being given work tasks that were aimed to progressively develop my capacity as a pattern maker, I spent about 3 months working in the production line (i.e. sitting on a sewing machine, performing standard production tasks), progressing through the trouser, vest and jacket plants so that I came to understand and could perform all the operations that were used to make the garments from the patterns I would make. Hence, a process of gradual engagement in activities that are increasingly demanding, and knowing the familiarity of the worker with these activities, comprise one of the classical models of apprenticeship (Gott, 1989).

So, for me, this was a highly invitational workplace, perhaps because I was a salaried staff member. Certainly, it is unlikely that a commencing storeperson, cutter or machinist would have been granted such affordances. On the other hand, it was important for my work performance to be provided with such experiences as my errors could be extremely expensive.

It follows, therefore, that, depending on the workplace's affordances, individuals will be either guarded against error making in a productive and learning-centred way, and guided to learn from any errors as they arise, or potentially be stigmatised and humiliated. Clearly, the avoidance of errors through effective preparation, orientations and even clear and helpful explanations would be a feature of a workplace that is properly managed. The degree of tolerance to errors is likely to be premised on their impact on work and the time taken by others or the novice to remedy them. Certainly, it would be mistaken to idealise the outcomes of errors and their apportionment as workplaces are far from benign environments, and the contestations that comprise so much of workplace relationships and the exercise of power within them can determine what constitutes an error and the opportunities for productive learning. However, for productive outcomes to arise from errors that have deleterious impacts on the goods and services in the workplace, these impacts can be used to further develop the capacities of those whose mistakes led to them in the first place, thus leading to their understanding something of what were the inadequacies of the task, the consequences and how they might be avoided. Moreover, and where appropriate, such mistakes might be used as instances for others to learn from. For instance, as often with safety issues and violations of safe working practice, instances can be used in discussion to understand what occurred, how it could be avoided and where else similar errors could arise.

Consequently, it is important to understand further about the ways in which the different kinds of workplace affordances assist or inhibit productive learning arising from errors. Investigations are required that would likely need to account for the relationships among the kinds of errors made, by whom, and how workplaces respond to them.

Personal Bases

Beyond the degree to which workplace affordances are supportive of learning through errors, it is important how individuals take up what is afforded directly or indirectly by the workplace. Central here is the degree to which individuals engage in the process of learning from what they or others perceive to be errors. Given that constructing new knowledge, its organisation and utilisation is likely to be effortful, the degree of effort individuals direct towards learning (i.e. their intentionality) as a result of what they or others perceive to be errors is central to the learning that arises through their engagement. This engagement also includes the degree to which they elect or are able to engage with others (e.g. more expert partners) to further develop their capacities. Doubtless, learning will arise, as it is not separable from thinking and acting. However, the important point is what learning arises. Individual personal ruminations may be quite unproductive, e.g. leading to unhelpful and restrictive personal criticisms, and that might limit further opportunities. Alternatively, considered and intentional personally based learning might be quite powerful and even emanicipatory. However, as stated, because what constitutes errors is socially shaped, and much of the knowledge required to learn from them is socially driven, the willingness for individuals to engage with social partners or social forms (e.g. texts, etc.) is likely to be important to their construction of knowledge. So, beyond the engaging in personally based learning is how individuals elect, and are permitted, to learn from errors. Moreover, whatever learning arises from errors will be mediated by personal construals and constructions.

Hence, we need to understand more about the ways in which personal epistemologies shape individuals' learning through errors, and in particular how best that learning can be directed in productive rather than in unproductive directions.

References

Anderson, J. R. (1982). Acquisition of cognitive skill. *Psychological Review, 89*, 369–406.

Anderson, J. R. (1993). Problem solving and learning. *American Psychologist, 48*, 35–44.

Bauer, J., & Drechsel, B. (2010). *Types of engagement in learning from errors at work – A person-centered view.* Paper presented at the 91st AERA annual meeting, Denver.

Bauer, J., & Mulder, R. H. (2007). Modelling learning from errors in daily work. *Learning in Health and Social Care, 6*, 121–133.

Bernhardt, A. (1999, March). *The future of low-wage jobs: Case studies in the retail industry* (Institute on Education and the Economy Working Paper 10). Teaching College, Columbia University.

Billett, S. (2001). Knowing in practice: Re-conceptualising vocational expertise. *Learning and Instruction, 11*, 431–452.

Billett, S. (2003). Sociogeneses, activity and ontogeny. *Culture and Psychology, 9*, 133–169.

Billett, S. (2009). Workplace competence. In C. R. Velde (Ed.), *International perspectives on competence in the workplace: Implications for research, policy and practice* (pp. 33–54). Dordrecht, the Netherlands: Springer.

Brown, J. S., Collins, A., & Duguid, P. (1989). Situated cognition and the culture of learning. *Educational Researcher, 18*(1), 32–34.

Collins, A., Brown, J. S., & Newman, S. E. (1989). Cognitive apprenticeship: Teaching the crafts of reading, writing, and mathematics. In L. B. Resnick (Ed.), *Knowing, learning and instruction* (pp. 453–494). Hillsdale, NJ: LEA.

Darrah, C. N. (1996). *Learning and work: An exploration in industrial ethnography.* New York: Garland Publishing.

Darrah, C. N. (1997). Complicating the concept of skill requirements: Scenes from a workplace. In G. Hull (Ed.), *Changing work, changing workers: Critical perspectives on language, literacy and skills* (pp. 249–272). New York: CUNY Press.

Ellstrom, P. E. (1998). The meaning of occupational competence and qualification. In W. J. Nijhof & J. N. Streumer (Eds.), *Key qualifications in work and education* (pp. 39–50). Dordrecht, the Netherlands: Kluwer Academic Publishers.

Ericsson, K. A. (2006). The influence of experience and deliberate practice on the development of superior expert performance. In K. A. Ericsson, N. Charness, P. J. Feltovich, & R. R. Hoffman (Eds.), *The Cambridge handbook of expertise and expert performance* (pp. 683–703). Cambridge, UK: Cambridge University Press.

Filliettaz, L., de Saint-Georges, I., & Duc, B. (2010). Skiing, cheese fondue and Swiss watches: Analogical discourse in vocational training interactions. *Vocations and Learning, 3*, 117–140.

Gartmeier, M., Bauer, J., Gruber, H., & Heid, H. (2008). Negative knowledge: Understanding professional learning and expertise. *Vocations and Learning: Studies in Professional and Vocational Learning, 1*, 87–103.

Gott, S. (1989). Apprenticeship instruction for real-world tasks: The co-ordination of procedures, mental models, and strategies. *Review of Research in Education, 15*, 97–169.

Hodges, D. C. (1998). Participation as dis-identification with/in a community of practice. *Mind, Culture and Activity, 5*, 272–290.

Lave, J. (1990). The culture of acquisition and the practice of understanding. In J. W. Stigler, R. A. Shweder, & G. Herdt (Eds.), *Cultural psychology* (pp. 259–286). Cambridge, UK: Cambridge University Press.

Martin, L. M. W., & Scribner, S. (1991). Laboratory for cognitive studies of work: A case study of the intellectual implications of a new technology. *Teachers College Record, 92*, 582–602.

Searle, J. R. (1995). *The construction of social reality*. London: Penguin.

Valsiner, J. (2000). *Culture and human development*. London: Sage.

Chapter 3
Tracing Outcomes of Learning from Errors on the Level of Knowledge

Martin Gartmeier and Elke M. Schüttelkopf

Introduction

At most weddings, a professional photographer is hired to capture the celebratory moments of the carefully planned and long awaited event. Especially during the church ceremony, it is crucial that some moments are shot nicely, e.g., when the bride and groom exchange the wedding rings. This means that the photographer mostly operates very close to the bridal couple and is therefore inside the area on which the attention of the whole wedding party is centred. For this reason, the photographer's dress needs to be somewhat festive during such an occasion. Inexperienced photographers often make typical mistakes when dressing to shoot a marriage. Firstly, it is important to wear clothes that are not hindering in terms of freedom of movement: the photographer may have to kneel down or climb onto a small stool in order to quickly bring the camera into promising positions and angles. Thereby, a long or rather tight skirt is very disadvantageous. In addition, slippery or high-heeled shoes are a 'no go'. Secondly, a photographer exhibiting underwear in front of a wedding party when kneeling down around the bridal couple to get a good shot is disturbing for a wedding ceremony. Therefore, the photographer should take care not to wear too tight or too short clothes which tend to slip easily.[1]

Imagine an inexperienced photographer making one of the above-described 'rookie mistakes' when shooting a wedding. When the photographer hears about the

[1] This example is a summary of an informal conversation between the first author of this chapter and a professional photographer.

M. Gartmeier, Ph.D. (✉)
TUM School of Education, Munich, Germany
e-mail: martin.gartmeier@tum.de

E.M. Schüttelkopf, Mag. M.Sc. MBA
Elke Schüttelkopf Consulting, Vienna, Austria
e-mail: elke.m.schuettelkopf@fehlerkultur.at

J. Bauer and C. Harteis (eds.), *Human Fallibility: The Ambiguity of Errors for Work and Learning*, Professional and Practice-based Learning 6,
DOI 10.1007/978-90-481-3941-5_3, © Springer Science+Business Media Dordrecht 2012

error—maybe through a subsequent complaint by the client—it is too late to do something about what happened. The situation has already passed; it can only be hoped that the mistake has no further harmful effects. A proximate question is: Why should precious time and energy be invested in pondering an event which itself is already over? This question is even more salient, as thinking about one's own errors may be time consuming and possibly connected with unpleasant insights into one's own fallibility.

The obvious—albeit not trivial—answer to this question is as follows: The primary motivation to concern oneself with one's own errors is to improve skills and knowledge in ways which allow for the future avoidance of the same or of similar errors (Barach & Small, 2000). With regard to research on learning from errors, this chapter argues that it is important to focus more strongly on the outcomes brought about by error-related learning. Thus, the first assumption of this chapter is as follows:

(i) *Researching outcomes of error-related learning is a sensible and necessary, but hitherto widely neglected, perspective.*

Drawing upon educational theorisation, the example discussed above can basically be described as a glimpse into a photographer's experiential knowledge (Waibel, 2002). Various contributions to the ongoing discourse around workplace learning (Billett, 2001a, 2001b; Boud & Gerrick, 1999; Gruber & Palonen, 2007; Harteis & Billett, 2008; Smith, 2003; Stenström & Tynjälä, 2009) have conceptualised employees' experiential knowledge as an important source of their professional competence (e.g., Eraut, 2000). As will be shown in this chapter, various interrelationships between the experience of errors and experiential knowledge are plausible: Experiential knowledge may result from error-related learning and may be a helpful basis for not repeating errors. Moreover, existing experiential knowledge may also influence any future (error-related) learning processes.

One interesting aspect about the initial example is that it involves rather specific recommendations about how a photographer should *not* dress while shooting a wedding ceremony. These may be very valuable for a professional photographer, because they pinpoint certain mistakes and hence allow for their purposeful avoidance. This assumption relates to the concept of negative knowledge (Gartmeier, Bauer, Gruber, & Heid, 2008; Minsky, 1994; Oser & Spychiger, 2005; Parviainen & Eriksson, 2006). Negative knowledge is focused on what not to do in a certain situation, on what assumptions are wrong with regard to a certain problem or on limitations in one's own or somebody else's skills or knowledge. As will be shown here, this concept offers a promising way to conceptualise and research outcomes of error-related learning. This point foreshadows the present chapter's second key assumption:

(ii) *The theory of negative knowledge represents a promising perspective for researching outcomes of error-related learning.*

A critical issue related to negative knowledge can again be exemplified by drawing upon the initial example: A photographer may become aware about how *not* to dress when shooting a wedding. However, this insight may leave open the question of which clothes to actually choose when doing so. In other words, negative knowledge may be helpful for avoiding mistakes. In some situations, however, it may provide little information about how to actually solve a given problem. This has conceptual and methodological consequences which future studies on knowledge as an outcome of error-related learning should consider: Two main points are, firstly, to pay attention to the embeddedness of negative knowledge in more general structures of experiential knowledge, and secondly, to use research methods which allow for obtaining more information on the process of constructing knowledge from an encountered (error) episode. This relates to the third point this chapter seeks to make:

(iii) *Future studies on knowledge as an outcome of error-related learning processes should seek to shed light on the embeddedness of negative knowledge in structures of experiential knowledge.*

The present chapter's line of argument follows the three key points advanced in this introductory section. In addressing some 'blind spots' of existing research on learning from errors, we outline the need to put a stronger focus on researching its outcomes in general. We will introduce the theory of negative knowledge as a recent theoretical approach engaging in this perspective, and outline challenges for research on this issue. In this way, we draw conclusions on future inquiries concerning negative knowledge as an outcome of learning from errors.

Processes, Prerequisites and Outcomes of Learning from Errors

A body of literature has evolved over the past years which focuses on the investigation of learning from errors in professional contexts (for an overview, see Bauer & Mulder, 2008). These works share the basic conjecture that errors at work, although being adverse events, bear significant potential for professional learning and innovation. Beyond their agreement upon this basic assumption, we argue that scholars have hitherto mainly analysed error-related learning processes from two different perspectives, focusing on prerequisites of such learning as well as on the learning process itself:

(1) The initiation and success of error-related learning processes depend upon individual and social variables, which can hence be regarded as prerequisites of such learning (Bauer, 2008). Individual-level variables assumed to influence how employees cope with occurring errors were introduced by Rybowiak, Garst, Frese, and Batinic (1999). Under the label *error-orientation*, the authors focus on different individual beliefs related to errors at work. Error-competence, for example, addresses the extent to which individuals believe in being able to cope with errors they are faced with at their workplace. Another facet, error-anticipation, addresses employees' expectation that errors will happen from time to time. One central assumption pursued by Rybowiak et al. is that

individuals who are persuaded of their ability to resolve upcoming problems or to thereby learn important things will more likely be able to cope effectively with error situations. In terms of sociocultural prerequisites for learning from errors, Edmondson (2004) has found team climate variables, namely the degree to which errors are openly discussed in a work-group, to be influential for employees' ability to identify and resolve mistakes and problems at work.

(2) In addition to these prerequisites, researchers have focused on error-related learning processes, which may involve both individual and social activities. Authors adopting this perspective research the efficacy of different activities in which individuals engage after an error at work has happened. Typical goals of such activities are cause analysis and the development of alternative action strategies (Bauer & Mulder, 2008). Therefore, reflective activities in particular have been identified as crucial (Van Woerkom, 2003). Due to the fact that errors at work are frequently described as potentially hazardous and hence stressful events (Perrow, 1984), activities taken up after an error has occurred might furthermore range from intentional ignorance to covering up errors (Rybowiak et al., 1999). On the social level, different error-related learning activities were described by Bauer and Mulder (2007), including the exchange of experiences, seeking advice from more experienced colleagues or root cause analysis in conversation with the supervisor.

Both introduced perspectives are important for understanding error-related learning processes at work. However, they still only provide an incomplete picture of the phenomenon. We hypothesise a third research perspective to be crucial: the perspective of outcomes of error-related learning processes, especially those occurring at the cognitive level.

What Can Be Learnt from Errors? Existing Results and Open Questions

The importance of the outcome-perspective can be substantiated in two different ways: firstly, in terms of its value for better explaining the results of existing studies, and secondly, through its potential for closing gaps in existing research on learning from errors.

Outcomes of learning from errors are traced in two recent studies. In a cross-sectional study conducted in two European countries, organisational error-management culture was found to be positively interrelated with performance measures of the organisations under investigation (Van Dyck, Frese, Baer, & Sonnentag, 2005). To explain these results, the authors argue that a more error-friendly organisational culture may, e.g., foster error-related communication, experimentation and innovativeness—all of which are plausible facilitative factors with regard to company performance. However, the "quantitative findings do not reveal the precise mechanisms by which error management culture translates into better performance" (Van Dyck et al., 2005, p. 1237).

In the latter respect, another study is interesting, as it investigated the effects of an innovative approach to skills training. In *error management training* (Frese et al., 1991), trainees autonomously work on challenging tasks—which makes the frequent occurrence of errors during the training process probable. In order to improve the trainees' skills for coping with errors and to prevent frustration, the trainees are instructed in how to learn from errors. Moreover, they are informed about the positive effects that making errors and learning from them may have on the learning processes as a whole (Keith & Frese, 2008). Different studies show that error management training—in certain respects—leads to better training outcomes than error-avoidance training (e.g., Chillarege, Nordstrom, & Williams, 2003; Nordstrom, Wendland, & Williams, 1998). For the heuristic task at hand, the most relevant study on error-management training (Keith & Frese, 2005) investigates psychological mechanisms responsible for its superiority compared to error-avoidance training. Error management training positively influences participants' emotional control, as well as their metacognitive skills. Both of these self-regulatory processes were shown to be significantly related to training outcomes.

In the reported studies' results, the different conclusions are similar: Not only does learning from errors have a significant impact on performance measures, both on the individual and on higher-order levels, but these effects can also be traced according to the level of individuals' cognitive processes, offering a plausible explanation for improvements in performance.

The reported results on self-regulatory mechanisms do not provide a sufficient explanation for how individuals profit from error-related learning. We argue that knowledge concepts have an increased explanatory power in this respect. To substantiate this claim, we subsequently outline three different challenges for research on learning from errors which make the necessity to trace its outcomes on the level of knowledge plausible. Engaging in this perspective allows for explaining employees' ability to anticipate errors, shedding light on how lessons learned from errors are transferred into future practice, and researching potentially counter-productive effects of learning from errors.

Knowledge-Based Error Anticipation

Research on learning from errors mainly focuses on employees' reactions to errors which have occurred in their professional practice. Von Weizsäcker and von Weizsäcker (1984) state that the handling of episodes which deviate from the usual course of things is not limited to just reacting to errors taking place. Beyond that, knowledge about possible errors can play an important role when making up plans about how to solve a task at hand. Similarly, Rybowiak et al. (1999) argue that the ability of employees to anticipate errors is an important cornerstone of their performance. If errors are anticipated, they may be avoided entirely or better coped with when they do occur. Different explanations may account for an employee recognising an error's leading signs, having a gut feeling or other ways of anticipating errors. One proximate approach is that earlier, error-related learning experiences have given an employee the opportunity to construct knowledge which entails experience-based error anticipation. This has two important consequences.

Firstly, from this perspective, anticipated errors can also be opportunities for learning from errors. It is an open question in which way the processes and surrounding conditions are different in the case of learning through error-anticipation. However, it can be said that here, thorough reflection and proactive planning of problem-solving strategies, and especially their limitations, there seem to be crucial prerequisites for identifying possible error-sources and for acting accordingly. In this respect, it is especially interesting to focus on proactive behaviours such as personal initiative (Frese & Fay, 2001), as these aim at tackling errors and problems before they occur and have a negative impact.

Secondly, it seems plausible that error-anticipation strongly depends upon an employee having had earlier error-related learning experiences. These may allow for the construction of specialised knowledge which, e.g., entails an employee's raised awareness about situations that bear a high risk of errors taking place. Yet, it is not understood that learning from errors fosters an individual's error-anticipative capacity. In this respect, the next point might be significant.

Transfer of Lessons Learned from Errors

As mentioned above, the interest of educational researchers in learning from errors currently focuses strongly on actions and action strategies carried out after an error has occurred, as well as on relevant surrounding conditions. As a legitimation of this interest, scholars assume that learning from errors entails valuable results which positively influence the competence of professionals or the design of work processes (Edmondson, 2004; Hofmann & Stetzer, 1998). From this point of view, research on learning from errors mainly focuses on actions or action strategies taken up after an error has occurred, but draws its legitimacy from the long-term beneficial effects of such learning.

The latter, in turn, has not yet been thoroughly studied in research on learning from errors. Doing so would mean focusing on results of learning from errors, which go beyond things like the mere correction of the error or the removal of possible damage induced by the incident. Questions relating to this perspective are what results learning from errors yields and how these are transferred to other situations. Key concepts in research on transfer are near versus far, as well as positive versus negative transfer (Yamnill & McLean, 2001). With regard to the quality of error-related learning processes, a possibly interesting measure could be whether resulting learning outcomes can only be transferred to very similar situations or if far transfer is also possible, because, e.g., a thorough analysis leads to deeper insights into an error's genealogy. Focusing on the positive/negative distinction, it might be asked whether certain error-related learning experiences, e.g., being assigned blame for an error one does not feel responsible for, impede learning from other, similar situations—this would be a case of negative transfer. This aspect is also discussed below.

Counter-Productivity of the Results of Learning from Errors

On the one hand, researchers draw upon the assumption that learning from errors contributes to improving employees' competence and companies' productivity. On the other hand, scholars have argued that certain lessons may be learned from errors which—from the perspective of personal and organisational development—have to be described as being adverse: Error-related experiences may lead to employees showing defensive behaviour, like covering up errors or avoiding the development of innovative problem-solving strategies (Rybowiak et al., 1999; Van Dyck et al., 2005). Other, different approaches are also relevant at this point: firstly, the concept of *defensive routines* (Argyris, 1986a). This concept focuses organisational habits which aim at the avoidance of critical and open discourses and which are counter-productive with regard to innovation and organisational learning. Secondly, the idea of employees' showing 'skilled incompetence' (Argyris, 1986b; Holmer, 2001) assumes that skills and knowledge can also be used for achieving undesirable or counterproductive learning outcomes. One such outcome of learning from errors may be knowledge about how best to cover up one's own mistakes or to embellish inadequate work results successfully. The described concepts relate to what Schüttelkopf (2008) conceptualises as *regressive*—as opposed to *progressive*—learning from errors. A case of regressive learning from errors would occur when employees decide to reduce or withdraw their participation in situations which they perceive as being error critical, e.g., team meetings or open discussions with supervisors. In contrast, the idea of progressive learning from errors focuses on innovative strategies of error-avoidance, e.g., an active search for better problem-solving approaches or a purposeful modification of existing work processes.

The points made in this section can be regarded as challenges for research on learning from errors. In order to meet these challenges, we argue that it is promising to focus the outcomes of error-related learning on the level of individuals' knowledge. By means of knowledge concepts, employees' ability to anticipate errors can be explained. Moreover, knowledge can be transferred and applied to similar situations and may be used in ways which are not in line with a company's 'official' policies. With regard to the goal of better understanding outcomes of learning from errors on the level of knowledge, the aforementioned theory of negative knowledge is interesting. This theoretical approach will be illustrated more fully in the next section.

Negative Knowledge as an Outcome of Learning from Errors

From the initial episodic example in the photography context, a recommendation can be drawn which seems valuable for a professional photographer: *When shooting a wedding, avoid wearing clothes that overly hinder your movements or that tend to slip unwantedly!* This is a typical example of negative knowledge (Gartmeier et al., 2008; Minsky, 1994; Oser & Spychiger, 2005; Parviainen & Eriksson, 2006). Theoretical and empirical evidence suggest the plausibility of assuming negative knowledge to be an outcome of experiencing and learning from errors. Below, we will delineate the theoretical background of this concept. On this basis, some limitations of the approach will be discussed and used to develop perspectives for future research.

Theoretical Conception

Drawing upon existing approaches, the following, workplace-specific definition of negative knowledge is proposed:

> Negative knowledge is context- and task-specific experiential knowledge which contains insights into assumptions which are wrong, but tend to be considered right. Typically, negative knowledge is acquired through experiencing and learning from (others' or own) workplace errors, because such learning reveals wrong assumptions being pursued. As it comprises insights into instances and causes of bad practice, the relevance of negative knowledge lies in assisting an actor in developing better practices and thereby avoiding error repetition.

This definition integrates existing conceptions of negative knowledge which will be introduced below. In particular, we focus Oser's (1996) work in the context of moral education and Minsky's (1994) ideas on negative expertise used.

With his concept of negative moral knowledge, Oser (1996) pursues the assumption that a person's experience and knowledge about immoral behaviour, for example about stealing, can play an important role in the future prevention of this behaviour. This is because knowledge about what not to do may serve as a contrastive element to the 'right' behaviour. In other words, *knowledge* about what should not be done is conceptualised as an outcome of actually *doing* something wrong and experiencing unpleasant consequences. For example, imagine a child stealing something and being caught by his or her parents: The subsequent lecture the parents give makes the child feel guilty and ashamed about the wrongdoing. In the concept of negative moral knowledge, such a negative experience as a consequence of wrong behaviour is hypothesised to possess an emotionally impressive momentum which is a crucial aspect of the intention not to repeat the experience. In that sense, the statement 'You shall not steal!' may on its own not be a very effective imperative. However, it gains a higher level of relevance if understood as an essential part of the establishment of moral categories like 'right' and 'wrong' through processes of experiential learning.

Pursuing a similar idea, Minsky (1994) states that experts in a professional field "must know both how to achieve goals and how to avoid disasters" (p. 13). It is assumed that—besides taking positive measures—the primary way to avoid accidents is by avoiding actions that are known to cause trouble. Minsky makes two main points: firstly, a negative way to conceptualise expertise is to regard experts as persons who are able to deliberately avoid errors, and secondly, one plausible prerequisite of this ability is experts' negative knowledge. According to Minsky, negative knowledge can be conceived as a metacognitive resource helping to monitor action at work by reminding the actor of what to avoid. To further illustrate the concept of negative knowledge, we will briefly sketch how its acquisition, cognitive representation and application are conceptualised.

Acquisition of Negative Knowledge

Although educational settings can teach what should be avoided in the performance of a task, personal experience is potentially more powerful in the acquisition of negative knowledge (Oser & Spychiger, 2005). Hence, negative knowledge is basically a special form of experiential knowledge that is acquired through processes of learning from experience (Kolb, 1984). An experience may serve as a starting point for the acquisition of negative knowledge, especially in cases which raise an actor's awareness of having wrong assumptions or applying wrong strategies for solving a problem at hand. Typically, errors at work are seen as experiences that meet this description (Gartmeier et al., 2008). Errors are conceptualised as a category of adverse events that produce "stress, accidents, inefficient human-machine interaction, quality and performance problems, and a bad climate" (Rybowiak et al., 1999, p. 528). Nevertheless, errors provide opportunities to reflect on their causes and thereby gain insights that may allow for the avoidance of similar errors in future practice. While conducting error-related learning activities, professionals may become aware of having inadequate conceptions, such as lacking particular problem-solving strategies (Bauer, 2008; van Woerkom, 2003). The results of such reflective processes contribute to building a body of negative knowledge about what should be avoided in a given class of work situations.

Representation of Negative Knowledge

The concept of negative knowledge can be subsumed under more general conceptions of knowledge representation typically used in research on experts' knowledge. In particular, script theories have been useful for modelling the representation of experts' action-oriented knowledge (Schank, 1999). Scripts are generalised action schemata which guide action in specific situations (e.g., the typical sequence of actions when visiting a restaurant) and which may comprise elements of declarative as well as procedural knowledge (Anderson & Lebiere, 1998). Scripts may change dynamically with the experience of new episodes. An important script modification practice is the integration of deviant episodes into existing scripts (Kolodner, 1983; Schank, 1999). Hence, learning from errors can be interpreted as a process of extending an existing script with instances where its application was unsuccessful, and with possible explanations for this deviance (Bauer, 2008). These extensions may assist professional action in future, similar situations by reminding the actor of the failed episode, possible explanations for the failure and alternative ways of acting. As has been suggested above, the idea of negative knowledge fits neatly into the theory of scripts as a more comprehensive framework to represent action-oriented knowledge. One could conceive of negative knowledge as represented in those parts of scripts that refer to conditions which would probably cause failures in task attainment.

Application of Negative Knowledge

Negative knowledge has a valuable problem-solving function in specific task situations because it reminds employees of potential error sources and is therefore valuable to avoid errors (Oser & Spychiger, 2005). The advantage of having negative knowledge may be summarised in the popular idiom 'forewarned is forearmed'. Being aware of what things can go wrong when working on a certain task is a plausible precondition for being able to purposefully avoid these errors (Oser & Spychiger, 2005). We assume that professionals in any given domain have a situation-specific repertoire of negative rules that makes them anticipate particular errors and is thus helpful for the avoidance of errors (Gartmeier et al., 2008; Kolodner, 1983; Minsky, 1994). Being aware of what actions are inappropriate in a given context is useful to ensure successful action, especially in situations that carry a fair chance of making errors or in which doing something wrong may result in serious consequences (Reason, 1990). This assumption is consistent with arguments from research on case-based reasoning showing that analogies from cases experienced earlier are helpful when it comes to mastering subsequent, similar situations (Kolodner, 1983). An example from the domain of chess illustrates the propositions made above: A chess rule of thumb says, 'A knight on the rim is grim.' This rule explicitly tells a player not to move a knight into a disadvantageous position where it has limited influence on the game. Although novice players may easily learn this rule, understanding its implications and the underlying rationale requires deeper insight into the game. Nevertheless, in representing an experienced player's knowledge, this simple formula may be helpful for inexperienced players as a guideline preventing them from getting into a disadvantageous position. In other words, in adhering to the exemplified rule and in seeking to understand the rationale behind it, a player is encouraged to anticipate possible negative consequences of a certain move.

This idea is also relevant for workplace contexts, because to "reduce disruptions, employees need to be able to sense problems and act proactively about them before they occur" (Baer & Frese, 2003, p. 46). The concept of negative knowledge offers a plausible explanation for this ability: Along with growing professional practice, an employee accumulates experience in handling errors. As the condensed result of such experiences, negative knowledge represents generalised guidelines for practice that make an employee aware of possible or, especially, typical errors for a particular task. Knowing what not to do in order to avoid such errors is an important precondition for acting in proactive and error-preventative ways.

We argue that negative knowledge provides a promising approach with regard to researching outcomes of error-related learning. Yet, researching employees' negative knowledge is a challenging task, especially due to two issues: firstly, the formal restrictedness of negative knowledge, and secondly, its primary focus on avoiding actions or disqualifying assumptions. These issues will be discussed below.

Challenges for Research on Negative Knowledge

To make the first point, it may sometimes be difficult to unambiguously identify negative knowledge in verbal data. For instance, the initially exemplified photographer could verbalise negative knowledge in stating, 'If you're dressing to shoot a wedding, take care not to wear unpractical clothes'. Yet, the photographer could also make the very same point in saying, e.g., 'If you're shooting a wedding, take care to wear clothes in which you can move easily'. The former exemplified statement would meet the definition of negative knowledge, whereas the latter would not.

This poses a challenge for research upon negative knowledge which is connected to the formal restrictedness of this concept. Firstly, participants in a study on negative knowledge might deliberately formulate certain statements in a negative way so that the relative importance of negative knowledge is overestimated. Secondly, it is possible that employees express knowledge which they see as being very relevant and helpful for avoiding errors and which is strongly connected to error experiences, but which does not meet the idea of negative knowledge, being focused on what is wrong. It has been argued that the negative knowledge approach provides a way to research the knowledge-based aspect of employees' error-avoidance capacity (Gartmeier et al., 2008). Yet, it can also be assumed that not all employees' error-related knowledge is necessarily negative knowledge. Future studies should hence seek to achieve a more complete picture of which type of knowledge employees use to avoid errors. Among other issues, this challenge will be addressed in the final section of the present chapter.

The second challenge for research on negative knowledge lies in this approach yielding a very plausible explanation for not acting incompetently, but offers no immediate explanation for competent behaviour.

Given the assumption that "the things we do not do far outnumber the things that we do" (Tykocinski & Pittman, 1998, p. 607), the value of negative knowledge might be estimated to be very high. This also ties in with other sources: Minsky (1994) assumes that a large part of expertise—as we can observe it, e.g., in the performance of an experienced professional—is actually negative expertise; i.e., the effect of cognitive agencies which deliberately focus on avoiding things like detours or inefficiencies, asking the wrong questions and making mistakes. Pursing a similar idea, Oser (1996) advances the hypothesis that half of aeroplane pilots' professional competence is built on negative knowledge because, "especially in situations of danger, the pilot alone must be able to perform without the slightest failure"

(Oser, 1996, p. 69). Interestingly, this quotation stresses the importance of negative knowledge, but at the same time highlights a limitation of the concept: In order to perform competently, problems have to be solved by actually *doing* the right things at the right time—not by avoiding actions. One aspect which many definitions of professionals' competence draw upon is their capacity to solve problems at work (Weinert, 2001); yet, the theory of negative knowledge offers only an indirect explanation of how problems are actually solved.

Here, the differentiation advanced above between regressive and progressive learning from errors (Schüttelkopf, 2008) comes into play: As was argued, negative knowledge is focused upon what *not* to do. Hence, such knowledge is useful as a basis for innovative behaviour only to the extent that it allows for avoiding errors which have occurred earlier. This means that the concept of negative knowledge provides an explanation for *regressive* learning from errors, i.e., for avoiding erroneous behaviour. Yet, it offers only an indirect explanation for *progressive* learning from errors, i.e., for using errors as starting points for the development of innovations. Entirely focusing upon the avoidance of problems does not tie in with the notion of modern work environments requesting employees to be dynamic and innovative, show personal initiative (Frese & Fay, 2001) and adapt quickly to workplace changes that occur (Bauer & Gruber, 2007). In such situations, doing nothing may even be the worst of all possible mistakes.

To sum up, it is our position that researching outcomes of learning from errors is worthwhile and that knowledge concepts provide a valuable basis for doing so. One open question is how future studies can research knowledge-based results of error-related learning and thereby deal with the challenges discussed above. This question will be discussed in the following section.

Researching Employees' Error-Related Knowledge: Conceptual and Methodological Conclusions

As the main difference between Einstein and an amoeba, Popper (1972) identifies Einstein's quality to purposefully strive for the avoidance of errors. In the present chapter, it has been argued that one resource which may be helpful for Einstein in his ambition to avoid errors is specialised knowledge resulting from experiencing and learning from errors. In this chapter's final section, we will firstly discuss the relationship between employees' experiential and negative knowledge. We will then draw conceptual conclusions which may be valuable for future studies on these issues.

Negative knowledge allows for avoiding actions which are known to yield poor outcomes (Gartmeier et al., 2008; Oser & Spychiger, 2005). Yet, to actually solve a problem, it may sometimes not suffice to have relevant negative knowledge. This may be the case for two reasons: After eliminating wrong ways to solve a given problem based on negative knowledge, either *several* plausible ways or *no* plausible problem-solving strategy may remain. We hence argue that it is important to research negative knowledge in its embeddedness in structures of error-related, experiential knowledge (Staw & Barsade, 1993).

This is plausible, as experiencing and learning from an error may allow an employee to gain insights into a large variety of aspects connected to the episode. Insights may be gained, e.g., into an error's enabling conditions and its immediate consequences within the work environment. Moreover, an employee may learn about things to be done to resolve the problem: own feelings or personal and social resources to cope with errors (Meurier, 2000). Briefly stated, errors can be eminently rich learning experiences; as incidents of failed practice, they are not merely opportunities to develop negative knowledge. Experiencing an error episode allows for the acquisition of a wider repertoire of very specific and differentiated experiential knowledge (Van Woerkom, 2003).

The importance of experiential knowledge as an outcome of error-related learning is apparent in the literature from different disciplines. For instance, a study conducted in the medical context raises the question of whether blogs are useful tools for improving the extent to which health care professionals collect and share medical error knowledge (Swain, 2007, p. 303). The quoted author does not further define or specify her theoretical reference point concerning knowledge. Yet, the concept of experiential knowledge is implicitly addressed in the cited contribution. It is hence in line with other studies that stress the organisational relevance of preserving employees' error-related, experiential knowledge (Barach & Small, 2000; Dovey & Phillips, 2004; Uribe, Schweikhart, Pathak, & Marsh, 2002).

The previously mentioned study on the effects of companies' error management culture (Van Dyck et al., 2005) is also relevant here. The authors argue that a positive error management culture "encompasses organisational practices related to communicating about errors, to sharing error knowledge, to helping in error situations, and to quickly detecting and handling errors" (Van Dyck et al., 2005, p. 1229). Speaking of *error knowledge*, the authors describe a form of knowledge which is informally shared and negotiated. This ties in well with established concepts of experiential knowledge: Such knowledge is formed during the process of performing the very actions for which it is helpful. Briefly stated, experiential knowledge is action-oriented knowledge structured in ways which are convenient for solving common problems at work (Gruber, 1999).

One central aspect of error episodes is that they are often experienced as being stressful and difficult (Bauer, 2008). This is an optimal precondition for the establishment of experiential knowledge: Scholars stress that such knowledge is often constructed from experiences which are personally meaningful and challenging (Kolb, 1984). An actor's experiential knowledge may incorporate information about the whole process of experiencing and learning from an error. In contrast, negative knowledge rather represents quintessences drawn from such a learning process—like in the initial photography example: The exemplified negative knowledge '*Don't wear too tight clothes when shooting a wedding*' is a general rule which could also appear in a practically oriented guidebook for professional photographers. Our assumption here is that experiential knowledge can have a descriptive, but also a rule-like, character, whereas negative knowledge most often has a rule-like, stronger quintessential character. For understanding why a (positive or negative) rule is relevant, it is necessary to gain insight into the contextual conditions under which it has been established or is applied. Hence, for fully understanding the relevance of negative knowledge, its embeddedness into structures of experiential knowledge needs to be researched.

We assume negative knowledge to be inextricably entangled within structures of experiential knowledge. In other words, negative knowledge represents an aspect of experiential knowledge which expresses a genuine characteristic of error-related learning, i.e., the effort to learn something in order to prevent the same (or reasonably similar) incidents from happening in the future.

From what has so far been advanced in this section, three conclusions for future studies on employees' knowledge as an outcome of learning from errors are put forward: (1) negative knowledge should be researched in its embeddedness in structures of experiential knowledge; (2) future studies should make use of a combination of knowledge-analytical methods and direct observations in realistic tasks; and (3) longitudinal research designs should be applied to research the evolvement of employees' error-related knowledge:

Consider the Embeddedness of Negative Knowledge in Structures of Experiential Knowledge

Future studies should apply knowledge elicitation techniques which allow the respondents to give insights into contextual and episodic reference points of their knowledge. This means that semi-structured or explorative techniques lend themselves to this application, e.g., the critical incident technique (Flanagan, 1954; Norman, Redfern, Tomalin, & Oliver, 1992). In this way, the interviewer possesses enough degrees of freedom to pose targeted questions which aim at shedding light on how error-related knowledge is acquired and the influence of relevant contextual elements.

Another relevant approach would be to conduct longitudinal studies with a repeated measurement of selected subjects' error-specific, experiential knowledge. Such an approach is particularly promising during phases of professional life when vocational experience is collected within a new or a radically changed work environment. In the sense of an initially peripheral (Billett, 2001a; Lave & Wenger, 1991), yet centre-oriented participation, it is plausible that in these cases the development of expertise depends upon a continued accumulation of workplace-specific knowledge through a large number of micro-learning processes. These reflect how the new professional environment and its challenges are tackled.

The research techniques described would allow to be shed light on how employees come from the experience of a concrete incident to hypotheses and insights into how the incident came about, its effects and consequences, ways to limit its harmfulness and its future avoidance. On this episodic basis, various more abstract components of employees' error-related knowledge may be theorised: Generalising over a larger number of error episodes, an employee may acquire knowledge about typical sources of errors and about which different forms of errors occur in the respective work environment. Moreover, it seems helpful to know about how best to discover errors—maybe there are certain points in work processes which offer better opportunities to install control routines than others. Then, employees may have knowledge about what can best be done in the case of different errors or in finding out which colleague may offer helpful support in the case of certain error situations.

Consider the Embeddedness of Error-Related Knowledge in a Particular Sociocultural Context

In most cases, an error is related to the (partial) frustration of certain human intentions or expectations (Rasmussen, 1987). This means that whether something is judged as being an error or not does not depend only on attributes of the phenomenon itself. Instead, such judgments are delivered with reference to certain normative criteria: For example, when shooting a wedding, the primary and most important criterion for the photographer is to satisfy the wishes of the customer. To achieve this primary goal, various other criteria have to be adhered to, e.g., technical or aesthetic criteria.

In general, these criteria reflect (implicit or explicit) rules and practices which pertain to a certain (work-)context (Bauer, 2008; Heid, 1999). As argued above, negative knowledge is strongly related to experiencing and learning from errors at work. Hence, to fully understand the rationale behind negative knowledge, it is very helpful to also gain insights into the conditions relevant in the particular context in which it is researched.

As was advanced, the sentence 'Don't wear too tight clothes when shooting a wedding!' represents a photographer's negative knowledge. To fully appreciate the relevance of this statement, understanding several contextual aspects is helpful. Firstly, as was described above, the photographer's primary goal is to satisfy the customer. This goal would be missed if the customer's wedding party is upset. Secondly, it is helpful to understand why this goal is relevant in the first place: Of course, a photographer who does not manage to satisfy customers might have trouble surviving economically.

From exemplifying these criteria, we conclude that, when researching employees' error-related knowledge, it is illuminative to systematically research the local, contextual conditions of the respondents' work environment. In that way, the situatedness of knowledge in a particular sociocultural context can be taken into account. This means that individual and organisational knowledge is constructed inside a framework which incorporates and reflects local practices of sense-making. The mutual relationships between local conditions prevalent at a certain workplace and different individuals' error-related experiential knowledge may reveal interesting differences between individual patterns of sense-making (Billett, 2001a; Waibel, 2002).

Comparatively Focus on Two Ways to Externalise Knowledge: Verbalisation and Application in Practical Tasks

A lucky person may solve a problem correctly without really being able to tell how the success came about. On the other hand, a problem may be solved by means of very purposefully planning and carrying out a certain course of actions. For this differentiation, Heid (1996) has coined the terms trivial and nontrivial competence. Now, one interesting aspect about the application of negative knowledge is that it results in *not* doing something. Applying this differentiation, it is apparent that it makes a big difference whether a person performs without making errors just because of being lucky or because of purposefully avoiding disadvantageous ways to act. However, what somebody does *not* do only appears in behaviour if the person *verbalises* the decision to avoid a certain actions. Hence, in order to differentiate between acts of trivial and nontrivial competence, future studies should make use of a combination of knowledge-analytic methods and direct observation techniques in realistic tasks (Gruber, 1999; Rothe & Schindler, 1996).

This could resolve the problem described above connected to the formal restrictedness of negative knowledge. In this context, it was argued that the identification of negative knowledge depends upon possible incidental variations in formulation. The essential idea of the theory of negative knowledge is that being aware of wrong assumptions is valuable because it may be helpful for not acting wrongly or committing errors. Yet, how can this awareness be captured?

Above, we argued that a respondent may formulate a statement in a negative way. Vice versa, a respondent could also possess negative knowledge, but formulate statements in a positive way. Hence, several questions remain open: Is an actor aware of certain possible mistakes when performing a certain task? Is an actor aware of the wrong assumptions or wrong actions which lead to these mistakes? As suggested, these questions could be answered by combining knowledge elicitation techniques with performance measures obtained in challenging tasks.

References

Anderson, J. R., & Lebiere, C. (1998). *The atomic components of thought*. Mahwah, NJ: Lawrence Erlbaum.

Argyris, C. (1986a). Reinforcing organizational defensive routines: An unintended human resources activity. *Human Resource Management, 25*, 541–555.

Argyris, C. (1986b). Skilled incompetence. *Harvard Business Review, 64*(5), 74–79.

Baer, M., & Frese, M. (2003). Innovation is not enough: Climates for initiative, psychological safety, process innovation and firm performance. *Journal of Organizational Behavior, 24*, 45–68.

Barach, P., & Small, S. D. (2000). Reporting and preventing medical mishaps: Lessons from non-medical near miss reporting systems. *British Medical Journal, 320*, 759–765.

Bauer, J., & Mulder, R. H. (2007). Modelling learning from errors in daily work. *Learning in Health and Social Care, 6*, 121–133.

Bauer, J. (2008). *Learning from errors at work. Studies on nurses' engagement in error related learning activities*. Doctoral dissertation, University of Regensburg, Regensburg. Retrieved July 15, 2010, from http://www.opus-bayern.de/uni-regensburg/volltexte/2008/990

Bauer, J., & Gruber, H. (2007). Workplace changes and workplace learning – Advantages of an educational micro perspective. *International Journal of Lifelong Education, 26*, 675–688.

Bauer, J., & Mulder, R. (2008). Conceptualisation of learning through errors at work. A literature review. In S. Billett, C. Harteis, & A. Eteläpelto (Eds.), *Emerging perspectives of workplace learning* (pp. 115–128). Rotterdam, the Netherlands: Sense.

Billett, S. (2001a). *Learning in the workplace. Strategies for effective practice*. Crows Nest, Australia: Allen & Unwin.

Billett, S. (2001b). Learning through work: Workplace affordances and individual engagement. *Journal of Workplace Learning, 13*, 209–214.

Boud, D. J., & Gerrick, J. (1999). Understandings of workplace learning. In D. J. Boud & J. Gerrick (Eds.), *Understandings of workplace learning* (pp. S. 1–S. 11). London: Routledge.

Chillarege, K. A., Nordstrom, C. R., & Williams, K. B. (2003). Learning from our mistakes: Error management training for mature learners. *Journal of Business and Psychology, 17*, 369–385.

Dovey, S. M., & Phillips, R. L. (2004). What should we report to medical error reporting systems? *Quality and Safety in Health Care, 13*, 322–323.

Edmondson, A. (2004). Learning from mistakes is easier said than done. *The Journal of Applied Behavioral Science, 40*, 66–90.

Eraut, M. (2000). Non-formal learning, implicit learning and tacit knowledge in professional work. In F. Coffield (Ed.), *The necessity of informal learning* (pp. 12–31). Bristol, UK: Policy Press.

Flanagan, J. C. (1954). The critical incident technique. *Psychological Bulletin, 51*, 327–358.

Frese, M., Brodbeck, F. C., Heinbokel, T., Mooser, C., Schleiffenbaum, E., & Thiemann, P. (1991). Errors in training computer skills: On the positive function of errors. *Human-Computer Interaction, 6*, 77–93.

Frese, M., & Fay, D. (2001). Personal initiative (PI): An active performance concept for work in the 21st century. In B. M. Staw & R. M. Sutton (Eds.), *Research in organizational behaviour* (pp. 133–187). Amsterdam: Elsevier.

Gartmeier, M., Bauer, J., Gruber, H., & Heid, H. (2008). Negative knowledge: Understanding professional learning and expertise. *Vocations and Learning, 1*, 87–103.

Gruber, H. (1999). *Erfahrung als Grundlage kompetenten Handelns* [Experience as a foundation of competent behavior]. Bern, Switzerland: Verlag Hans Huber.

Gruber, H., & Palonen, T. (Eds.). (2007). *Learning in the workplace – New developments*. Turku, Finland: Finnish Educational Research Association.

Harteis, C., & Billett, S. (Eds.). (2008). Organisational and personal contributions to workplace learning environments. *Special Issue of the International Journal for Educational Research, 47*(4).

Heid, H. (1996). Erfordernis und Problematik einer Unterscheidung zwischen Verhalten und Verhaltensdisposition [The need and difficulty of a distinction between behavior and disposition of behavior]. In K. Beck, W. Müller, T. Deißinger, & M. Zimmermann (Eds.), *Berufserziehung im Umbruch* (pp. 79–85). Weinheim, Germany: Deutscher Studien.

Heid, H. (1999). Autorität—über die Verwandlung von Fehlern in Verfehlungen [Authority—The transformation of errors into misconducts]. In W. Althof (Ed.), *Fehlerwelten. Vom Fehlermachen und Lernen aus Fehlern* (pp. 129–136). Leverkusen, Germany: Leske + Budrich.

Hofmann, D., & Stetzer, A. (1998). The role of safety climate and communication in accident interpretation: Implications for learning from negative events. *The Academy of Management Journal, 41*, 644–657.

Holmer, L. (2001). Will we teach leadership or skilled incompetence? The challenge of student project teams. *Journal of Management Education, 25*, 590–605.

Keith, N., & Frese, M. (2005). Self-regulation in error-management training: Emotion control and metacognition as mediators of performance effects. *Journal of Applied Psychology, 90*, 677–691.

Keith, N., & Frese, M. (2008). Effectiveness of error management training: A meta-analysis. *Journal of Applied Psychology, 93*, 59–69.

Kolb, D. (1984). *Experiential learning. Experience as the source of learning and development.* Upper Saddle River, NJ: Prentice-Hall.

Kolodner, J. (1983). Towards an understanding of the role of experience in the evolution from novice to expert. *International Journal of Man-Machine Studies, 19*, 497–518.

Lave, J., & Wenger, E. (1991). *Situated Learning. Legitimate Peripheral Participation.* Cambridge: Cambridge University Press.

Meurier, C. E. (2000). Understanding the nature of errors in nursing: Using a model to analyse critical incident reports of errors which had resulted in an adverse or potentially adverse event. *Journal of Advanced Nursing, 32*, 202–207.

Minsky, M. (1994). Negative expertise. *International Journal of Expert Systems, 7*, 13–19.

Nordstrom, C. R., Wendland, D., & Williams, K. B. (1998). To err is human: An examination of the effectiveness of error management training. *Journal of Business and Psychology, 12*, 269–282.

Norman, I., Redfern, S., Tomalin, D., & Oliver, S. (1992). Developing Flanagan's critical incident technique to elicit indicators of high and low quality nursing care from patients and their nurses. *Journal of Advanced Nursing, 17*, 590–600.

Oser, F. (1996). Learning from negative morality. *Journal of Moral Education, 25*, 67–74.

Oser, F., & Spychiger, M. (2005). *Lernen ist schmerzhaft. Zur Theorie des negativen Wissens und zur Praxis der Fehlerkultur* [Learning is painful. On the theory of negative knowledge and the practice of error culture]. Weinheim, Germany: Beltz.

Parviainen, J., & Eriksson, M. (2006). Negative knowledge, expertise and organisations. *International Journal of Management Concepts and Philosophy, 2*, 140–153.

Perrow, C. (1984). *Normal accidents: Living with high risk technologies.* Princeton, NJ: University Press.

Popper, K. R. (1972). *Objective knowledge: An evolutionary approach.* Oxford, UK: Clarendon.

Rasmussen, J. (1987). The definition of human error and a taxonomy for technical system design. In J. Rasmussen, K. Duncan, & J. Leplat (Eds.), *New technology and human error* (pp. 23–30). Chichester, UK: Wiley.

Reason, J. (1990). *To err is human.* Cambridge, UK: University Press.

Rothe, H.-J., & Schindler, M. (1996). Expertise und Wissen [Expertise and knowledge]. In H. Gruber & A. Ziegler (Eds.), *Expertiseforschung. Theoretische und methodische Grundlagen* (pp. S. 35–S. 57). Leverkusen, Germany: Westdeutscher.

Rybowiak, V., Garst, H., Frese, M., & Batinic, B. (1999). Error orientation questionnaire (EOQ): Reliability, validity and different language equivalence. *Journal of Organizational Behavior, 20*, 527–547.

Schank, R. C. (1999). *Dynamic memory revisited.* Cambridge, UK: University Press.

Schüttelkopf, E. M. (2008). Erfolgsstrategie Fehlerkultur. Wie Organisationen durch einen professionellen Umgang mit Fehlern ihre Performance optimieren [Error culture as a success strategy: How organizations optimize their performance by means of a professional error handling]. In G. Ebner, P. Heimerl, & E. M. Schüttelkopf (Eds.), *Fehler Lernen Unternehmen. Wie Sie die Fehlerkultur und Lernreife Ihrer Organisation wahrnehmen und gestalten* (pp. 151–314). Frankfurt, Germany: Peter Lang.

Smith, P. J. (2003). Workplace learning and flexible delivery. *Review of Educational Research, 73*, 53–88.

Staw, B. M., & Barsade, S. G. (1993). Affect and managerial performance: A test of the sadder-but-wiser vs. smarter but-happier hypotheses. *Administrative Science Quarterly, 38*, 304–331.

Stenström, M.-L., & Tynjälä, P. (2009). *Towards integration of work and learning. Strategies for connectivity and transformation.* Dordrecht, the Netherlands: Springer.

Swain, D. (2007). Can blogging be used to improve medication error collection as part of health informatics knowledge management? In S. Hawamdeh (Ed.), *Creating collaborative advantage through knowledge and innovation* (pp. 301–313). Singapore: World Scientific.

Tykocinski, O., & Pittman, T. (1998). The consequences of doing nothing: Inaction inertia as avoidance of anticipated counterfactual regret. *Journal of Personality and Social Psychology, 75*, 607–616.

Uribe, C. L., Schweikhart, S. B., Pathak, D. S., & Marsh, G. B. (2002). Perceived barriers to medical-error reporting: An exploratory investigation. *Journal of Healthcare Management, 47*, 264–279.

Van Dyck, C., Frese, M., Baer, M., & Sonnentag, S. (2005). Organizational error management culture and its impact on performance: A two-study replication. *Journal of Applied Psychology, 90*, 1228–1240.

Van Woerkom, M. (2003). *Critical reflection at work. Bridging individual and organisational learning*. Enschede, the Netherlands: PrintPartners.

Von Weizsäcker, C., & von Weizsäcker, E. U. (1984). Fehlerfreundlichkeit [Error-friendliness]. In K. Kornwachs (Ed.), *Offenheit – Zeitlichkeit – Komplexität. Zur Theorie der offenen Systeme* (pp. 168–201). Frankfurt, Germany: Campus.

Waibel, M. (2002). Lokales Wissen in der betrieblichen Lebenswelt [Local knowledge in work settings]. In *Harburger Beiträge* (Sonderband, Vol. 2). Hamburg-Harburg, Germany: Technische Universität.

Weinert, F. E. (2001). Concepts of competence – A conceptual clarification. In D. S. Rychen & L. H. Salyanik (Eds.), *Defining and selecting key competencies* (pp. 45–65). Göttingen, Germany: Hogrefe.

Yamnill, S., & McLean, G. N. (2001). Theories supporting transfer of training. *Human Resource Development Quarterly, 12*, 195–208.

Chapter 4
Towards a Theory of Negative Knowledge (NK): Almost-Mistakes as Drivers of Episodic Memory Amplification

Fritz K. Oser, Catherine Näpflin, Christine Hofer, and Philipp Aerni

Over the past decade, educational psychologists (Bauer, 2004; Dörner, 2003; Harteis, Bauer, Festner, Gruber, & Heid, 2005; Meyer, Seidel & Prenzel, 2006; Oser & Spychiger, 2005; Osten, 2006; Zapf, Frese, & Brodbeck, 1999), educational philosophers (Benner, 2005; Heid, in press; Koch, 1955), researchers in the field of pedagogical content knowledge and practitioners in education (Blanck, 2001; Gebauer, Groth, & Simon, 2004; Kahl, 1995) made attempts to circumscribe, conceptualize and operationalize the phenomenon and function of Negative Knowledge (NK). Most of these attempts, however, do not address how NK is retrieved and actualized in structurally similar but new situation, even though actualization seems to be a key issue related to the concept. To date, the reconstruction of NK is understood in the context of special situational elements, like the fear of committing the same mistake again and/or the apprehensibility of suffering from consequences of similar mistakes.

F.K. Oser, Ph.D. (✉)
Department of Educational Science, University of Fribourg, Fribourg, Switzerland
e-mail: Fritz.Oser@unifr.ch

C. Näpflin, M.Sc.
University of Fribourg, Fribourg, Switzerland
e-mail: Catherine.Naepflin@unifr.ch

C. Hofer, M.Sc.
Fribourg, Switzerland
e-mail: christine.e.hofer@bluewin.ch

P. Aerni, Ph.D.
ETH Zurich and the World Trade Institute, Bern, Switzerland
e-mail: aernip@ethz.ch

J. Bauer and C. Harteis (eds.), *Human Fallibility: The Ambiguity of Errors for Work and Learning*, Professional and Practice-based Learning 6,
DOI 10.1007/978-90-481-3941-5_4, © Springer Science+Business Media Dordrecht 2012

In this chapter, we explore the phenomenological possibilities on NK and introduce the concept of almost-mistakes (nearby-mistake or near-miss) and its nonlinear relationship to NK as a new important dimension by means of a qualitative small pilot study. In this survey, we asked subjects to remember what kind of almost-mistakes they experienced, what they learned and how they felt about them. For that purpose, we used a semi-standardized questionnaire to interview children, adolescents and adults. In addition we planned to design a special internet platform where people, especially medical staff, talk about their nearby-mistake situations without any risk of feeling ashamed, blamed or similar. As we know from experience in the health sector, any mistake can have fatal consequences. For nursing staff and doctors, it is not easy to talk about a mistake, even if it is "only" a near-miss. If a platform gives them the possibility to discuss their concerns while remaining anonymous, this might help them to overcome the reluctance to discuss these negative experiences. A second study that we will present in this chapter deals with personality traits that influence the coping with nearby-errors and the respective NK.

Negative Knowledge: To Know What Is Wrong Helps in Understanding What Is Right

Negative knowledge (NK) refers to memories related to events, things, procedures or strategies that are experienced as false, inadequate or even ineffective. It also refers to the respective consequences linked to such falseness and the connected memories such as feeling ashamed, and being blamed, punished or exposed in one's own intimacy.

But this remembering is also of importance to epistemic understanding. To know that a simple mathematical operation is right means to know all the possibilities of its falseness. If someone knows what a money exchange rate is, negative knowledge is a kind of opposite index, which cannot be used as an exchange rate. If someone knows how to use the gear in speeding up a car, it is helpful to know what endangers the engine, namely putting in the reverse gear while driving forward. As Heid (in press) shows, for the constitution of truth, the opposite of it is necessary, the non-truth; the constitution of a theory is its falsification. The philosophical constitution of truth includes its epistemological counterpart (false, right; good, bad; light, dark; appropriate, not appropriate; purposive, non-purposive); the psychological functions are control, orientation security, protection from committing mistakes again, and operational handsomeness. Or more precisely: We think that NK helps

(a) to create a useful alert against committing the same mistake again (protection),
(b) to distinguish between contrasts (bad and good),
(c) to find orientation between opposite characteristics (high versus low), and
(d) to produce certainty in addressing a problem following a particular procedure.

Interestingly, different authors define similar, but not the same, functions. Schumacher (2007), for instance, names a kind of pedagogical/learning functions such as (1) orientation for teachers (they know more about the way their pupils think), (2) motivation to learn in order to overcome the false, (3) mistake analysis in order to prevent them in future, (4) learning within mistake groups (groups with similar strengths and weaknesses for progress), and (5) occasion and time for self-correction as a fundamental epistemological endeavor. Whereas the functions that we formulate refer to NK in itself, Schumacher's concept is related to what we call a mistake culture in schools. Bauer (2008) sees the function rather in the sense of reflection pragmatics; he thinks that NK stimulates meta-cognition, action regulation, memory sensitivity, and new situational framing.

Almost-Mistakes/Nearby-Mistakes/Near-Misses: A New Learning Framework

What exactly is an almost-mistake? It occurs in a situation in which a subject managed to prevent a potential failure, catastrophe, or accident that logically should have taken place, but did not because of chance, grace, or protection from an unseen or unexpected person or force, or from a last moment reflection and respective reaction. The main criteria for an almost-mistake is that the subject in this situation has already produced, in other similar situations, a similar mistake, building up NK, and that he/she knows how critical or how consequential the respective mistake can be. In education, it can also be that an apprenticeship trainer in certain situations stops the intended behavior of a learner (for instance, when he/she tries to manipulate an engine in a certain dysfunctional way). We know – in education the trainer knows – the possible consequences that we have NK already in us. For example, if we just managed to escape from being hit by a car by linking previous personal experiences or advocatory experiences like seeing things in films, television shows, or from stories, etc., this link to past experiences prevents us from doing it again. These consequences can be felt bodily, financially, or with respect to wasted time. Thus, almost-mistakes are an actualization of NK in the sense that we become aware of risks, consequences, and pains of something negative that happened once before, in another time in a similar situation. We feel the peril of recalling a past uncontrollable incident.

Previous Research

The article "Near-Miss Analysis" (Aspden, Corrigan, Wolcott, & Erickson, 2004) is one of the few contributions to the concept of "almost-mistakes", which proposed so called near-miss systems with systematic near-miss reports for preventing real adverse events. The author discusses such security controls for hospitals and health care centers on regional and national scales. His concern is guided by a couple of normative demands, collecting and classifying such events from which others can learn. The interesting aspects of his presentation, however, are a few additional observations, namely (1) that near misses in the medical field are until 100 times more frequent than real adverse events, (2) that the three goals for near-miss systems according to Van der Schaaf (1991) such as "*modeling* – to gain a *qualitative insight* into (small) failures or errors developing into near misses and sometimes into adverse events", "*trending* – to gain a *quantitative insight* into the relative distribution if failure and recovery factors by building a database of underlying root causes of a large number of near misses", and "*mindfulness.../alertness* – to maintain a certain level of alertness to danger..." are central for understanding the tendency to prevent from adverse events, (3) that the "causal continuum assumption" that states that "the causal factors of consequential accidents are similar to those of non-consequential incidents or near misses" (p. 219) is important to understand the role of the functions of near misses, and (4) that a dual pathway of near-miss reporting, namely the direct analytical pathway in which we ask what the near-miss and the real adverse event have in common, and a second, indirect cultural pathway in which the learning effect of the reporters are taken into consideration, helps to understand the prevention mechanisms. These ideas are, of course, helpful even if the main concept of what psychologically happens if we commit an almost-mistake is less considered and the notion of the above-mentioned negative knowledge is not yet developed. The work on the definitions is especially interesting for our concept. For example, "a near-miss is an occurrence with potentially important safety-related effects, which, in the end, is prevented from developing into actual consequences" (p. 227), or, "a near-miss is defined as an act of commission or omission that could have harmed the patient but did not cause harm as a result of chance, prevention, or mitigation." (p. 227), or "according to the incident causation model, near-misses are the immediate precursors to later possible adverse events" (p. 227). The whole concept presented by Aspden et al.(2004) could have been developed into a new research program, but probably was not mature enough at this stage.

What Aspden and colleagues (2004) also did not see was that the almost-mistake has a different procedural phase structure than the happening of a real mistake. The subject sees with open eyes that through his/her intention and behavior something negative arrives, and it is too late to stop it. Most typical is the near-miss where people often close their eyes. But just before it arrives, things turn around and the shock turns into a relief and discharge of the respective fear; as we mentioned before, we go away without the realization of the event. But now begins the imaging of the consequences, and, because in a former similar event we had already built up NK, we now actualize it and even anticipate consequences beyond the possible reality. We have feelings of gratefulness combined with a full imaging of possible outcomes. Nearby-mistakes are thus motivators for a strong reanimation of NK. In addition, we are ready to confabulate on it; we tell stories of what could have happened, and in this sense we retrieve the NK that was already built up long before. Seen psychologically, it is interesting to examine how a similar situation actualizes the prior NK and thus again obtains the protection from it.

As mentioned before, we conducted a small pilot study to gain insight about peoples' reaction to near-misses. In addition to personal data (age, sex, education), the respondents of the questionnaire were asked to describe one or two "near-miss situations" including the real and imagined consequences they suffered (emotionally and materially), the way they tried to cope with the situation, and the form and intensity of remembering it (NK). One interesting interview question was also about the difference between a real mistake and a near-miss situation. Finally, questions on sharing this experience with someone (*kids, grandchild or friends*), and the effects and functions of the almost-mistake for the future continuation of work and life purposes closed the interview process. The first group of people we asked on the street told us stories from everyday life, without any specification. For the second group, we interviewed people from a specific field, namely the medical area *(W = Women, G = Girl, M = Men, B = Boy)*. Whereas children mostly described situations in school, teenagers also mentioned near-miss situations on a moral level, like friendship risks and that it is important to deliver on a promise. Adults often told their experience with near-misses in their job or leisure activities. Below, are some selected examples:

G: 10: "*It was during an English test. Before rendering it, I noticed some words written in capital letters, as I am used to doing it in German. I got very anxious and I did not know what to do. Fortunately, I was able to correct it in the last minute. The same thing happens in math, too.*"

G: 16: "*My friend (X) asked another girl of my class (Y) if she would join him after school. Yet, at the same time, Y asked me to go out with her after school. She even called me after school again. I didn't know that Y had already turned X down. At the very last moment, I decided not to go out with Y. I was right, because if I would have done this, X would have felt betrayed by his friend.*"

W: 56: "*It often happens when I am about to pass someone on the highway that all of a sudden a car turns up in the rear almost causing an accident. Fortunately, I am able to respond quickly and cancel the maneuver at the last moment. That is really shocking!*"

W: 65: *(worked in a travel agency):* "*Once I prepared a flight ticket for the wrong date and time. I only realized it once the customer arrived to pick it up, together with other documents. Since it was not yet printed, I still managed to change it at the very last second. But I didn't mentioned my mistake to the customer (laugh).*"

All in all, these examples are not very "dangerous". Consequently, almost everyone admitted that the imagined consequences would not have been serious. Nevertheless, everyone was also aware that it was pure chance that prevented the mistake. The "shock" by these near-misses – even if not very impressive – produced a great number of imagined consequences, probably more than in reality would have been possible. In their mind, they imagined what else could have happened, playing through all possible scenarios with their expected outcomes. Here are two examples about imagined consequences from different subjects:

G: 10: "*The teacher would have given me a bad mark and I would have had to explain it to my parents*"

M: 63: He was hiking without any safety arrangements, and then said*: "Only when I was back, I realized how careless I was and imagined what could have had happened to me and how my friends would have responded to my foolishness*"

By imagining the consequences, subjects often refer to the delicacy of the possible justification of the near-miss to others, such as parents and friends. The fear of not being able to do so seems to be a driver for the actualization of NK. Because of this, it seems that the theory has to be enlarged in the sense that the awareness of what could have happened is stronger in the moment of the transition from shock to relief. All in all, these examples may be real but not very deep. Bauer (2008), referring to Reason (1990, 1995), distinguishes between slips/lapses and knowledge/rule-based errors. He believes that only the second type is relevant for learning. Oser and Spychiger (2005, p. 29) developed a whole taxonomy of mistake or NK intensity (level 1, fast adaptations; level 2, knowledge about contrasts; level 3, delineation- and protection knowledge; level 4, important personal episodic protection knowledge; level 5, important protection knowledge as cultural inventory). And, of course, they believe that the deeper the NK is experienced, the more important it is for the history of personal feelings of security. Once almost-mistakes are elicited in daily life situations, their effectiveness is enhanced.

Let us have a look at two more profound and touching near-miss examples from a specific vocational field, namely the medical domain:

M: 49: Internist / Rheumatologist with 24 years of working experience: "*Once I prescribed a drug to a patient that turned out to be a mistake because, as is well known, if this drug is taken in combination with another one then it could cause a serious adverse reaction. Since I did not bother double-checking, I gave the specific drug to the patient. Usually, it should have shown really bad side effects and enhance the effect of the first medicament.*

I always imagine the worst case, especially when there is no way to correct the mistake. But I also try everything in my power to prevent the worst. It sounds weird, but in such moments not only the patient is important but also my personal life, my professional life."..."Of course I felt very bad... And this also had negative consequences on my private life because I kept my mind busy all the time. It would also be terrible if the patient was not here, and I become aware of the problem, but I cannot act; he/she is maybe home and it is a long way to go..."

W: anesthesiologist: *"For the local anesthesia (leg, arm), we always mix two different medicaments to enhance the effect. I was under time pressure and quickly took the bottle with the local anesthetic, mixed it with the other medicament and placed it on the worktable. Then I realized that the mixture does not have the usual color. In the last moment, I took the bottle away and verified the labels again. I saw that it was not the anesthetic but the blood pressure medicament. That really could have resulted in very, very bad consequences.*

At that moment I felt very bad, and shivers went down my spine. In the next second, I prayed to thank God that I had realized my mistake at the very last second."

These professional examples elicit very profound responsibilities and reactions. It seems that they connect a deep commitment with the wish not to fail, but to do the best for each patient. The higher the stakes, the deeper the experience and the less the re-actualized NK becomes.

Negative Knowledge: A Remembering Task

As already indicated, one condition for the functioning of NK is remembering and thus knowing how we changed; this implies mentally re-actualizing what is false in order to prevent it from re-occurring in reality. Because NK is central for controlling, coordinating, and stimulating epistemic and procedural activities (inner and outer) on the one hand, knowing the false, the dysfunctional, and the disturbing impact on the other hand, leads to a higher appreciation of what it means to remember. For understanding the concept of NK, the theory of episodic memory with its known–remember distinction may be of substantial help (Baddeley, Aggleton, & Conway, 2002; Tulving, 2001). This distinction states that there is a difference in *knowing that* $A^2+B^2=C^2$, and in remembering *how we learned* this formula, e.g., by making a calculating error and then being called stupid or similar. It makes a difference whether we know and reflect a fact or whether we remember the experience how we learned about it. "A crucial feature of the concept of episodic memory is the role of the remembered" (Baddeley, 2002, p. 6). And this is why this concept helps to shape the understanding of learning from mistakes and the theory of NK. We remember the circumstances of how a mistake happened, as well as the subsequent shock, the immediate consequences, and the long-term impact. In the case of almost-mistakes, we postulate that this shock is followed by a moment of relief, but also imagining at the same time all the possible contingencies. In accordance with the importance of the violated norm, we can remember this event as strongly as or even stronger than if the mistake had actually occurred. Why is this so? If the event actually happens, then our mind is engaged in deliberations on how to overcome the mistake situation ("negative anchor"; Oser & Spychiger, 2005), as well as how to justify our actions and save our face. If the event (only) happens nearby, we have time to observe all the terrible consequences and we envision the hurting, the punishment, the discrimination, the scandal, etc., all this by not changing the path of production, reaction, or advancement. We therefore argue that almost-mistakes may produce an episodic negative memory trace "in a better way" than real mistakes, especially with respect to dangerous situations. We survived an unimaginable situation and associate it with terrible negative feelings of potential guilt and very positive feelings of relief. To become mentally aware of a mistake in the past helps to avoid its repetition in the future. This is related to the ability of traveling back mentally and using personal memory to prevent the same mistake or error from happening again (cf. Wheeler, Stuss, & Tulwin, 1997). Tulving and Craig (2000) calls this "autonoetic" remembering: "Episodic remembering is closely related to other higher order mental achievement that is not typically considered to be related to acts of memory. Individuals with autonoetic awareness are capable of reflecting their own experiences in the past, the present and the future. Reflecting on past happenings is episodic memory. The ability to introspect upon present experiences, and also to anticipate or imagine future experiences through imagination, daydreams and fantasies is also related to autonoetic awareness " (p. 598). The application of these mistakes and errors leads to our notion of NK, whereas the difference lies in the fact that we only reconstruct this remembering if we are in danger of falling into the same trap. NK is only active if the new situation recalls the mistaken one and thus protects us from a new similar case. Almost-mistakes produce the same activity but with protected agitation and projected consequences. There is no linear reaction for what happens, but a curvilinear situatedness in relation to special events, special remembering, and special NK elements. If the norm to which the mistake relates is important (personally and/or publicly), the remembering is strong; if not, we adapt ourselves without further consequences.

Here, some everyday, unspecific examples of episodic memory-functions from our pilot study: Everyone remembers near-miss situations very well and mostly in a profound way. But in the majority of cases, if they found themselves in a similar situation, they seldom talk about this near-miss in a deliberate way. They thought that it is not important, because nothing happened; they were only ashamed of themselves.

M: 63: *"Oh no, I never told anyone of my near-miss. As an officer in the military, I behaved very carelessly instead of being a good example of responsible behavior in the army. I felt personally ashamed and angry, being aware that I was teaching soldiers all the time to never go to the mountains alone and without any safety arrangements!!"*

M: 10: *"I remember all the time when I am in English class or when I am writing a test. I told my friends to be careful about writing in English and that they always have to reread it before rendering it."* (warning a third party)

M: 16: *"Every time when my friend is asking me to do something together, I check first if there is someone else asking her already. I do not want anyone to be angry because of me. It is important to be honest with your friends".*

These examples demonstrate the ambiguity mentioned before. On the one hand, things seem not to be so important (the mistake did not happen); on the other hand, no one does forget. Everyone said that a near-miss is like an *alarm clock*. It tells you that you were not attentive enough. It is like a *last chance* that you can do it better next time. So it is important that you will remember this near-miss for a very long time, in order to prevent it from happening again. What about the special functions? Do we recognize the direction of change from insight to remembering, and its respective protection from repeating a near-miss, as fruitful? Already in the last examples we meet the message "don't do it again". And here is another example:

W: 56: *"It was a shocking moment and it is still in my bones when I am driving and want to pass. It is like an alarm system. It has a protective function".*

Do people feel similar kinds of functions in the specific medical field in a near-miss situation?

M: 49: Internist / Rheumatologist: *"This mistake won't happen again. From now on, I always look twice if I apply something."*

W: Anesthesiologist: *"Maybe the function is to protect us against carelessness and against too much felt security and realized routine. If you rehabilitate and discuss such situations, they can be helpful for the whole team. That is how I feel about that. But unfortunately, almost-mistakes were not always discussed in the team; I depend on the administration, the team and the working collaboration."*

Negativity in Itself: Some Anthropological Considerations

One of the central dimensions in NK is the creating of an experience that contradicts acquired knowledge being generalized until now. The typicality of such knowledge becomes de-typicalized through it. It was the philosopher Gadamer (1986) in his "*Truth and Method*" who first stated this contradiction. He analyzed the impact of an experience that is not compatible with daily thinking and routine. He states: "Thus, the real experience is always a negative one. If we experience an object, it means that, until now, the reality was not seen the right way, and we do better understand once we make the real experience. The negativity of an experience discloses thus a special productive meaning. It is not just a beguilement that now becomes visible but consequent knowledge affirmation that is acquired (p. 359)". He also explains that these things do not happen by chance but through an experience of something that we believed before to be right, but which was wrong and now receives a different shape. He calls this negation a special negation because the experience that underlies it is what he calls dialectical.

Concerning almost-mistakes negativity in experience in the sense of Gadamer discloses a remembering of one's experienced transformation, its re-actualization, and a strong transformation of an, until now, secure behavior set. The nearby-fault is a chance to transform oneself by reanimation of experienced negative consequences that have happened before, without all the consequences and often even disturbing power. But this is only an application of Gadamer's thinking. The limits of Gadamer's dialectic become immediately visible, because nobody changes solely because of a negative experience; it needs a motivational guiding moment, which is shown by Benner (2008), who gives the experience being discussed a specific content form, namely morality. For Benner (p. 166) the primary goal of moral education is not positive moral behavior but rather a much more restricted task, namely to inform the next generation on negative immoral behavior and thus to sensitize children and adolescents for moral questions. Thus, Benner puts himself in the tradition of J. Korczak, the Polish Pestalozzi, whose educational strategies started from the concept that a child that never lied, never stole, never behaved unfairly, etc. cannot be a moral person. In this concept, negativity acquires a different meaning, it is not just experimentation of the unknown, rather it is a content-specific and compulsory process from the mistake to the experienced negativity, and then through reflection, shame, forgiveness, and change towards a new understanding of a norm. In our work, we can demonstrate that children who did not encounter this negative "going through experiences" show less moral identity, less security, and less oppositional understanding (Oser & Spychiger, 2005).

Almost-mistakes in this sense clearly have a different and enlarged function as compared to mistakes. They stimulate repeating the mistake experience inside us in immediately bringing to mind an inflation of possible consequences and mostly a feeling of going from guilt to be shocked to a feeling of gratefulness that they did not appear. These consequences are often derived from advocatory mistake making: we have seen others making this mistake and earning the respective consequences, we have read about others being in the terrible situation, or we have seen films that precisely elicit the consequences that we missed by making the mistake as a near accident. Advocatory mistakes represent a treasure of cultural experiences that lead us to what we call negative knowledge. Each scandal is a good representation of what we should not do and would not experience. And even if we think that we, in the same situation, would have been more careful, we are happy not to be trapped into this situation. For the issue of almost-mistakes, advocatory experiences and real experiences are, according to the respective "extent of conditional touching", the same sources for the reanimation of old and building up of new protective NK.

One of the major contributions to the philosophical groundwork of the epistemological functioning of making mistakes (and thus to build up NK) is done by Heid (in press). He speaks about the necessary conditions that mean we see a behavior as a mistake; these conditions lie in the fact that we must build a judgment of sufficient negative but not absolute negative accuracy. If we can think of or create a deficit status of a concept, a process, or a strategy, then we are sure to know its rightness or the right process or right strategy. Finally, possible mistakes serve as quality assurance of these categories; speaking about mistakes means speaking about the lack of quality. Sentences without having the possibility to be false have no informational content and no epistemological earnings. This includes, first, the weight of importance someone gives to the mistake (see importance of the respective norms, in Oser & Spychiger, 2005, p. 90 f.), and second, the reasons someone gives for having made the mistake. NK in this sense is knowledge about a competence deficit that helps to build up competence functioning. This knowledge is based on remembering. It leads to the control of success, and control of success is a measure of having the false possibilities in mind by doing the right thing. With respect to this argumentation, almost-mistakes are situations in which humans experience the near loss of competence control, and thus mostly react by making provisions that the respective real mistake does not recur. Almost-mistakes enlarge the repertoire of NK elements by important new characteristics – imagining on the one hand and advocatory remembering on the other.

However, people often prefer not to tell others about their almost-mistakes, because sharing such experience is still perceived to be ambiguous. In our pilot study, elderly persons keep the near-misses to themselves, but they nevertheless share means to divide and to learn. Most of the elderly people argue that sharing would not help. They think in a functional mode. That is why for them a near-miss situation cannot be shared with others. It is something everyone should experience for him or herself; it has some kind of personal protective function. They see no need to tell their experience, for example to the child or grandchild. But sometimes they give advice. For younger persons, sharing has a different meaning. It is just telling. Here are some examples from the first, unspecific group of not sharing:

W: 65: *"No I do not tell my near-miss. I think, everyone has the right to make his own experience. Even in the office, I never gave any advice or such."*

W: 85: *"No, I do not share my near-miss. I think today's young people won't listen anyway since they are not interested in them. They have enough problems."*

M: 63: *"If it is a near-miss like mine, which can end with your death, then you should maybe explain or tell how you should do it better. If someone really listens I don't know. In the end, everyone will make his own experience."*

These examples have of course – like the ones above – only an exploratory character. They can help to start a new research direction for elucidating in a more differentiated way the function of an almost-mistake. (We know, of course, many situations in which people tell stories about near-misses in which they escaped from some forces like the police. A good example would be someone who drank a little bit too much and escaped the control just at the last moment.)

How is it in the specific medical field? Do they talk about their mistakes? The two following examples show that it is very important to discuss near-miss situations. And we understand better why Aspden et al. (2004) speak about a protected reporting system that should be installed to promote a collection of near- misses helping others to prevent them. The taboo not to speak about them should be broken:

M: 49: Internist / Rheumatologist: "*The hospitals now have this CIRS-System*[1] *where you can report your mistakes or propose how to avoid such mistakes in future. Even with this new CIRS System, I think it is still a taboo and nobody talks openly about it. I believe, too, that people only note the mistakes with no real bad consequences. They were afraid of losing their anonymity.*

For myself, I can say, if there was no real bad consequence, as in my first example, then I do not talk about it – after all, the situation has been resolved. But when we worked in a team, and there was such a situation, we try to discuss it together. It depends on the chief you have, if he shows comprehension or not".

---

[1] CIRS = critical incident reporting system: Based on the experiences from the Australian Incident Monitoring Study (Runciman et al., 1993; AIMS), they create an international forum where they collect and distribute critical incidents that happened in daily anesthetic practice. This program not only allows the submission of critical incidents that happened at the place but also serves as a teaching instrument: share the experiences and have a look at the experiences of others by browsing through the cases. CIRS© is anonymous.

W: anesthesiologist: "*We always talked about such mistakes. In the morning, we always had an 'early meeting' to split the working areas. By this chance, when we were all together, we talked about our almost-mistakes or mistakes we made. I think that is a way to sensitize each other. The more routine someone has, the higher is the danger of making mistakes. To make mistakes is human and it could happen to everyone. I learned the experience that discussing your own mistakes is a good sensitizing for others.*"

Applauding Mistakes or Almost-Mistakes: On the Necessity of Demythologizing the "Right" Mistake

The stream of pedagogical reflection, in which the making of mistakes is applauded, easily accepted, or even striven for, cannot be stopped. We exercise overall this pedagogical mythologizing of constructs that have a motivational effect. If we consider the grades of seriousness of mistakes and the societal importance of the related norm, the three dimensions of such norms have to be taken into account: (1) how important they are in a respective field, (2) who is setting and controlling them, and (3) what are the known consequences in trespassing the norm. All three criteria must be interpreted differently if the mistake maker sees himself in a learning situation (professional school, music lesson, research institute), or in a production/performance situation (firm, workplace, health care, administration). Nevertheless, the principal goal is not to make mistakes anymore, to prevent all kind of mistakes, or to keep mistakes out of human activity, but if they occur, to use them for learning purposes, to work with them to transform approaches, techniques, strategies, and concepts into an adequate norm fulfilling or creating more effective functional ways. This ambiguity to fight against mistakes on the one hand, but on the other to create a positive learning and change-accepting climate, is paramount for understanding the motivational tension with respect to transformational cognitive activities. It is like a secret apriority of a paradigm. Just as for Einstein the secret apriority was that in nature all forces are finally in equilibrium, here the apriority is that we do not want and should not make a mistake, but mistakes are the only way of being able to learn, to change, and to grow. We have to accept this correct incorrectedness.

Whereas in the European tradition the value of making mistakes and building up negative knowledge is largely estimated (especially from the viewpoint of learning), in the US tradition, psychologists have a much stronger adherence to not making mistakes, preventing mistakes and event fighting against mistakes. In his book "*Error nomics – Why we make mistakes and what we can do to avoid them*", Hallinan (2009) asks not how we can learn from mistakes and build up NK, but how can we prevent their appearance. There are at least three elements that lead humans to make errors or mistakes. First, there is the false belief that we can do different things at the same time, the so-called multitasking. " 'Multitasking' is a term cribbed from the computer world; it describes a technique by which a computer can split its work into many processes or tasks. This allows us to, say, run Microsoft Word while downloading something from the Internet. Most of us believe that our brains work the same way. Indeed, multitasking has become the hallmark of the modern workplace. But multitasking is one of the great myths of the modern age. Although we think we are focusing on several activities at once, our attention is actually jumping back and forth between the tasks." (Hallinan, 2009, p. 78). The author demonstrates that, because we lose a lot of energy in going back and forth, many of the mistakes in the traffic are due to this belief. In addition to losing energy, we also forget what we did before. We lose track of our actions and thoughts because our brain works "like water in the desert"; it just disappears. He cites data from the National Highway Traffic Safety administration that states that 78% of all crashes and 65% of the near crashes happened because the drivers were multitasking, meaning that they were, for instance, entering numbers in their mobile phones.

Hallinan, in the same book, enumerates other reasons why we run into serious mistake troubles by distorting information, framing information wrongly, like thinking that we are above average, not introducing constraints in limiting our alternatives, inferring from good looking persons to their competences, and also wrongly predicting what others feel, and taking higher risks if we are fatigued, etc. A whole bunch of these heuristic effects are analyzed and illustrated with good examples and stories. But encompassing the main points of his thinking direction is not learning from mistakes and not building up NK but blaming the wrong cause of the mistake. In this case, the distinction between nearby-mistakes and real mistakes gets lost because the viewing direction is not towards remembering for being protected but psychologizing for avoidance. We believe that knowing about how heuristics can mislead our judgment goes beyond that. It fosters a culture of being morally vigilant.

Fostering the Error Culture Through Near-Miss in Firms

Above we learned that persons often do not talk about mistakes and especially not about near-miss situations. This has to do with the error culture of a firm or institution. A positive error culture would be one in which the responsible for a work unit gives apprentices the occasion to learn from almost-mistakes. They cry "stop" and explain the danger of a possible error. A negative mistake culture is one in which the apprentice is only ashamed, and of course not controlled respectively stopped from committing a possible error. There is no occasion for redoing the situation in order to learn.

The following little study aims at disclosing the effects of the firm-error-culture of retail business apprentices and of commercial apprentices. While some studies about error culture in general-education schools exist (cf. Oser & Spychiger, 2005), there is little known about error culture in companies. Thus, the super-ordinate target of this study is to analyse how (1) personality traits, (2) self-efficacy, (3) achievement motivation, (4) professional self-esteem, and (5) personal handling of errors are correlated with the firm-error-culture. To answer this research question four hypothesizes were formulated:

- The firm error culture and personal handling of errors are positively correlated
- The firm error culture and professional self-esteem are positively correlated
- The firm error culture and achievement motivation are positively correlated
- The internal error culture[2] and self-efficacy are positively correlated

A total of 455 apprentices (most of them were retail business and commercial apprentices) were surveyed by means of a semi-standardized questionnaires. For measuring internal error culture the well-known questionnaire from Spychiger, Oser, Hascher, and Mahler (1998) was adapted; some items of the internal error questionnaires were also newly formulated and complemented with near-miss examples. The same was done with the items of the 'personal handling of errors' questionnaire. For the achievement motivation the questionnaire from Schuler and Prochaska (2001) was chosen. This questionnaire was constructed to measure the achievement motivation in a professional context. Professional self-esteem was measured using the questionnaire designed by Sonntag and Schäfer-Rauser (1993). Self- efficacy was measured by the questionnaire of Scharzer and Jerusalem (1999). In this case the items of this questionnaire were reformulated. (e.g. "I can always manage to solve difficult problems if I try hard enough", was reformulated to "I can always manage to solve difficult mistake problems at work if I try hard enough"), this because self-efficacy should be measured in a professional context.

The relationship between firm error culture and personality traits was investigated using Pearson product-moment correlation coefficient. Not surprisingly, we found indeed positive correlations between firm error culture and the chosen personality traits, these were revealed especially for the male participants but not for the female ones. The following tables show the results in detail:

Table 4.1 shows that the better the firm error culture is, the better apprentices can handle their own mistakes. Nevertheless there is a strange difference between men and women. Men in the commercial training do react more sensitive to the firm error culture.

In Table 4.2 this difference looks even stranger: the relationship between self-esteem and error culture counts only for men, but not for women. What does this mean? It is important to consider that women do not react to what we call a firm error culture strengthening their self-esteem whereas men do. For men, the higher they rate the firm culture of learning from mistakes, the stronger their self-esteem.

Table 4.3 explicitly demonstrates that there is no relationship between firm error culture and achievement motivation. Both are independent from each other, both have – it seems – different forms of sources for its development.

[2] The idea of internal error culture goes back to Oser and Spychiger. The authors hold that persons (in their case primary students) are dealing with errors they have made in a different way. E.g., some students / apprentice think that they can learn from errors they have made, so they are trying to understand why they have made a certain error. This variable should measure how apprentice are dealing with errors they have made.

Table 4.1 Person product-moment correlation between measures of personal coping with errors and firm error culture

	Men all	Women all	Women commercial	Women business	Men commercial	Men business	All
EC9[a]	.41**	.21**	.16*	.26*	.48**	.26	.28**
	(*N*=153)	(*N*=272)	(*N*=173)	(*N*=84)	(*N*=87)	(*N*=22)	(*N*=431)

*p<.05, **p<.01

Scale firm error culture: 35 items, Cronbach's Alpha: .80

Scale personal coping with errors: 6 items, Cronbach's Alpha: .53

[a]"Error Culture" measured with 9 items, followed by Spychiger et al. (1998)

1. If I have made a mistake my instructor is talking nasty behind my back to my peers
2. If I have made a mistake my instructor informs also third parties, who are not involved by my mistake
3. If I have made a mistake they are yelling at me
4. If my instructor has made a mistake, he talks himself out of way
5. If something didn't worked my instructor would explain it calmly to me again and seeking for a solution
6. Sometimes I am criticized for my behavior, without knowing that this behavior is bad/unwanted
7. With my instructor I can reflect, what I could learn by my mistakes
8. If I had made a mistake my instructor would cold-shoulder me and take care of the customer
9. If I have made a mistake I am sanctioned more hard than my graduate colleagues

Table 4.2 Person product-moment correlation between measures of professional self-esteem and firm error culture

	Men all	Women all	Women commercial	Women business	Men commercial	Men business	All
EC9[a]	.36**	.005	.09	–.103	.34**	.47*	.14**
	(*N*=129)	(*N*=252)	(*N*=165)	(*N*=73)	(*N*=72)	(*N*=22)	(*N*=386)

*p<.05, **p<.01

Scale: self-esteem: 9 items, Cronbach's Alpha: .80

[a]"Error Culture" measured with 9 items, followed by Spychiger et al. (1998)

Table 4.3 Person product-moment correlation between measures of achievement motivation and firm error culture

	Men all	Women all	Women commercial	Women business	Men commercial	Men business	All
EC9[a]	.16	–.05	–.03	–.14	.13	.25	.02
	(*N*=138)	(*N*=258)	(*N*=169)	(*N*=74)	(*N*=78)	(*N*=23)	(*N*=403)

Scale achievement motivation: originally 30 items, Cronbach's Alpha: .91

[a]"Error Culture" measured with 9 items, followed by Spychiger et al. (1998)

Table 4.4 finally makes the gender aspect even stronger because women feel that the firm error culture is negatively related to the self- efficacy belief, whereas with men the relation is highly positive. For women there is no positive relatedness of these two constructs. It seems that women feel not good with mistakes, and even the mistake culture does not relate positively to their felt success.

Table 4.4 Person product-moment correlation between measures of self-efficacy and internal error culture

	Men all	Women all	Women commercial	Women business	Men commercial	Men business	All
EC9[a]	.33** (*N*=147)	–.06 (*N*=267)	.06 (*N*=172)	–.27** (*N*=82)	.40** (*N*=88)	.33 (*N*=23)	.09 (*N*=421)

**p<.01
Scale self-efficacy: 10 items, Cronbach's Alpha: .73
[a]"Error Culture" measured with 9 items, followed by Spychiger et al. (1998)

The results of this little study where the error culture in companies was estimated by the participants (and not by other persons like heads of the companies) is interesting in the sense that building up NK is related to personality traits and gender aspects; men react completely different with respect to such traits than women. Male apprentices are more sensible towards a bad error culture within their companies than their female counterparts. One reason for this issue could be that the apprenticeship itself as an opportunity to learn is more important for males than for females. Males take criticism after a mistake more seriously and this could affect the personal traits.

The only small critical shortcoming of this study is that the difference between real mistakes and near- miss cannot be calculated because the items of the scales contain both, and scales are holistic concepts. Further research is necessary to investigate this interesting distinction. Taking into account some of Schoy-Lutz's (2005) findings, namely that there is no correlation between mistake culture in classroom and cognitive activation of students, it is necessary to look again closer at the stimulation mechanism caused by NK.

Discussion

Almost mistakes are drivers for the reanimation and amplification of NK. The question of how we re-actualize the NK in a similar situation is accompanied by the question of how strong we are touched by the near-miss, how important the respective norm is and how much the escape from a real mistake is felt as an alleviation. Humans have to live with NK, and the more someone has collected from it without being taped in, as more positive knowledge (wisdom) is possible. Almost mistakes are always related to real mistakes, and the experience of an almost mistake needs as a precondition the NK in relation to a real mistake. Thus almost mistakes cannot be a surrogate for real mistake, but an educational mean that helps preventing a repetition of the same mistakes and filling out and substantiate NK. As seen in the previous paragraphs almost-mistakes are effective means for extending NK, but also for generating it in a tense situation in order to prevent the same mistake from happening again.

There are a couple conclusions to be drawn from our presentation. First, almost mistakes refer always to a prior event in which the adverse incident was either realised or experienced advocatory by seeing others doing the same or similar errors.

That means in a near miss situation we have already the NK about the respective norm, and we remember and project at the same time what could have happened with all the terrible consequences. With this in mind we argue that almost mistakes actualize and deepen the respective NK. – Second, in daily life we often cannot speak about very serious almost mistakes; whereas in professional settings, within a reporting system, in a trustworthy context of course, very serious situations are presented, reflected and used to protect us from doing such things again. Thus reporting systems are especially fruitful for near misses. – Third, the emotional reaction to almost mistakes can be even stronger than the reaction of real adverse mistake events. This is given by the fact that the feelings are double bounded, namely positive and negative. The positive side is that we feel happiness that the event didn't occur (I was so happy, I prayed in my thankfulness as I saw myself being spared from a terrible accident etc.), the negative one is the feeling of horror of the imagined consequences (I saw this patient dying, I felt certain to lose my job and expected all the newspaper to report on my failure to act responsibly etc.). – Fourth, concerning the results of the error culture study with apprentices, it seems that females in a professional setting react less sensitive to a full mistake culture than males. For males the relationship between self-efficacy belief and mistake culture or between professional self-esteem and mistake culture is a highly positive one, females seem not to be too much touched by real mistakes and by near misses. They correct without being affected, or they even feel negatively in certain cases.

References

Aspden, P., Corrigan, J. M., Wolcott, J., & Erickson, S. M. (2004). *Patient safety*. Washington, DC: National Academies Press.

Baddeley, A. (2002). The concept of episodic memory. In A. Baddeley, J. P. Aggleton, & M. A. Conway (Eds.), *Episodic memory: New directions in research* (pp. 1–10). Oxford, UK: Oxford University Press.

Baddeley, A., Aggleton, J. P., & Conway, M. A. (Eds.). (2002). *Episodic memory: New directions in research*. Oxford, UK: Oxford University Press.

Bauer, J. (2004). Fehlerkultur und epistemische Überzeugungen als Einflussfaktoren individuellen Kompetenzenerwerbs am Arbeitsplatz. In H. Gruber, C. Harteis, H. Heid, & B. Meier (Eds.), *Kapital und Kompetenz – Veränderung der Arbeitswelt und ihre Auswirkungen aus erziehungswissenschaftlicher Sicht* (pp. 59–75). Wiesbaden, Germany: VS Verlag.

Bauer, J. (2008). *Learning from errors at work, studies on nurses' engagement in error-related learning activities*. Doctoral thesis, Regensburg.

Benner, D. (2005). Über pädagogisch relevante und erziehungswissenschaftlich fruchtbare Aspekte der Negativität menschlicher Erfahrung. In D. Benner (Ed.), *Erziehung – Bildung – Negativität. 49. Beiheft der Zeitschrift für Pädagogik* (pp. 7–21). Weinheim, Germany: Beltz.

Benner, D. (2008). *Bildungstheorie und Bildungsforschung*. Paderborn, Germany: Schöningh.

Blanck, B. (2001). *Erwägungsorientierung, Entscheidung und Didaktik*. Stuttgart, Germany: Lucius & Lucius.

Dörner, D. (2003). *Die Logik des Misslingens* (3rd ed.). Reinbek, Germany: Rowohlt.

Gadamer, H.-G. (1986). *Hermeneutik I. Wahrheit und Methode. Grundzüge einer philosophischen Hermeneutik*. Tübingen, Germany: Mohr.

Gebauer, A., Groth, T., & Simon, F. (2004). Aus Fehlern lernen – Scheitern als Chance. Denkanstösse zum lernförderlichen Umgang mit Fehlern und Misserfolgen in Unternehmen. *Personalführung, 37*(6), 72–80.

Hallinan, J. T. (2009). *Error nomics. Why we make mistakes and what we can do to avoid them.* London: Ebury Press.

Harteis, C., Bauer, J., Festner, D., Gruber, H., & Heid, H. (2005). *Learning from mistakes. Results of an interview-study in German enterprises.* Paper präsentiert auf der 86, Jahreskonferenz der American Educational Research Association in Montreal, Kanada.

Heid, H. (in press). *Der Fehler – eine Konstitutionsbedingung des Richtigen.*

Kahl, R. (1995). *Lob des Fehlers. Eine Sendereihe.* Hamburg, Germany: Pädagogische Beiträge Verlag.

Koch, L. (1955). *Bildung und Negativität. Grundzüge einer negativen Bildungstheorie.* Weinheim, Germany: Deutscher Studienverlag.

Meyer, L., Seidel, T., & Prenzel, M. (2006). Wenn Lernsituationen zu Leistungssituationen werden: Untersuchung zur Fehlerkultur in einer Videostudie. *Schweizerische Zeitschrift für Bildungswissenschaften, 28*(1), 21–41.

Oser, F., & Spychiger, M. (2005). *Lernen ist schmerzhaft. Zur Theorie des Negativen Wissens und zur Praxis der Fehlerkultur.* Weinheim, Germany: Beltz.

Osten, M. (2006). *Die Kunst, Fehler zu machen.* Frankfurt am Main, Germany: Suhrkamp.

Reason, J. T. (1990). *Human error.* Cambridge, UK: Cambridge University Press.

Reason, J. T. (1995). Understanding adverse events: Human factors. *Quality in Health Care, 4*, 80–89.

Runciman, W. B., Sellen, A., Webb, R. K., Williamson, J. A., Currie, M., Morgan, C., et al. (1993). The Australian incident monitoring study. Errors, incidents and accidents in anaesthetic practice. *Anaesthesia and Intensive Care, 21*, 506–519.

Schoy-Lutz, M. (2005). *Fehlerkultur im Mathematikunterricht.* Hildesheim/Berlin, Germany: Verlag Franzbecker.

Schuler, H., & Prochaska, M. (2001). *Leistungsmotivationsinventar.* Göttingen, Germany: Hogrefe.

Schumacher, R. (2007). Der produktive Umgang mit Fehlern. Fehler als Lerngelegenheit und Orientierungshilfe. In R. Caspry (Ed.), *Nur wer Fehler macht, kommt weiter. Wege zu einer neuen Lernkultur* (pp. 49–71). Freiburg, Germany: Herder/Spektrum.

Scharzer, R., & Jerusalem, M. (Eds.). (1999). *Skalen zur Erfassung von Lehrer- und Schülermerkmalen. Dokumentation der psychometrischen Verfahren im Rahmen der Wissenschaftlichen Begleitung des Modellversuchs Selbstwirksame Schulen.* Berlin, Germany: Freie Universität Berlin.

Sonntag, K.-H., & Schäfer-Rauser, U. (1993). Selbsteinschätzung beruflicher Kompetenzen bei der Evaluation von Bildungsmaßnahmen. *Zeitschrift für Arbeits- und Organisationspsychologie, 37*, 163–171.

Spychiger, M., Oser, F., Hascher, T., & Mahler, F. (1998). *Der Fragebogen S-UFS: Entwicklung und erste Ergebnisse.* Schriftenreihe zum Projekt: "Lernen Menschen aus Fehlern?", Nr. 4. Pädagogisches Institut der Universität Fribourg.

Tulving, E. (2001). Episodic memory and common sense: How far apart? *The Royal Society, 356*, 1505–1515.

Tulving, E., & Craig, F. I. M. (2000). *The Oxford handbook of memory.* Oxford, UK: Oxford University Press.

Van der Schaaf, T. W. (1991). A framework for designing near miss management systems. In T. W. Van der Schaaf, D. A. Lucas & A. R. Hale (Eds.), *Near miss reporting as a safety tool* (pp. 35–57). Oxford: Butterworth-Heinemann Ltd.

Wheeler, M. A., Stuss, D. T., & Tulwin, E. (1997). Toward a theory of episodic memory: The frontal lobes and autonoetic consciousness. *Psychological Bulletin, 121*, 331–354.

Zapf, D., Frese, M., & Brodbeck, F. C. (1999). Fehler und Fehlermanagement. In C. Hoyos & D. Frey (Eds.), *Arbeits- und Organisationspsychologie* (pp. 398–411). Weinheim, Germany: PVU.

Chapter 5
Professional Knowledge Is (Also) Knowledge About Errors

Hans Gruber and Michael Mohe

Knowledge Is Power

One of the key findings of research on expertise (Ericsson, Charness, Feltovich, & Hoffman, 2006) is that the outstanding performance of experts in any complex professional domain is related to their outstanding domain of knowledge. Experts excel by a great amount of knowledge and advantageous knowledge organisation in order to make functional and efficient use of their knowledge. Thus, it is appropriate to state that "knowledge is power". In his seminal work, De Groot (1965) analysed cognitive structures and information processing of chess players. By comparing chess players of different performance levels, De Groot identified the experts' ability to remember domain-specific information faster and more effectively, and to recall domain-specific information more accurately, than novices when they were presented chess positions for a few seconds and then immediately asked to remember them. The experts' superior recall is explicable by the specific perceptual structures they held in memory, which were closely related to their domain-specific knowledge. Similar evidence was found in many different domains, such as music, sports, physics, medicine, history, and many others (Degner & Gruber, 2011).

Many studies confirm the eminent role of a large base of declarative knowledge for expert problem-solving (Simon & Simon, 1978). In most professional fields, many expert actions are highly automated. Theories exist, which describe how declarative knowledge is transformed into procedural knowledge through practice

H. Gruber, Ph.D. (✉)
Institute of Educational Science, University of Regensburg, Regensburg, Germany
e-mail: hans.gruber@paedagogik.uni-regensburg.de

M. Mohe, Ph.D.
Department of Technics, University of Applied Sciences Bielefeld, Bielefeld, Germany
e-mail: michael.mohe@fh-bielefeld.de

J. Bauer and C. Harteis (eds.), *Human Fallibility: The Ambiguity of Errors for Work and Learning*, Professional and Practice-based Learning 6,
DOI 10.1007/978-90-481-3941-5_5,

(e.g. ACT model; Anderson, 1982). That means that different kinds of knowledge have to be distinguished. The distinction between declarative knowledge and procedural knowledge is the most prominent one, but other classification systems are much more fine-grained. De Jong and Ferguson-Hessler (1996) proposed a 4×5 matrix, in which four different kinds of knowledge (situational, conceptual, procedural, and strategic) and five different criteria of knowledge (superficial vs. deep, isolated vs. linked, explicit vs. complied, visual or analytic, and general vs. domain-specific) are differentiated. They address different aspects of the acquisition, storage, retrieval, application, and transformation of knowledge. In terms of learning and professional development, the transformation of knowledge through professional practice is the most crucial aspect. Such transformations are described in the encapsulation theory and in the dynamic memory theory.

The transformation of knowledge during practice is at the core of the encapsulation theory (Schmidt & Boshuizen, 1993). This model, which was developed in the domain of medicine, postulates that acquisition of expertise leads to an integration of declarative and experiential knowledge in encapsulated knowledge. Through professional activity and experience of real cases, declarative knowledge about diseases is developed into knowledge structures called illness scripts. These are generalised over cases, but are nevertheless closely related to application contexts, because they are based on episodic experiences with real cases. The use of illness scripts leads to quick action without the need to effortfully activate declarative knowledge. The declarative knowledge remains available if necessary, but can be neglected in most cases, because the knowledge encapsulated in clinical experience is sufficient. Empirical evidence for the encapsulation model is based on findings that medical experts improve their performance if presented with additional case data about patients – such information is useless for novices who depend on abstract declarative knowledge. Additionally, experts' descriptions of clinical phenomena of diseases contain much more information about cases than novices' descriptions. Connecting declarative knowledge with case experience is obviously a crucial component of the acquisition of expertise in medicine.

The experience of real professional episodes and their conscious reflection plays an important role in the acquisition of expertise. In the model of dynamic memory, Kolodner (1983) explained how episodes are represented in memory and how episodic experiential knowledge can be applied. Knowledge is regarded as episodic definitions that include the subjective relevance and perception of episodes as well as knowledge about the applicability and application of errors. Since experts' episodic definitions are superior to novices', the acquisition of expertise can be interpreted as a continuing refinement of episodic definitions based on the experience of repeated application of knowledge. Episodic definitions are represented in Episodic Memory Organisation Packets (E-MOPs). An E-MOP can be described as generalised episode; it contains both information that is common across episodes and deviations of particular episodes from this general information. Thus, E-MOPs include applicable episodic knowledge in which the subjects' own experiences are integrated. Two classes of events trigger learning from experience: generalisation across episodes and analysis of errors. After the occurrence of an error in a particular episode, the deviations of this episode from the generalised one are explicitly stored. Such knowledge about errors can later be used to avoid further errors. In educational theory, the explicit use of errors during learning has been controversially discussed. However, since errors inevitably occur in complex domains, dealing with them is very important in order to enable subjects to cope with new errors.

Complex Professional Activities Are Not Free from Errors

In many professions, like business management, it is not trivial to define "correct" (and useful) knowledge. Sometimes, it is even difficult to evaluate whether an undertaken activity is correct or erroneous. The problems to be solved are complex and often cannot be successfully approached by applying simple algorithms. Voss, Blais, Means, Greene, and Ahwesh (1989) showed, more than 20 years ago, that in domains like economics, formal training does not play such a major role during the acquisition of expertise as in other domains and professions. Individuals develop concepts of the field mainly through real-world experience, but not through pure cumulation of a large number of knowledge units. It is possible that veridical concepts and misconceptions simultaneously exist in the subjects' knowledge and sometimes it is difficult to distinguish them (Mandl, Gruber, & Renkl, 1993). This is particularly true in modern knowledge-intensive professions, which usually develop rapidly, depending on the changing information technologies that include fallible interaction and co-operation. They require processes of complex problem-solving which are known to be prone to errors (Dörner & Schaub, 1994).

In such professions, knowledge thus plays a double-edged role: On the one hand, they heavily depend on the existence of abounding knowledge, and on the other, they often provoke employees to commit errors, to possess incorrect knowledge, to be unsettled about the nature of knowledge, etc. Stollfuß, Sieweke, Mohe, and Gruber (2011) argue that, in such domains, employees are unlikely to commit no errors, and organisations are forced to deal with errors in order to reduce potentially negative outcomes. Therefore, these professions put much effort into the development of error management strategies, which either try to minimise the negative potential of errors (Van Dyck, Frese, Baer, & Sonnentag, 2005) or lead to learning from errors (Gartmeier, Bauer, Gruber, & Heid, 2008).

Several barriers impede error management in organisations. Cognitive abilities determine to which degree individuals are able to correctly identify errors within complex cause and effect chains. Many employees hide their own errors rather than reporting them, because they are afraid of motivational or even monetary drawbacks (Zhao & Olivera, 2006). Working conditions influence what kinds of challenges an employee faces while trying to fulfill a task and thus these working conditions influence the potential to discover and report errors (Sasou & Reason, 1999). Such working conditions may refer to environmental (physical appearance of the workplace, e.g. darkness in the laboratory), intra-individual (e.g. provocation of excessive fatigue) and social (e.g. lack of communication opportunities) performance-shaping factors. Reason (1990) found that a lack of motivation has a significant influence on employees' errors. In many cases, system failures are rather induced by employees' lack of willingness to fulfill a certain task according to some well-known rules than by lack of skills.

Barriers of an effective error management may thus be based on the detection, the communication, or the handling of errors (Stollfuß & Sieweke, 2010). Difficulties in the detection of errors may be provoked when the correctness of an action cannot be precisely evaluated, or when different aims which are conflicting have to be simultaneously reached. In many modern professions, it is far from trivial to understand the nature of dynamic decision-making processes even if clearly defined outcomes are observable. Constraints at the workplace might help to miss the detection of error (Sellen, 1994). Lack of communication can cause information asymmetries about specific errors. Subjects, who assume that these errors cannot be detected by someone else, conclude a variety of reporting and non-reporting behaviours (Zhao & Olivera, 2006). There exists a dynamic interrelationship among the different barriers that prevent employees from successfully accomplishing a task. Employees' workflows are often disrupted because problems, which have to be dealt with, occur, e.g. if a construction worker is missing the optimal tool to fulfill a certain task. Barriers, therefore, often prevent task completion.

Among intra-individual determinants of barriers, employees' abilities and motivation play a major role. Attribution theory suggests that individuals' abilities to detect their own errors are constrained because they tend to be unconsciously biassed while attributing the causes of negative outcomes to their own welfare in order to protect their self-esteem (Argyris, 1991). Employees are often not willing to communicate their own errors when reporting behaviour causes higher costs – emotional as well as monetary – than not reporting the behaviour (Bauer, 2008).

The domain of company consultation can serve as an example of how difficult it is to adequately reflect on the error-proneness of professional behaviour in real professional contexts. Most research on organisational error management does not take the specific characteristics of profit-oriented consultations into account, whereas research specifically on profit-oriented consultations tends to neglect dealing with errors. Because of the characteristics of consultations, such as the intangibility of the product (Lowendahl, Revang, & Fosstenlokken, 2001), a special set of latent conditions is present in companies that diverge from those of other organisations. These companies rely, to a vast amount, on clients' trust in the consultancy itself. This implies that a consultancy's reputation may be assumed as an extremely important tangible asset for them, which is revealed by its importance in the purchasing of consultancies (Dawes, Dowling, & Patterson, 1992).

Research on consultancies has shown that they often operate under conditions of uncertainty and ambiguity (Alvesson, 1993; Glückler & Armbrüster, 2003). Consultants are supposed to be regularly confronted with the lack of rules about how to act correctly. The degree and the variety of actions that cannot be ex ante classified as being right or wrong are rather high (Stollfuß et al., 2011). Accordingly, many actions cannot be aligned to predefined patterns of behaviour. Even though higher-level goals might be familiar (e.g. curing a patient; improving the strategy of the client organisation; increasing the profitability of the company), employees often have to decide ad hoc which action is most likely to reach these higher-level goals. If employees face a lack of knowledge about cause-and-effect chains of these ad hoc actions, possibilities for action-based error detection are considerably constrained. Evaluating the outcomes of consulting is constrained because the professional contexts surrounding their service is usually ambiguous, comprises many social interactions, and leads to partially invisible side effects (Clark & Salaman, 1998). Uncertainty about the effects of one's actions, however, reduces the possibilities of outcome-based error detection and thus constrains attempts to prevent future errors.

Many employees of consultations operate under conditions that are likely to encourage their willingness to engage in internal impression management rather than in error management (Stollfuß, 2011). Top management consultancies tend to apply rigid human resource management systems in which employees, within frequent intervals, are either promoted to a higher rank or laid off from the company (Greenwood & Empson, 2003). Alvesson and Kärreman (2004) provide evidence that, under those working conditions, employees' loyalties belong to the team rather than to the organisation while dealing with errors in trade-off situations. The costs of error communication are quite high within consultations because reporting one's own errors might reduce the chances for promotion. Therefore, the probability of reporting the error is reduced.

It is thus not surprising that Argyris (1991) observed a defensive way that consultants deal with their own errors. They "projected the blame for any problems away from themselves and onto what they said were unclear goals, insensitive and unfair leaders, and stupid clients" (p. 101). Consultants tend to attribute the origin of errors to other persons. As a detrimental consequence, they have difficulties in correctly detecting and attributing their own errors. These specific conditions in consultation contexts provoke difficulties in realising attempts to improve error management. We will return to such attempts in the last paragraph of this chapter.

According to Stollfuß (2011), it can be concluded from the example of company consultations that organisations often face many trade-offs, because, often, a stimulation of a factor that takes forward specific aspects of error management (e.g. increasing the willingness to handle one's own errors quickly) cannot be separated from a stimulation of other factors that hinder error management (e.g. decreasing the willingness to communicate about one's own errors). The appropriate use of options for error management in consultations is therefore difficult to anticipate; job-rotation, transparent architecture of the office building, group reflection, teamwork, etc. The installation of teamwork does not conflict with the specific characteristics of consultations, but it cannot be seen as panacea either. Even though teamwork is said to induce many positive effects, research also identified several serious problems related to teamwork. Implications of research thus cannot be easily adopted by managers in consultations in order to improve the ways their organisations deal with errors.

How Knowledge Is (Undesirably) Affected: Inert Knowledge – Problems of Knowledge Application

Even in domains in which veridical knowledge can be reliably identified, evidence was found that the availability of a large knowledge base is not necessarily connected with high-level performance. The problem of "inert knowledge" was identified as a major challenge for instructional research (Bransford, Goldman, & Vye, 1991).

Stark, Mandl, Gruber, and Renkl (1999) report that, in various domains, a similar phenomenon could be observed: Learners have considerable problems with successfully applying acquired knowledge to relevant problem situations in real settings. Advanced students of business management had great difficulties in applying their conceptual knowledge to controlling a complex computer-based simulation of a company. On the one hand, they were able to communicate domain-specific aspects in a rather professional way and they generated differentiated mental models. But on the other hand, in achieving business profits, which is certainly an important aspect of business management, they were even less successful than novices.

During their reasoning, the advanced students considered more content aspects than they were able to structure and integrate in order to come to a functional decision. The content aspects expressed were veridical with regard to economic theories, but not always relevant to the simulated market situations. Their reasoning was thus complex, but did not meet the specific constraints of the situation at hand. As a matter of fact, it was not flexible enough. Thus, the students' knowledge remained inert. Starting from such a knowledge base, which clearly lacks functionality, failures in practice are pre-assigned, which cannot be easily detected and remedied.

As similar results were found in studies investigating the knowledge application of advanced medical students, it can be concluded that university students tend to learn much declarative knowledge, which, however, can often hardly be used in solving complex problems. The instruction, therefore, seems to be not appropriate for the development of flexible expertise in students, although much knowledge is acquired.

Although the very reasons for the difficulties of knowledge application vary across domains, there seems to be a common root: The lecture-like instruction formats that often predominate in higher education are not appropriate to equip the students with competencies needed for effective action, or, as Bransford, Franks, Vye, and Sherwood (1989) put it: "... wisdom can't be told" (p. 470). Students are not well-prepared for later job demands or for the acquisition of the kind of domain-specific expertise that is typical of practitioners in their respective community of practice.

In order to effectively deal with the inert knowledge problem, analyses of the underlying causes are necessary (Renkl, Mandl, & Gruber, 1996). Instruction can be designed, which allows learners to construct useful and broadly applicable knowledge, on the basis of the reasons of the insufficient transfer. Three kinds of explanations of the non-application of knowledge can be found in the psychological and educational literature: metaprocess, structure deficit, and situatedness explanations. Metaprocess explanations assume that the relevant knowledge is available, but it is not used because of disturbed access processes (e.g. lacking metacognitive control or low self-efficacy). Structure deficit explanations suppose that the deficit is rooted in the structure of the knowledge itself (i.e. the knowledge is not available in a form that allows its application). In situatedness explanations, the traditional concepts of knowledge and transfer are questioned. One basic assumption of this perspective is that knowledge is fundamentally situated and, therefore, context-bound.

Typical metaprocess explanations stem from research on metacognition and on the influence of non-cognitive factors (e.g. motivation, epistemological beliefs) on learning. Within metacognitive explanations, it is assumed that it is not sufficient for a person to have some knowledge of strategy in order to be a strategic learner. Paris, Lipson, and Wixson (1983) argue that conditional knowledge is necessary for effective metacognitive control of knowledge application processes. Conditional knowledge comprises the knowledge of "when" and "why" to access certain facts or strategies.

Structure deficit explanations typically assume that deficits in the to-be-applied knowledge are responsible for its missing application. They differ with respect to the specific aspect of knowledge that is made responsible for the inertia problem. Lacking knowledge application and transfer is often explained by lacking conceptual knowledge (i.e. deep-level understanding), missing knowledge compilation (i.e. transformation of declarative knowledge into procedural knowledge), or knowledge compartmentalisation (i.e. storage of information acquired in different contexts in separate memory parts, which lack connections).

Since the late 1980s, several researchers have postulated a fundamental situatedness of knowledge. Such situated cognition models criticise the traditional notion of knowledge, but do not form a uniform theoretical approach. Whereas metaprocess and structure deficit explanations assume that there is some knowledge which cannot be applied or transferred, some situated cognition proponents hold the radical position that there is no knowledge stored as an abstract-decontextualised entity that can be acquired in one context and applied in another. Clancey (1993) argues that the attribution of knowledge as an abstract entity to a person may just be the result of a sense-making process in which an observer (third-person) describes patterns of behavior of an intelligent agent. He says that reification of knowledge in the first person is a category error.

The overview shows that many factors can impede knowledge application. As a consequence, instruction has to be designed in a way that explicitly deals with this problem. There are several approaches that try to foster the applicability and the transfer of knowledge. The most influential approach is the situatedness explanation of inert knowledge, which triggered something like an educational turn in the psychology of knowledge. After some intensive debates between situated learning proponents (e.g. Greeno, Smith, & Moore, 1993) and cognitive scientists (e.g. Anderson, Reder, & Simon, 1997), most researchers agreed that the situated learning movement extended our view on how to foster professional learning processes. Situated learning was not considered as an alternative to the cognitive perspective on individual determinants of skill acquisition, but rather as a theory of learning environments that helped to understand how to embed individual learning processes in learning environments, which adequately reflect relevant social, cultural and technological contexts.

Models of situated learning are, therefore, promising supplements for traditional forms of instruction, regardless of which theoretical explanation for the inert knowledge problem is adopted. The most prominent instructional models are cognitive apprenticeship (Collins, Brown, & Newman, 1989), anchored instruction (Cognition & Technology Group at Vanderbilt, 1997) and random access instruction (Spiro, Feltovich, Jacobson, & Coulson, 1991). Although the models differ in detail, they have some pivotal instructional principles in common. One important feature is that learning should be motivated by an interesting to-be-solved problem (problem-oriented learning). Knowledge is then acquired in the context of immediate application to a problem solution and not in an abstract, decontextualised way. Furthermore, the problem should be authentic or, at least, close to reality. This means that the problems are usually complex and ill-defined as it is typical of non-trivial problems of vocational and everyday life.

Within the anchored instruction approach, for example, a series of video-presented adventures was developed with open-ended problems to be solved. In one story that was constructed for mathematics learning at the fifth and sixth grade level, the anchor for further learning is a challenge to save a wounded eagle. A cover story made it plausible that the ultralight of Jasper, the "hero" of the video series, had to be used. The rescue of the eagle is, however, impeded by many factors, such as the limited payload and the fuel capacity of the ultralight and the relatively long distances to overcome. Hence, in order to plan the rescue, many mathematical tasks have to be performed and corresponding knowledge has to be acquired and applied. The students cooperated to solve these Jasper problems, of course with the support of a teacher. Evaluations of the Jasper series were very promising.

This type of learning environment fits the principle of similarity between the learning and the application context derived from the situated cognition assumptions. Although the student will probably never be in a situation where they have to save an eagle, this Jasper problem shares many features with realistic problems of vocational and everyday life. It is rather complex and ill-defined, and students are cooperating and are using tools (e.g. maps) as in real worklife settings.

But also from the view of the discussed metaprocess and structure deficit explanations, Jasper-type anchor problems for learning seem to be useful. They stimulate interest and motivate students to acquire mathematical knowledge (Cognition & Technology Group at Vanderbilt, 1997). In addition, students can learn about the application conditions of the to-be-learned mathematical concepts (conditional knowledge, knowledge compilation). Furthermore, school matter is brought into contact with everyday knowledge and some real-world-type phenomena. The student can experience that mathematical rules do not merely constitute the rules of a game, but are connected to things like distances or fuel consumption. A restriction of such learning environments is that they are still "instant realities." Despite that restriction, they constitute a helpful intermediate stage between abstract learning of theoretical concepts or principles and problem solving in real-world contexts.

Analysing such models in depth, a number of similarities can be found in theories about experience-based acquisition of expertise mentioned in the first paragraph of this chapter. Both the model of encapsulation and the theory of dynamic memory imply consequences for the instructional support of the acquisition of expertise that are based on the implementation of case-based reasoning during learning. As learning by experience with cases alters knowledge structures, instructional consequences are evident: The acquisition of expertise can be supported didactically by fostering reflective application of knowledge through the presentation of complex learning environments in which real application situations occur. Case-based learning is a preferable mode of learning to reach these goals.

Case-based learning conceptions stress, like situated learning models, the similarity between learning situation and application situation. By dealing with complex initial case problems, learners get a notion of the relevance of the knowledge to-be-learned. Authenticity and situativity of cases enable learners to make experiences in complex episodes of learning. Multiple perspectives on the same subject matter help to avoid oversimplifications and to enhance the transferability of the knowledge to-be-learned. It is not random that the random access instruction (Spiro et al., 1991) focusses on the development of cognitive flexibility through multiple perspectives during advanced learning processes. Employing multiple perspectives aims at making knowledge more transferable. Learners should deal with concepts at different times, in different contexts, with different purposes, and with different roles. Thus, oversimplification and too narrow ties to specific contexts are avoided.

Cognitive flexibility theory stresses the importance of multiple contexts in which the knowledge to be acquired is embedded. The theory is particularly relevant for research on expertise because it mainly deals with advanced knowledge acquisition in ill-structured domains. Such domains can be described by the complexity of concepts and cases and by irregularity and large variability of cases. Instruction, following the theory of cognitive flexibility, aims to induce multiple and, as a consequence, flexible representations of the knowledge, which can be applied in many different contexts. An instructional means to induce this is the technique of landscape criss-crossing in which the conceptual map is explored in many different ways. As a consequence, many facets of the concepts are learned so that they can be applied in a variety of contexts. Thus, expert flexibility can be enhanced.

Using Errors and Ambiguities as Starting Point to Reconsider the Concept of Knowledge

We have argued above that errors and ambiguities are inevitably part of professional activities in most modern professions. Errors at work are incidents that interrupt the workflow, cause stress, and pose challenges to employees' competencies. However, they have the potential to serve as opportunities for learning and for the development of performance as well as for organisational innovation. Obviously, individual attitudes towards errors, e.g. error orientation and organisational error climate play a central role. To illuminate and critically appraise the potential benefits of errors and ambiguities, we argue that the concept of knowledge has to be reconsidered. It has to be acknowledged that knowledge is not only an individual property and a cognitive entity. From the assumption of the situatedness of knowledge it can be derived that the conditionalisation of knowledge and the social nature of knowledge have to be taken into account, if the role of knowledge for professional activity is be adequately investigated. Both aspects are treated in some detail in this section. Another conclusion about the nature of knowledge that can be drawn from the analysis of errors and ambiguities is that "negative knowledge" is of eminent importance. This conclusion is not elaborated in this chapter, as it is treated in this volume in two separate chapters (see Chaps. 3 and 4 in this book).

Mandl et al. (1993) described the concept of knowledge compartmentalisation based on the analyses of inert knowledge by concluding that, in many cases, individuals' knowledge structures about a specific domain are composed of several separate, not intertwined, parts. For example, implicit or procedural knowledge that gets automatically activated in everyday routines often operates somewhat independently of more explicit forms of knowledge. Three types of knowledge compartmentalisation can be distinguished, which differ with regard to their consequences concerning further learning and knowledge application: namely, the compartmentalisation of (1) incorrect and correct concepts, (2) several correct concepts, and (3) symbol systems and real world entities.

In particular, the lack of mapping between symbol systems and real-world entities affects education. For instance, children who have learned that thermometers measure temperature do not connect this knowledge with their own experience of hot and cold. They expect that thermometer readings should be of a different nature. Thus, they expect that a doubled temperature results when two cups of water at the same temperature are poured together. The common sense knowledge that the poured water will be of the same temperature is not considered. The rules of physics are treated like the rules of a game that have nothing to do with real-world entities and processes (Perkins & Simmons, 1988). Similarly, students often lack comprehension mapping between the reference domain and the symbol system in the domain of mathematics. This kind of knowledge compartmentalisation causes students to perform meaningless symbol manipulations without understanding the relevance to their everyday life. This leads to the situation that, on the one hand, real-world knowledge is not used in solving arithmetic problems in school, and on the other hand, that the kind of mathematics taught in schools is not used in everyday activities.

Conditionalisation of knowledge refers to the information about the conditions and constraints on its application. It is knowledge that is triggered by three components that interact in problem solving: salient conditions of the problem situation, goals within the problem situation, and predictable consequences of operators. The term "salient conditions" refers to the situation and to the aspects of the task that are integrated by the problem solver into her/his initial problem definition. The problem solver's level of expertise as well as the goals involved determine which situational features will become salient conditions. The goal is not only important for the selection of relevant features: Situational features may reciprocally lead to (re)definitions of the goals. If knowledge is conditionalised, operators, which are combined with the salient conditions given and the actual goals, are activated. During the operator activation process, several possible operators and their consequences are evaluated in an anticipatory way. Particularly, situation-specific side effects are considered because they set important constraints for efficient operator selection.

The concept of conditionalisation of knowledge is based on the assumption that knowledge as an important building block of expert performance is inevitably situated in specific professional contexts, which thus have to be taken into consideration in the analysis of professional learning and performance (Gruber, Palonen, Rehrl, & Lehtinen, 2007). Expertise in organisational settings evolves as a result of the acknowledged achievements of individuals and groups. Its value is always related to its viability and usefulness. This implies that members of a social system with shared practices and common goals are sufficiently capable of reliably nominating experts. It has been observed repeatedly that these nominees do not necessarily correspond with the formal leaders in the system (Stein, 1995). As a consequence of their formal or informal centrality, experts do not only possess more and better knowledge than those with whom they interact but they are also able to manage the transfer of knowledge. Individual strength and group acknowledgment are thus intrinsically related. Expertise can then be denoted as a stable description of cognitive skills emerging through interactive processes. It reflects both social relationships in practice and adequate (or even excellent) individual attributes (knowledge, skills, etc.), which in turn emerge through intensive interaction at work.

Experts thus become experts by receiving the attribution of being an expert from others. The definition of expertise can then be based on social acknowledgment, where being regarded as an expert means receiving a nomination from people with whom one interacts. Mieg (2001) argued that an expert is a role or a form of interaction rather than a particular individual. According to a cognitive approach, the ascription of expert status is based on an individual's knowledge. The value of such knowledge, however, depends on the knowledge of other members within a shared context. Expertise then arises from the "goodness of fit" between the knowledge and skills of the expert on the one hand and the expectations and attitudes of people belonging to the expert's social context on the other hand.

An indirect acknowledgment of the role of professional social networks has for long been provided by research on expertise: In defining the level of expertise of their subjects, the authors of many studies relied on peer judgments and other classifications by professionally-related persons, such as supervisors or principals (Berliner, 2001). Trusting those people to reliably determine a subject's level of expertise in research on expertise clearly indicates that the social network's assessment of individual excellence plays an important part in the definition itself. Other researchers stress that social scaffolding is necessary for individuals to proceed to increasingly complex levels of expert behaviour (Yan & Fischer, 2002). Efforts have been made to explicitly analyse the mutual impact of individual attributes and network relationships in the growth of expertise. Initial attempts have been made in order to design empirical studies that simultaneously integrate the development of cognitive capacities or skills and the taking over of powerful positions within social communities.

In exploring the social recognition of individual expertise, it is important to go beyond the formal status of an individual within social and professional communities or organisations. However, it is more important to focus on informal status in terms of professional respect among colleagues as well as the actual functioning of the individual as a member of an expert network or community. As the acquisition of specific expertise is bound to the experience domain, the analysis of situational contexts of the domain is important. Acquisition of expertise can be viewed as a process of enculturation and of becoming a full participant in a community of practice. Participation denotes the process by which individuals are working together and working with experts in a social setting. Acquisition of expertise thus depends on interactions within a particular social context. Lave and Wenger (1991) conceived learning as legitimate peripheral participation by which newcomers become enculturated into a community of practice and acquire expertise.

The process by which a newcomer becomes a full participant or an expert is both individual and social. In addition, there are artefacts and physical and symbolic tools that originate from a broad cultural context, which is historically constructed and developed. Further, learning as enculturation comprises more than merely the acquisition of knowledge; it concerns many social aspects, such as ways of speaking, belief systems, social customs, and tricks of the trade. The concept of "communities of practice" is widely used, yet rarely defined precisely. Brown and Duguid's (2001) definition emphasises the aspect of "communities" in the sense of group membership instead of focusing on the shared practice itself. On the other hand, as practical work is managed in division, an organisation might be regarded as a community of communities of practices. It is important to specify the criterion of a shared context because even subjects in the same job category within a large organisation do not necessarily participate in a particular community of practice. Many modern workplaces are organised in such a way that they increasingly lose their continuity and clear-cut boundaries, although the organisations are certainly not devoid of boundaries (Cross, Yan, & Louis, 2000).

A community of practice has been defined as a group of persons with particular individual attributes (skills, knowledge, etc.), who either formally interact within an organisation or who informally interact in a network while following shared goals (Hakkarainen, Palonen, Paavola, & Lehtinen, 2004). However, at the same time, we have to consider that workers are affiliated with more than one community of practice, depending on how the communities are defined and how professional expertise is formed. Consequently, we argue that, in the case of rapidly changing knowledge-based professions, which is the focus of this volume, the concept of "networks of practice" might be preferable to the concept of "communities of practice". This also includes the notion that the relationships among network members might be significantly more flexible than those within communities of practice.

In such networks of practice, other persons play a crucial role in designing practice activities, goal-setting, motivating (often: forcing) individuals to engage in practice and breaking down complex performance into smaller units to be practiced. Such persons are trainers, coaches, teachers, mentors or parents. Up to now, only few studies in expertise research have pointed out the important role of particular social contacts for the long-term development of individuals.

One reason might be that these persons usually are "persons in the shadow" (Gruber, Lehtinen, Palonen, & Degner, 2008) who tend not to be in the public front line of the expertise development of their "fosterlings".

Implications for the Practice of Knowledge-Intensive Professions

In this chapter, we have argued that there is convincing evidence that "knowledge is power", but the power is often limited because people cannot make adequate use of their knowledge so it remains inert. Reasons for the inertness can be found within the individuals, in the design of their learning and development processes, and in the nature of the workplace. The paradox arose that particularly in knowledge-intensive professions, the veridicality of knowledge is often unreliable, unstable, or generally doubted. One reason is that the unreflected application of knowledge, without taking into account its conditionalisation and its social nature, often leads to errors or to ambiguous situations. All this has to be taken into account if implications for professional practice are drawn, in particular, concerning error management and the application of knowledge.

Stollfuß et al. (2011) concluded that a variety of mechanisms can be found that are related to (in)effective error management. A drawback of many research attempts is that they focus on isolated mechanisms of (in)effective error management (e.g. the impact of a non-punishment culture on employees' willingness to share knowledge about own errors). In professional practice, however, complex interactions of a large number of such mechanisms are the normal case. It is argued how managers can be motivated to engage in the reflection on how to consider these complex relations. Instruments that, on the one hand, do not directly create an impression for employees about being mistrusted by the organisation and that, on the other hand, increase social monitoring are regarded as being worthwhile. However, the effects of instruments such as job-rotation, transparent architecture of the office building, group reflection, and teamwork have to be the object of on-going reflection processes.

Three implications for improving organisations' error management are mentioned most often, introducing safe environments, installing incentives and rewarding systems, and introducing team work and team training. However, Stollfuß et al. (2011) argue that the suitability of the recommendations in the literature to improve error management is limited for knowledge-intensive professions.

Concerning safe environments, the finding that fear of punishment encourages employees not to honestly communicate about errors, inspired researchers (e.g. Tynan, 2005) to suggest to organisations that they provide their employees both psychological safety in order to overcome communication barriers, which is a sort of immunity against punishment, and safe communication channels.

Psychological safety (Edmondson, 1999) is based on employees' respect among themselves and it is characterised by employees' shared beliefs that they will not be rejected, embarrassed, or punished by their colleagues for speaking up. These working conditions are closely related to a proactive feedback-seeking that encourages learning because employees are more likely to engage in social learning activities by sharing their knowledge about their own errors with their colleagues if they do not have to fear any social punishment for revealing their own errors (Bauer, 2008). It is still unresolved, however, how demands on employees for being promoted might limit organisations' possibilities to nurture psychological safety. Stollfuß (2011) assumes that competition among employees for limited chances of being promoted to a higher rank might decrease employees' freedom to speak up among their colleagues about their own errors, because employees might want to create the impression of being the one that deserves to be promoted. Accordingly, the suggestion to provide a sort of immunity in order to increase employees' communication about errors (Van Dyck et al., 2005) is interesting and problematic. Even if organisations forbear from using social sanctioning among employees, it is still unclear how far direct and immediate sanctioning is similarly affected as long-term implicit punishing. It is still underspecified under which conditions a non-punishment culture might conflict with working conditions, in which employees compete against each other for their own reputation and/or their own chances of being promoted to a higher level, as is the case in many company consultations.

Enhancing employees' communication about errors seems to be the most promising. However, this instrument requires quite different practices in different professions. Weinberg (2002) showed that establishing reporting systems in hospitals encouraged employees to communicate openly about their errors. Sucov, Shapiro, Jay, Suner, and Simon (2001) reported that the implementation of an anonymous error-reporting system in a medical institution significantly improved error detection compared to traditional incident reporting systems.

In a similar vein, researchers argue about the usefulness of incentive and rewarding systems. For example, Weick and Sutcliffe (2001) postulate that installing a system to reward communication about one's own errors – even in those cases in which the error causes severe costs for the organisation – might lead to positive outcomes for both the individuals and the organisations. There are limits to such rewards, of course, e.g. when the same error is committed repeatedly, or when the error caused injuries or damages.

The relationship between individuals and the organisation is obviously of utmost importance. Most prominent in research are studies on the value of teamwork and team training. Much evidence exists that teamwork has a huge potential to prevent errors and to improve error management. For example, Barach (2007) found positive effects of teamwork on dealing with risks in health care professions. By introducing monitoring functions, which can displace the boundaries of communication from the individual level to the team level, teams can develop a shared responsibility for work processes. In addition, teams usually have a back-up function, e.g. through double-checking in relevant safety processes. Teamwork does not function per se; however, it instead has to be the object of permanent training and reflection. This seems to be a crucial feature of all attempts to improve the practice of knowledge-intensive professional work.

References

Alvesson, M. (1993). Organizations as rhetoric: Knowledge-intensive firms and the struggle with ambiguity. *Journal of Management Studies, 30*, 997–1015.

Alvesson, M., & Kärreman, D. (2004). Interfaces of control. Technocratic and socio-ideological control in a global management consultancy firm. *Accounting, Organizations and Society, 29*, 423–444.

Anderson, J. R. (1982). Acquisition of cognitive skill. *Psychological Review, 89*, 369–406.

Anderson, J. R., Reder, L. M., & Simon, H. A. (1997). Situative versus cognitive perspectives: Form versus substance. *Educational Researcher, 26*(1), 18–21.

Argyris, C. (1991). Teaching smart people how to learn. *Harvard Business Review, 69*(3), 99–109.

Barach, P. (2007). A team-based risk modification programme to make health care safer. *Theoretical Issues in Ergonomics Science, 8*, 481–494.

Bauer, J. (2008). *Learning from errors at work. Studies on nurses' engagement in error-related learning activities*. Doctoral dissertation, University of Regensburg, Regensburg, Germany.

Berliner, D. C. (2001). Learning about and learning from expert teachers. *International Journal of Educational Research, 35*, 463–482.

Bransford, J. D., Franks, J. J., Vye, N. J., & Sherwood, R. D. (1989). New approaches to learning and instruction: Because wisdom can't be told. In S. Vosniadou & A. Ortony (Eds.), *Similarity and analogical reasoning* (pp. 470–497). Cambridge, UK: Cambridge University Press.

Bransford, J. D., Goldman, S. R., & Vye, N. J. (1991). Making a difference in people's ability to think: Reflections on a decade of work and some hopes for the future. In R. J. Sternberg & L. Okagaki (Eds.), *Influences on children* (pp. 147–180). Hillsdale, NJ: Erlbaum.

Brown, J. S., & Duguid, P. (2001). Knowledge in organization: A social practice perspective. *Organization Science, 12*, 198–213.

Clancey, W. J. (1993). Situated action: A neuropsychological interpretation response to Vera and Simon. *Cognitive Science, 17*, 87–116.

Clark, T., & Salaman, G. (1998). Creating the "right" impression: Towards a dramaturgy of management consultancy. *Service Industries Journal, 18*(1), 18–38.

Cognition and Technology Group at Vanderbilt. (1997). *The Jasper project: Lessons in curriculum, instruction, assessment, and professional development*. Mahwah, NJ: Erlbaum.

Collins, A., Brown, J. S., & Newman, S. E. (1989). Cognitive apprenticeship: Teaching the crafts of reading, writing and mathematics. In L. B. Resnick (Ed.), *Knowing, learning, and instruction* (pp. 453–494). Hillsdale, NJ: Erlbaum.

Cross, R. L., Yan, A., & Louis, M. R. (2000). Boundary activities in boundaryless organizations: A case study of a transformation to a team-based structure. *Human Relations, 53*, 841–868.

Dawes, P. L., Dowling, G. R., & Patterson, P. G. (1992). Criteria used to select management consultants. *Industrial Marketing Management, 21*, 187–193.

De Groot, A. D. (1965). *Thought and choice in chess*. The Hague, the Netherlands: Mouton.

De Jong, T., & Ferguson-Hessler, M. G. M. (1996). Types and qualities of knowledge. *Educational Psychologist, 31*, 105–113.

Degner, S., & Gruber, H. (2011). Persons in the shadow: How guidance works in the acquisition of expertise. In B. Weber, E. Marsal, & T. Dobashi (Eds.), *The politics of empathy. New interdisciplinary perspectives on an ancient phenomenon* (pp. 103–116). Münster, Germany: Lit.

Dörner, D., & Schaub, H. (1994). Errors in planning and decision-making and the nature of human information processing. *Applied Psychology: An International Review, 43*, 433–453.

Edmondson, A. (1999). Psychological safety and learning behavior in work teams. *Administrative Science Quarterly, 44*, 350–383.

Ericsson, K. A., Charness, N., Feltovich, P. J., & Hoffman, R. R. (Eds.). (2006). *The Cambridge handbook of expertise and expert performance*. Cambridge, UK: Cambridge University Press.

Gartmeier, M., Bauer, J., Gruber, H., & Heid, H. (2008). Negative knowledge: Understanding professional learning and expertise. *Vocations and Learning: Studies in Vocational and Professional Education, 1*, 87–103.

Glückler, J., & Armbrüster, T. (2003). Bridging uncertainty in management consulting: The mechanisms of trust and networked reputation. *Organization Studies, 24*, 269–297.
Greeno, J. G., Smith, D. R., & Moore, J. L. (1993). Transfer of situated learning. In D. K. Dettermann & R. J. Sternberg (Eds.), *Transfer on trial: Intelligence, cognition, and instruction* (pp. 99–167). Norwood, MA: Ablex.
Greenwood, R., & Empson, L. (2003). The professional partnership: Relic or exemplary form of governance? *Organization Studies, 24*, 909–933.
Gruber, H., Lehtinen, E., Palonen, T., & Degner, S. (2008). Persons in the shadow: Assessing the social context of high abilities. *Psychology Science Quarterly, 50*, 237–258.
Gruber, H., Palonen, T., Rehrl, M., & Lehtinen, E. (2007). Understanding the nature of expertise: Individual knowledge, social resources and cultural context. In H. Gruber & T. Palonen (Eds.), *Learning in the workplace – New developments* (pp. 227–250). Turku, Finland: Finnish Educational Research Association (FERA).
Hakkarainen, K., Palonen, T., Paavola, S., & Lehtinen, E. (2004). *Communities of networked expertise: Educational and professional perspectives*. Amsterdam: Elsevier.
Kolodner, J. L. (1983). Towards an understanding of the role of experience in the evolution from novice to expert. *International Journal of Man-Machine Studies, 19*, 497–518.
Lave, J., & Wenger, E. (1991). *Situated learning: Legitimate peripheral participation*. Cambridge, UK: Cambridge University Press.
Lowendahl, B. R., Revang, O., & Fosstenlokken, S. M. (2001). Knowledge and value creation in professional service firms: A framework for analysis. *Human Relations, 54*, 911–932.
Mandl, H., Gruber, H., & Renkl, A. (1993). Misconceptions and knowledge compartmentalization. In G. Strube & K. F. Wender (Eds.), *The cognitive psychology of knowledge* (pp. 161–176). Amsterdam: North-Holland.
Mieg, H. A. (2001). *The social psychology of expertise: Case studies in research, professional domains, and expert roles*. Mahwah, NJ: Erlbaum.
Paris, S. G., Lipson, M. Y., & Wixson, K. K. (1983). Becoming a strategic reader. *Contemporary Educational Psychology, 8*, 293–316.
Perkins, D. N., & Simmons, R. (1988). Patterns of misunderstanding: An integrative model of science, math, and programming. *Review of Educational Research, 58*, 303–326.
Reason, J. (1990). *Human error*. New York: Cambridge University Press.
Renkl, A., Mandl, H., & Gruber, H. (1996). Inert knowledge: Analyses and remedies. *Educational Psychologist, 31*, 115–121.
Sasou, K., & Reason, J. (1999). Team errors: Definition and taxonomy. *Reliability Engineering and System Safety, 65*, 1–9.
Schmidt, H. G., & Boshuizen, H. P. A. (1993). On acquiring expertise in medicine. *Educational Psychology Review, 5*, 205–221.
Sellen, A. J. (1994). Detection of everyday errors. *Applied Psychology: An International Review, 43*, 475–498.
Simon, D. P., & Simon, H. A. (1978). Individual differences in solving physics problems. In R. S. Siegler (Ed.), *Children's thinking: What develops?* (pp. 325–348). Hillsdale, NJ: Erlbaum.
Spiro, R. J., Feltovich, P. J., Jacobson, M. J., & Coulson, R. L. (1991). Cognitive flexibility, constructivism, and hypertext: Random access instruction for advanced knowledge acquisition in ill-structured domains. *Educational Technology, 31*(5), 24–33.
Stark, R., Mandl, H., Gruber, H., & Renkl, A. (1999). Instructional means to overcome transfer problems in the domain of economics: Empirical studies. *International Journal of Educational Research, 31*, 591–609.
Stein, E. W. (1995). Social and individual characteristics of organizational experts. *International Journal of Expert Systems, 8*, 121–143.
Stollfuß, M. (2011). Dealings with errors under conditions of competition among employees. Revealing the social dynamics of consultancies' up-or-out practices. In IPOB (Ed.), *The future of knowledge-intensive service work. Theory and practice of managing human and organisational resources* (pp. 91–125). Marburg, Germany: Metropolis.

Stollfuß, M., & Sieweke, J. (2010). Discussing mechanisms of intra-organizational transparency about errors. In S. Behrends, A. Bloemen, B. Mokwinski, & W. Schröder (Eds.), *Wissen und Wissensmanagement – Chancen in der Wirtschaftskrise* (pp. 101–116). Oldenburg, Germany: BIS.

Stollfuß, M., Sieweke, J., Mohe, M., & Gruber, H. (2011). Dealings with errors in professional service firms. In M. Reihlen & A. Werr (Eds.), *Handbook of research on entrepreneurship in professional services*. Cheltenham, UK: Elgar.

Sucov, A., Shapiro, M. J., Jay, G., Suner, S., & Simon, R. (2001). Anonymous error reporting as an adjunct to traditional incident reporting improves error detection. *Academic Emergency Medicine, 8*, 498–499.

Tynan, R. (2005). The effects of threat sensitivity and face giving on dyadic psychological safety and upward communication. *Journal of Applied Social Psychology, 35*, 223–247.

Van Dyck, C., Frese, M., Baer, M., & Sonnentag, S. (2005). Organizational error management culture and its impact on performance: A two-study replication. *Journal of Applied Psychology, 90*, 1228–1240.

Voss, J. F., Blais, J., Means, M. L., Greene, T. R., & Ahwesh, E. (1989). Informal reasoning and subject matter knowledge in the solving of economics problems by naive and novice individuals. In L. B. Resnick (Ed.), *Knowing, learning, and instruction* (pp. 217–249). Hillsdale, NJ: Erlbaum.

Weick, K. E., & Sutcliffe, K. M. (2001). *Managing the unexpected: Assuring high performance in an age of complexity*. San Francisco: Jossey-Bass.

Weinberg, J. K. (2002). Medical error and patient safety: Understanding cultures in conflict. *Law & Policy, 24*(2), 93–113.

Yan, Z., & Fischer, K. (2002). Always under construction. Dynamic variations in adult cognitive micro-development. *Human Development, 45*, 141–160.

Zhao, B., & Olivera, F. (2006). Error reporting in organizations. *Academy of Management Review, 31*, 1012–1030.

Part II
Methodological Strategies

Chapter 6
Research on Errors and Learning from Them: Methodological Perspectives

Klaus Mehl and Theo Wehner

Introduction

Factors such as "unexpected events", "unplanned actions" and "mistakes" represent a challenge as well as a special opportunity for gaining scientific insight. Such events provoke the search for an explanation that does not simply dismiss them as "a deviation from the norm" but can integrate their occurrence in a theory of normality. In this sense, errors are, as Norman (1981) has put it, "windows to the mind". Almost a 100 years earlier, Meringer and Mayer (1895, p. VII) formulated the problem as follows: "One has to avoid mistaking an error (of speech/writing) for something pathological. In the case of an error (of writing), only the attention actually fails while the typewriter runs without guidance and is left to itself. And what makes an error instructive for science is the fact that when it occurs the situation seems like a clockwork stripped out of its case that allows a glimpse into its mechanics."

For us, too, examining action-based human errors is and has been an instructive and challenging analytical approach. When studying the amalgamation of partial actions with whole motor-system-based actions, we used the analysis of action-based human errors as a methodological vehicle (see Wehner, Stadler, & Mehl, 1983; Wehner, Stadler, Mehl, & Kruse, 1985). These works focused on an aspect that two authors writing about conferences on "human error" in 1980 and 1983 found to be of such vital importance that they decided to emphasize it in their preface: "Progress in the study of error is slow – the topic is not a simple one" (Senders & Moray, 1991, p. xii). Why is that the case? Why should research into human errors

K. Mehl, Ph.D. (✉)
Department of Education, Carl von Ossietzky University, Oldenburg, Germany
e-mail: klaus.mehl@uni-oldenburg.de

T. Wehner, Ph.D.
Zentrum für Organisations- und Arbeitswissenschaften, Swiss Federal Institute of Technology (ETH), Zurich, Switzerland
e-mail: twehner@ethz.ch

J. Bauer and C. Harteis (eds.), *Human Fallibility: The Ambiguity of Errors for Work and Learning*, Professional and Practice-based Learning 6,
DOI 10.1007/978-90-481-3941-5_6,

be more difficult than any other psychological topic? The image given by Meringer and Mayer provides a first clue: the faulty functioning of a watch becomes obvious when the position of the hands fails to correspond to expectations about what time it is or to the hands of other watches. However, since there are different time zones and since some people deliberately alter the time on their watches (e.g., setting it some minutes ahead in order to avoid being late), the "true" reference for judging the watch as "faulty" is the first problem. Given agreement on these basics, the question follows of how to infer the mechanics of the clockwork from the position of the hands, and also how to deduce the cause of the fault. A watchmaker needs exact knowledge about the logic of the given functions of the clockwork as well as instruments to measure and test its precision, etc. So what kind of information, what measurements and what strategies are appropriate for an analytical–methodological approach to "action-based human errors"?

On Difficulties About Coping with Erroneous Functioning and Errors: The Tricky Search for Reasons and Causes

In a synopsis, Senders and Moray summarize the discussion of the participating experts at the above-mentioned conference on the question about the causes of errors in the following way (1991, p. 99): "Whether we explain errors in terms of information-processing models such as those of Norman and Reason, or we invoke the theories of depth psychology, which are currently much less popular, all the accounts assume that a cause or a number of causes can be found for any error that a person makes". They repeatedly emphasize how important it is to recognize the causes of errors: "We need to understand causes if we are to understand how errors arise. This is important both so that errors can be prevented and also so that we can have a theory and explanation of error." (p. 108). Nevertheless, if there are a single or multiple causes for each and every error, why do they state that "the topic is not a simple one"?

To illustrate the central problems according to their point of view, Senders and Moray present three "causal chains" relating to a misspelling, a car accident, and an aircraft crash. The first of these is shown in the following figure (Fig. 6.1).

The erroneous typing of the "u" key while using the keyboard is put into focus: instead of typing the given word "color", the writer types "colour". Senders and Moray further specify and state: "In these examples, there are several events that can plausibly be considered to "cause" the outcome. Perhaps it is more accurate to say that there are several causal chains leading to the outcome, since it is always possible to work backwards in what appears to be an infinite regression from the outcome to more and more distant causes. It seems best, at least from a pragmatic point of view, to say that what is deemed to be the cause of an [..] error depends on the purpose of the inquiry. There is no absolute cause" (1991, p. 106). As well as: "Note that to adopt one of those causes as the cause does not in any sense rule out the validity of the others."

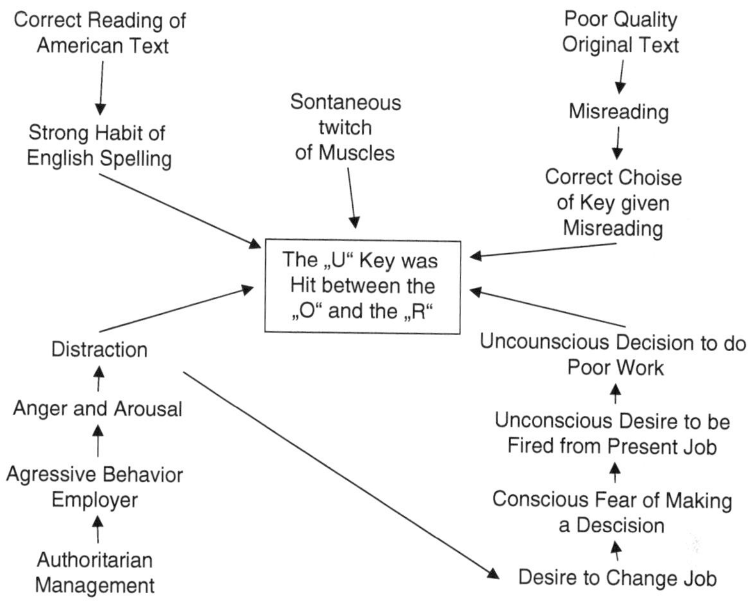

Fig. 6.1 "Why did the typist type "colour" and not "color"?" (Taken from Senders & Moray, 1991, p. 105)

Now, the occurrence of various hypotheses of causation (and the list of the authors in Fig. 6.1 is by no means complete and the causes are probably of a wider scope) is by no means an exclusive feature of psychological research into action-based errors. The formulation and verification of hypotheses is central to all scientific and research practice. This is also true for a disturbance or error expert whose qualifications rather comprise of the competence *to search* for the cause of an error – and ultimately to find that cause; in brief, to differentiate correct from incorrect hypotheses – than to formulate hypotheses of causation.

One of the most common ways of verifying such formulated hypotheses can essentially be described as follows: a criterion or dependent variable is related to predictors in order to test constellations in which correlations can be observed. This will inevitably yield insights into the conditions that affect or do not affect the criterion. The following procedure can then try to describe the seemingly relevant conditions in detail. This can go as far as determining thresholds for numeric predictors and categorical criteria (i.e. functions) if both predictors and criteria are numerical.

Seen from this perspective, the criterion of "misspelling" in Fig. 6.1 of this text is related to different predictors: a strong routine, inattention, the unconscious motive to produce poor work, a misreading of the guidelines as well as muscle twitching. As regards the misreading, one would have to determine what the writer had actually intended to put to paper. If he/she had intended to write "colour", one cannot speak of an error of typing. The attribute "strong" applied to routines refers to different degrees of specificity that can presumably also exist for inattention, the strength of unconscious motives and to a lesser degree also for the occurrence of muscle twitching. So the existence or strength of emotions such as anger and arousal can be provisionally deduced and related to the presence or absence of typing errors. A case like the one shown in Fig. 6.1 gives rise primarily to the following questions: Why are specifications about the state or degree of specificity of the listed predictors missing? How can differentiated insights into causation be found and how can decisions regarding the cause(s) be made if all possible predictors are equally weighted with respect to each other?

This brief outline of hypothesis verification can be modified by factors such as the nature of the error or the degree of damage. In the case of the "causal chain of typing errors", we do not only experience *that* an error has occurred but its *nature*. A script or characters possess meaning as well as structure as long as the writer is familiar with the sign system – they are not meaningless figures. Furthermore, in the case of a typing error, the configuration of the keyboard is known and it can be determined whether a deviation occurred "only" by typing the adjacent key. If an error occurs, it can be examined from this perspective under two aspects: (1) What contents-referred meaning can be inferred from the configuration of signs actually produced instead of the intended configuration (the perspective of "depth psychology" in Senders & Moray, 1991), and (2) did the sequence of signs stem from a common repertoire or was it produced for the first time. Referring to the example of Senders and Moray, where the British spelling "colour" was used instead of the intended U.S. spelling "color", questions like the following arise: Was the typist responsible for the misspelling in Fig. 6.1 of British or American origin? Was it perhaps an Englishman who posted letters to an American addressee in Colorado several times a day – someone who may have been thinking intensively of another letter while writing our example? But even from this perspective, insights can only be gained and hypotheses verified if the necessary information about the writer is provided.

Nevertheless, the example of misspelling leads to an even deeper question: Can the character of erroneous actions be found in random events which follow chaotic paths without any perceptible structure; or can an experienced American writer be observed to produce misspellings such as "v&ülq@ä" when he intended to write "color"? Or does a deviation always merely follow other predecessor structures; may it even be that the occurrence of action-based errors requires the existence of such specially primed pathways? And finally, do some reasons for a typing error, such as spontaneous muscle twitching, produce random sequences of signs whereas unconscious motives lead to erroneous actions and to the replacement of one ordered sequence by another?

Amazingly, no discussion or reflection about an adequate methodological approach to verifying hypotheses on the scope of this question can be found in the work of Senders and Moray. This is reason enough to consider this aspect of considerable importance and ask: How, with which methods, with what results and problems has this psychological research been conducted so far? What kinds of insights have been gained and what open questions remain? The limited scope of this work allows only a few contrasting snapshots to be taken. A number of important works, such as those of Schwarz (1927), Rasmussen (1982), and Reason and Mycielska (1982) as well as many others, have to be neglected.

At the beginning of each section, an action-based error is presented for speculation and reflection. It is subsequently analyzed and interpreted.

Older Strategies of Analysis and Associated Insights

> In a university library, a man – an academic judging by his appearance and habits – can be observed standing at a desk where he dips his quill not into the inkwell to his left but into an empty inkwell to his right.

Early works of psychological research into action-based human errors have overcome or rather bypassed the analytical–methodological problem of reliably assigning these errors to specific types in what seems quite an easy way. Keywords describing this seemingly easy path are:

- Restricting the scope of the analysis of action-based human errors to a clearly defined and structured but narrow range.
- Analyzing situations in which the action sequence of failure can be unambiguously perceived and judged with certainty.

One of the earliest works that used methods of analysis matching these keywords stems from Hugo Münsterberg (1892). He used cases of habit-based human errors as a methodological approach to studies of memory. He assumed that psychophysiological developments are mainly determined by arbitrary associations of sensations and impulses of movement that merge into involuntary actions. "The psychophysiological mechanism therefore relaxes (…) We walk, eat, play music and so on without volition of every separate act although initially we had to pay attention to each and every single action" (Münsterberg, 1892, p. 69). In the case of failure of a habituated action sequence, Münsterberg (in opposition to his colleague Weimer, 1925) did not focus on "failing instances" but simply analyzed the given action sequence with great care. For him, this sequence could reveal an impulse of movement that was in that exact instance bound to the circumstances of the given situation.

The question that led Münsterberg to his investigations was: What happens if "exactly the same imagination interacts with different mutually exclusive impulses of movement at the same time" (Münsterberg, 1892, p. 69)? That is how "a disposition that has not been erased from memory becomes associated with a new and voluntarily practiced impulse of movement, whereby the newly practiced association changes to an involuntary one. Are former associations erased from memory as soon as a new association, opposed to the first one, has been practiced so extensively that it is executed instinctively correctly without exception? Can one performance trace only become invariably correct by the disappearance of another?" (loc. cit., p. 70). In order to solve the methodological problems connected to his questions as well as to ensure that all mistaken actions were instantly recognized, Münsterberg made use of simple daily routines such as the seemingly mechanical movement of his quill towards the inkwell on the left of the desk. This involuntary action was triggered by realizing that the quill was about to run out of ink. The preparation for analyzing this habit-based action required Münsterberg to set up two identical inkwells, one of them full and the other empty. He placed the full inkwell alternately to his right and left. On the basis of writing for 7 h a day "The left inkwell had been forgotten (after 8 days of writing) and a fully automated move to the right set in every time the ink ran out" (loc. cit., p. 75). Up to this stage, he counted 64 false moves to the right. After about 3 weeks of using the inkwell on the right, Münsterberg returned to using the left one. It now took him only 25 false moves until he had accomplished his "re-habituation". The following changes of the inkwell took him 23, 13, 9 and finally 3 erroneous moves in order to adjust until no more false attempts occurred after the sixth change.

Moreover, Münsterberg's observations show that there was by no means a specific point in time when his moves towards the inkwell changed abruptly from the false to the correct side: "...after seven hours of writing, the move ended erroneously eight times, i.e. the quill really dipped into the empty inkwell. On seventeen occasions the beginning of the move went wrong, i.e. it went to the left side but was inhibited on its way by a more or less clear association that triggered the change to the correct movement" (Münsterberg, 1892, p. 75).

We are fascinated by the clarity of these experimental settings, which successfully gave an insight into the conditional and genetic parameters of the experiments. It has to be stressed that the given alternative actions were precisely determined in the error situation. Ink could be found in either the left or the right inkwell. Another remark concerns Münsterberg's use of a longitudinal design in combination with the systematic variation of the action conditions. This methodology allowed an overall picture to emerge.

Although Münsterberg's approach was not further explored at the time, we do find similar experimental strategies that also show a reference to everyday life and are therefore highly plausible in phenomenological terms, i.e. seem to have a high degree of ecological validity. Further explorations of this kind include studies concerning errors of speech, reading or writing. They made use of the fact that the flow of these actions (speech, reading or writing) is well documented, so that the analysis of any registered error could be evaluated with regard to the background of inter-individual conventions such as grammar or spelling.

Experimental Works Concerning the Topic

Ach and Lewin's Investigations into the Conditions of Erroneous Reactions

> Please read out loud the following syllables and then form a rhyming syllable that you read out loud as well!" Answer: "tuk – ruk; pal' -, lap'... (freely cited from Lewin, 1917).

Ach (1910) sought a suitable procedure for measuring volition from the perspective of association theory. His underlying theoretical assumption and experimental set-up were as follows: the participants initially created associations between a series of two meaningless pairs of syllables, for instance by learning them by heart. After this phase, they were instructed to carry out a specific activity while hearing certain other syllables (also meaningless ones), such as to make them rhyme by changing their first letters. If previously learnt syllables were mixed with those used in this latter process, the resulting situation may be understood as follows on the basis of association theory: the participant's response to this instruction produced a determining tendency to follow the presented syllable with a corresponding rhyme. However, this tendency is opposed by another one, namely of responding instead with the syllable to which an association had been formed in the learning phase. The participant's response consequently permits us to determine which is stronger, the habit of uttering the associated syllable or the will to produce a rhyme. If the association wins, Ach calls this an "intended false reaction" (from the experimenter's viewpoint). He calls the association strength sufficient to produce such a reaction an "associative equivalent". Association theory states that the association strength always results from the number of repetitions made in order to generate it. Ach used this "struggle" between habit and will to make the determining tendency of an act of will, and thus the individual's volition, accessible to measurement.

Lewin (1917, 1921, 1922), who initially accepted the viewpoint of association theory, made use of the experimental paradigm outlined above. The key parameters of his experimental set-up are as follows: his participant was initially instructed to practice saying a series of meaningless syllables until he could recite it *freely and fluently* (270 times in the event). He designated the syllables of this series as *g-syllables* ("learnt" syllables in German). But the participants also had to read n-syllables (neutral syllables), although these were presented to them in a continuously changing sequence so that no habit could be formed. This was followed by the test series shown below in which the two syllables were presented alternately:

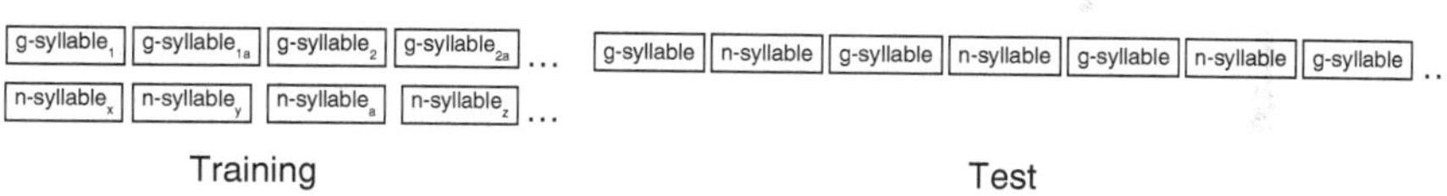

The participants were instructed first to read the syllable out loud, and then to exchange the first and last letters and repeat the altered syllable out loud. The association set up by this learning process to say the next syllable out loud was opposed by the instruction to change the letters around, and should, according to the theory, have led to an "intended false reaction" or to considerable retardations in making the changes. To his own surprise, however, Lewin found that: "Against my expectations, despite [...] the considerable number of preceding repetitions [...], despite the fact that the series were invariably so well learnt by heart that they could be spoken at top speed, on average no delay, or only a short one, was noted in the heterogeneous activity of the changeover, always remaining below the mean variation" (1921, p. 210). Variations in the experimental set-up, such as different numbers of repetitions in the association-forming phase, produced identical results.

These experiments and their results showed that the repeated succession of two experiences, and the resulting permanent association, is not a sufficient condition for producing intended false reactions. However, as the work of Ach as well as Lewin's preliminary work showed, highly striking reaction-time increases as well as intended false reactions, Lewin sought a "configuration that regularly generates false reactions or inhibitions" (1917, p. 220). "After trying out a large number of different configurations" (loc. cit.), he succeeded in his attempt. His experimental design was now as follows: only four syllables were now used in each case: they were either exclusively rhymed in the habituation phase, known as *cr-syllables* (constantly rhymed), or exclusively had their letters changed round, known as *cu-syllables* (constantly inverted in German). The position of the individual syllables in the presented series was varied. However, the repetitions were now clustered in this phase: each syllable was presented twice in direct succession.

The form and manner of presenting the test series also changed: after a relatively small number of repetitions (in general under 20) compared with the first experiments, test series were presented that typically had the following form (see Lewin, 1922, p. 71):

Training	Test
cu-syllable$_1$ cu-syllable$_1$ cu-syllable$_2$ cu-syllable$_2$ …	cr-syllable$_1$ cr-syllable$_2$ cr-syllable$_4$ cr-syllable$_3$ cr-syllable$_2$ cr-syllable$_3$ cu-syllable$_2$ …
cr-syllable$_1$ cr-syllable$_1$ cr-syllable$_2$ cr-syllable$_2$ …	

It is crucial to note that the test person was instructed to produce rhymes for all presented syllables. The syllables learned during the habituation phase were now presented in a different sequence than hitherto. As can be seen above, at some point a cu-syllable was introduced and, as expected, invariably led to a false reaction.

This corresponds to Lewin's earlier finding that: "with this configuration, […] invariably either a false reaction occurred, or, if the participant was very careful, at any rate a noticeable increase of the reaction time" (1917, p. 221). Lewin noted four repetitions as the smallest number, after which Ach's "associative equivalent" was exceeded and an intended false reaction occurred.

It thus became evident that the absolute number of repetitions was not a decisive factor for the occurrence or non-occurrence of false reactions. Lewin succeeded in showing that, in tackling the set tasks, it is essential to distinguish between two different types of activity. In one case, the second syllable in each case can be obtained by using the sequence given in the habituation phase. If, for instance, a syllable presented in the habituation phase is always followed by the same syllable in rhymed form, then in response to the "rhyme" instruction, the second syllable will be found to rhyme with no direct relationship to the task. Lewin calls this type of task performance "reproducing activity". He delimits it from "rhyming activity" where the presented syllable invariably leads to the formation of the required second rhyming syllable by a new rhyming process.

His key conclusion is: "The cause of the intended false reaction must be sought in the particular type of execution activity used" (Lewin, 1922, p. 75). "The non-occurrence or occurrence of the tendency to a false reaction depends on whether

[...] this is an [activity process] or [a reproduction activity process]. Only in the second case does a tendency to a false reaction occur." (1917, p. 228). Lewin's observation that even the strongest intention does not protect the subject reliably from committing an activity error, may be understood as follows: "The result depends not on the intensity of the resolution, but on the type of willingness to act that it creates. Even intensive resolutions to produce an intended false reaction give no assurance of avoiding further false reactions if, rather than changing the execution activity, a more intensive resolution occurs to produce a target activity that again uses the old error-generating execution activity" (1922, p. 102). So the crucial factor is to what extent the inappropriate activity can be changed or replaced (see Lewin, 1922, p. 93).

A final aspect is needed to round off the above discussion, namely the question as to how far the acting person is consciously aware of the processes of choice and use of the various types of activity outlined above. Some relevant indications may be found in Lewin's statements based mainly on the self-observed data of the test participants. This showed that both types of activity distinguished by Lewin could be differentiated empirically and unequivocally only at the beginning of the experiments. "With advancing automation, the empirical differences disappear with the decay of the experiences themselves, without the actual processes being the same" (1917, p. 225). "In the case of high automation, a reliable empirical distinction between the various types of activity is no longer possible" (1917, p. 227).

Sigmund Freud: The "Analytico-Methodical Turning Point"

> Apparently [..] a persistent misprint once found its way into a social-democratic newspaper. A report about a certain festive occasion noted that: Among those present his Majesty the Corn Prince was also seen. The next day a correction was attempted. The paper published an apology and wrote: it should of course have been the Corwn Prince (Freud, 1930, p. 25).

An important quasi-analytico-methodical turning point in psychological error research is closely linked to the famous works of Sigmund Freud (1981). The vehemence with which contemporary psychologists reacted to Freud's approach is evidence enough of this (cf. Ranschburg, 1911, p. 14). Various authors criticized his lack of "rigorous scientific proof": the typographical error described by Freud may be used to clarify this matter. He actually used this case to show that the error "is perhaps entitled to be considered as a fully valid mental act, which may also pursue its own goal, as an expression of content and significance" (Freud, 1930, p. 29). In Freud's view, the typo reveals the – certainly consciously – hostile attitude of the social-democratic typesetter to the monarchy. He uses this and a large number of other everyday events to show that what seem to superficial observation to be "apparently unintentional acts" turn out to be "well-motivated and determined by motives unknown to the consciousness" when the technique of psychoanalytical examination is applied to them (Freud, 1981, p. 189).

Seen from an analytico-methodical perspective, Freud failed in any way to back up his quite plausible analysis of causes in this, as in other, cases. Typos such as this could, as Meringer and Mayer (1923, p. 136) argue in another context, certainly have occurred as a result of other "error sources [..], partly optical ones, due to the shape of the letters, partly motoric ones, resulting from the similarity of the movements involved". Freud could easily have found ways of backing up his viewpoint, but he apparently neither sought nor used them. Thus the implied unconscious motive of "disparaging the monarch" would also have had to manifest itself on numerous other occasions available to a typesetter, assuming it to be stable between individuals and possibly even transcending them, for instance in expressions such as "His Modesty" or "His Majesty". Thus, Freud could have subscribed to this periodical – if he was interested in a causal explanation and not (only) in achieving a hermeneutic understanding – in order to collect such typos and examine them for their anti-monarchist content. In contrast, it would certainly be instructive to make a parallel study of pro-monarchy periodicals such as the *Neue preußische Zeitung* to see whether they reveal an over-proportional number of typos that in turn disparage social democracy. To avert an obvious misunderstanding, there is no attempt here to advocate a crude positivism. There can be no doubt about the justification and use of such case analyses – so long as ways to support the assumptions, such as varying the conditions, are sought and used.

However, the criticism of a lack of a rigorous scientific proof conceals a much more important aspect. Freud's highly popular work, which is now rightly considered as literature, marks a change of perspective with respect to activity errors. Whereas the "older" works examined earlier used errors as a methodical vehicle for a more precise analysis of the selected topic, the Freudian analysis and argument already constitute an established theory that is used to interpret such slips. Thus Freud does not allow the error to speak for itself, but "merely" talks about it instead. But it would also be instructive from a psychoanalytical perspective to analyze lapses in a systematic way in order to investigate this approach further. One more comment on this point: Freud assumes in his work "that the effect of the [typo] may perhaps be entitled to be considered as a fully valid mental act, which may also pursue its own goal, as an expression of content and significance. We have hitherto always spoken of lapses, but it now appears as if such a lapse is sometimes entirely appropriate and merely replaces another expected or intended one," (Freud, 1930, p. 29). It would be instructive in this context to examine more precisely the question as to whether the "motives unknown to the consciousness" (Freud, 1981, p. 189) that determine a lapse have to use existing established pathways, or whether they can also pursue their aims autonomously and freely away from the beaten track. The experimental design needed to clarify this aspect resembles the requirements already outlined above: analysis of the lapse against the background of the development and decay of existing activity routines (what, and how routinely, had previously been written? Do typos such as "Crqwn Prince" occur instead of "Crown Prince", some of which show no similarity to the usual spelling of other words?).

Action-Based Human Errors as Seen from an Updated Cognitivistic Point of View

> I went into my bedroom intending to fetch a book. I took off my rings, looked in the mirror and came out again – without the book. (Zhang, Patel, Johnson, & Shortliffe, 2002, p. 972)

One of the most influential contributions to research into human errors stems from Norman (Norman, 1981). It is written from a cognitivistic point of view and is headed: "Categorization of Action Slips". Its introductory statement is of special interest, namely that "It is indeed true that slips appear manageable and that they cry out for interpretation. [...] However, the meaning in them is not at all clear; their categorization and interpretation are theory dependent, yet contemporary theories of cognitive behaviour are not really up to the task" (loc. cit., 2). In order to fill this gap, Norman presented a classification system to which many authors refer and which is used to categorize applied issues.

Although not representative for the vast research area of human errors, the work of Zhang et al. (2002) is worth examining closely: Programmatically headed "Toward an action-based taxonomy of human errors [...]", the work of Zhang et al. has the objective "... to understand the fundamental causes of [...] errors such that [...] errors can be prevented or greatly reduced systematically on a large scale" (loc. cit., p. 970). The authors introduce their work as follows: "To understand the cognitive mechanisms underlying [...] errors, we first need to develop a cognitive taxonomy of [...] errors that can (1) categorize all types of [...] error along cognitive dimensions, (2) associate each type of [...] error to a specific underlying cognitive mechanism, (3) explain why and even predict when and where a specific error will occur, and (4) generate intervention strategies for each type of error" (loc. cit., p. 971). Furthermore, Zhang et al. distinguish that "according to Reason [1994], human errors are divided into two major categories: (1) slips that result from the incorrect execution of a correct action sequence, and (2) mistakes that result from the correct execution of an incorrect action sequence." This distinction is followed by an outline model referring to Norman's theory of action-based behavior which the authors describe with the aid of the scenario illustrated in Fig. 6.2.

According to Norman's model (see Fig. 6.2), all human actions follow seven steps or subdivisions. First of all, (1) a goal is established, and (2) a plan for its fulfillment is generated. This is followed by (3) specifying the manner in which the action will be executed. The fourth step is (4) the execution of the action itself. The action is then (5) perceived with regard to altered system states. The perception of the changed system state is followed by (6) its interpretation, and finally results in (7) the evaluation of the system state with regard to the fulfillment of goals and intentions.

Zhang et al. (2002) – inspired by the model mentioned above and differentiating between "mistakes" and "slips" according to Reason – conclude with 10 (!) sources of error ("places where mistakes and slips may occur") which are cited and additionally emphasized through arrows in Fig. 6.2 below:

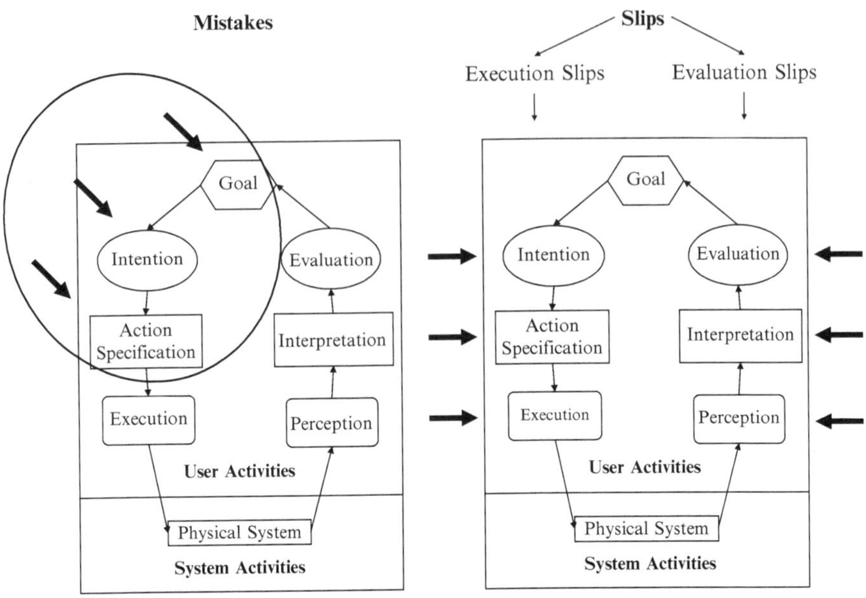

Fig. 6.2 "Slips can occur at all stages, whereas mistakes can only occur in the first three stages" (From Zhang et al., 2002, p. 972)

From the illustration above, it becomes clear that the category of "slips" is further subdivided into "execution slips" and "evaluation slips". Regarding the "execution slips", the authors assume that "a correct goal could be distorted due to its strongly shared schema with another irrelevant goal. A correct intention could be deactivated due to memory decay or swapped by another irrelevant intention due to similarity of schemas. A correct action specification could be distorted due to many factors such as attention shift, situational stimulation etc. The execution of an action sequence could misfire due to memory and attention problems or various environmental factors" (loc. cit. p. 973).

Interestingly, the assumptions made above are not followed by questions concerning *how* decisions about the classification of an individual case could be made. According to which criteria and based on what sources of information would cases of human error be classified? However, for every "type of error", Zhang et al. (2002) present examples as an illustration. One of these is cited in the introduction to this section and concerns the goal of fetching a book.

On the basis of the line of argument presented so far, the cited example could be discussed as follows: the case of a "mistake" can be excluded under the condition that the book was actually present in the bedroom. Given this condition, the plan to fetch it from the bedroom was in principle correct and was no mistake. It follows that attention should be paid to the different "types of slip". However, whether or not the example can be classified as a "goal slip" remains unclear, as nothing is said about the superordinated intention of the action and its context, which may well have influenced the act of fetching the book. So the authors must be criticized for apparently thinking that the context and intentions were irrelevant to the action. In the case of parallel goals, such as removing the rings from the fingers and looking in the mirror, the "goal slip" remains an imaginable cause. As the intention to fetch the book seems to have been correct in view of the overall context, its classification as an "intention slip" is illogical. Therefore, two other "types" remain: ritualized specifications of actions and the specific actions that accompanied the act of fetching the book seem probable, and the case described could be seen as an example of an "action specification slip". Nevertheless, the description of the case leaves no cues about the style and extent to which habits and rituals may have accompanied the action. Furthermore, it is worth mentioning that the non-intended actions of removing the rings and forgetting the book were realized at an unspecified time and place by the human agent. So we could just as well speak of "perception, interpretation and evaluation slips" until the agent realized that something had gone wrong or that the book had been forgotten.

However, the interpretation and classification of the cited case by the authors says "intention slip" without further differentiation.

A Methodical Conclusion

These "snapshots" show a picture already described concisely by Singelton (1973, p. 735): "there are many kinds of errors, many different causation factors, many relevant models or theories". At the same time, the suspicion arises that analytico-methodical problems are not wholly uninvolved in these distinctions: the questions addressed, the analytico-methodical perspectives and the procedures selected and used for them are so varied and so specifically oriented that basically only the view set up in each case is treated. In simpler terms, psychoanalytical approaches tend to ignore the possible role of fixed routines just as stubbornly as those with a different theoretical background tend to ignore conscious or unconscious motives.

Closer scrutiny shows that authors from the most diverse theoretical schools admit analytico-methodical difficulties, but fail to pursue their causes further or to develop an analytical or diagnostic concept for this purpose. Indeed, it gets worse: the initially raised question as to why theoretical and applied approaches in activity-error research fail to apply any verifiable predictors to the criterion of "error or no error" must be formulated as follows after considering these snapshots: why does more recent work merely formulate hypotheses and stop short of verifying them?

A rather technical answer to this question is: more recent work takes the perspective of starting from the end of an error and subsequently examining the preceding events. The contrary approach, namely to examine the occurrence of errors by starting from the events and conditions of the preceding situation, has disappeared for no apparent reason. But the events, conditions, and changes in the situation preceding an error are of crucial importance. A theory of activity errors is not particularly well developed if, like current cognitive theories, it merely classifies these errors but lacks any functional, conditional-genetic treatment or the formation of associated concepts (see Lewin, 1931). So a key requirement from a practical-prophylactic and theoretical perspective must be to acquire data of maximum reliability from the situation preceding any changes or divergences from intended actions. The results presented by Münsterberg and Lewin, as representative of a series of other findings, expressly confirm the effect of the preceding situation on the occurrence of activity errors.

A Proposed Analytico-Methodical Approach Appropriate to the Topic

We draw the following conclusion from the above findings and considerations:

> An analysis of activity errors must be oriented from the preceding situation to the error, and not inversely from the latter to the former. Even in the case of very promising analytical options, the contrasting consideration of erroneous and error-free activities is indispensable in differentiating error-generating conditions from others. Moreover, the changes that occur at motor and cognitive levels, and that are associated with the occurrence of errors, impede inferences from "ex-post" to "ex-ante" and thus also militate against a retrospective approach.

The conclusion can consequently be drawn that errors are accessible to analysis only in particular cases under natural, ecological conditions, so that "experimental laboratory techniques" (Norman, 1981, p. 13) are the sole solution to this analytico-methodical problem. At first sight, this realization would seem to reinforce a widespread skepticism with regard to the possibility of analyzing everyday errors, as especially in particularly relevant sectors such as nuclear energy, aviation, and shipping, investigations "within the experimental laboratory" are likely to be difficult. This is partly because the complexity of the demands is very high in such cases but also because a more differentiated analysis of the criteria for "reproducible" activities as well as recording their current details is likely to be possible, if at all, only under ecological conditions. It follows that:

> differentiated empirical data is required about a sequence of erroneous activities (i.e. what exactly was carried out, at what point in time, for how long, and with which dynamic character); of even more importance, and ultimately crucial, however, are data about a person's "willingness to act".

Thus, to investigate the causes of activity errors, it is not so important to collect as many errors as possible, and above all not from different persons and sectors, for different aims, in different situations. The essential aspect is to examine the scope of action – inclusive of its structure and origin – open to a person or group of people who must tackle highly standardized tasks that were acquired under comparable training conditions in response to equally standardized demands. The activity errors that occur can then be analyzed in view of this baseline data. So, to investigate a spelling mistake, as discussed above, in an appropriately analytico-methodical way, a very large number of ways of, for instance, writing the word in question, or the sequence of characters, must previously be compiled. This means that:

> psychological research into activity errors must be based mainly on developing activity complexes and secondarily on the application of these complexes in practice, and, naturally, investigate the errors occurring in both cases.

Therefore, approaches must be sought that combine the development of activity competences and their everyday practical application with experimental laboratory techniques of condition checks and differentiated modes of observation. The almost paradigmatic approach that we favor for this purpose is linked to the successful use of simulations as may be found in the work of Dörner (1989). He used the simulation of complex ecologically valid problem-solving tasks in networked intransparent and dynamic situations (such as the management of a development project) to examine the "logic of failure":

> Modern training simulators are *the prime analytical tools* for psychological research into activity errors. They virtualize practical demands and simulate them efficiently to create a synthetic environment into which education, testing, and training can be and are completely transferred. The crucial aspects of this context are the available options of standardization and systematic variation of parameters, observation, and running surveys. Moreover, log files in which all relevant activity and situation parameters are documented with high temporal resolution are recorded and are thus available for analysis. Thereby, psychological research into errors now has access to data that have been little used so far but deserve to be used extensively (see Mehl, 2008).

Let us finally supplement these more technical aspects of data acquisition and experimental control by highlighting the following points:

The analytical approach favored here can be utilized to acquire and manipulate parameters preceding an activity error on a broad empirical basis in order to determine their effect on the occurrence of errors. The search for "configurations that regularly generate false reactions" motivated by Lewin represents an important analytico-methodical complement in this case. Its use suggests a quasi-synthetic approach to error research in which analyses of "naturally" occurring constellations are flanked and complemented by synthetic "artificial" constellations that are modified prior to the occurrence of errors. Of equal importance as the publication of constellations recognized to be critical, i.e. error-producing, is that of conditions in which no such effect could be observed.

References

Ach, N. (1910). *Über den Willensakt und das Temprament*. Leipzig, Germany: Quelle & Meyer.

Dörner, D. (1989). *Die Logik des Misslingens*. Reinbek, Germany: Rowohlt.

Freud, S. (1930). *Vorlesungen zur Einführung in die Psychoanalyse*. Wien, Austria: Internationaler Psychoanalytischer Verlag.

Freud, S. (1981). *Zur Psychopathologie des Alltagslebens*. Frankfurt, Germany: Fischer.

Lewin, K. (1917). Die psychische Tätigkeit bei der Hemmung von Willensvorgängen und das Grundgesetz der Assoziation. *Zeitschrift für Psychologie, 77*, 212–247.

Lewin, K. (1921). Das Problem der Willensmessung und das Grundgesetz der Assoziation. I. *Psychologische Forschung, 1*, 191–302.
Lewin, K. (1922). Das Problem der Willensmessung und das Grundgesetz der Assoziation. II. *Psychologische Forschung, 2*, 65–140.
Lewin, K. (1931). Der Übergang von der aristotelischen zur galileischen Denkweise in Biologie und Psychologie. *Erkenntnis, 1*, 421–466.
Mehl, K. (2008). Simulation as a tool for training and analysis. In P. Dieckmann (Ed.), *Using simulations for education, training and research* (pp. 157–179). Lengerich, Germany: Pabst Science.
Meringer, R., & Mayer, K. (1923). Die täglichen Fehler im Sprechen, Lesen und Handeln. *Wörter und Sachen, 8*, 122–141.
Meringer, R., & Mayer, K. (1895). *Versprechen und Verlesen*. Stuttgart, Germany: Goeschen.
Münsterberg, H. (1892). *Beiträge zur Experimentellen Psychologie*. Freiburg im Breisgau, Germany: J. C. B. Mohr.
Norman, D. A. (1981). Categorization of action slips. *Psychological Review, 88*(1), 1–15.
Ranschburg, P. (1911). *Das kranke Gedächtnis*. Leipzig ,Germany: Ambrosius Barth.
Rasmussen, J. (1982). Human errors: A taxonomy for describing human malfunction in industrial installations. *Journal of Occupational Accidents, 4*, 311–335.
Reason, J., & Mycielska, K. (1982). *Absent-minded? The psychology of mental lapses and everyday errors*. Englewood, CO: Prentice-Hall.
Schwarz, G. (1927). Über Rückfälligkeit bei Umgewöhnung. 1. Teil. Rückfalltendenz und Verwechslungsgefahr. *Psychologische Forschung, 9*, 86–158.
Senders, J. W., & Moray, N. P. (1991). *Human error: Cause, prediction, and reduction*. Hillsdale, NJ: Lawrence Erlbaum.
Singelton, W. T. (1973). Theoretical approaches to human error. *Ergonomics, 6*, 727–737.
Weimer, H. (1925). *Psychologie der Fehler*. Leipzig: Julius Klinkhardt.
Wehner, T., Stadler, M., & Mehl, K. (1983). Handlungsfehler – Wiederaufnahme eines alten Paradigmas aus gestaltpsychologischer Sicht. *Gestalt Theory, 5*, 267–292.
Wehner, T., Stadler, M., Mehl, K., & Kruse, P. (1985). Action slips. In J. L. McGaugh (Ed.), *Contemporary psychology: Biological processes and theoretical issues* (pp. 475–487). Amsterdam: North-Holland.
Zhang, J., Patel, V. L., Johnson, T. R., & Shortliffe, E. H. (2002). Toward an action-based taxonomy of human errors in medicine. In W. Gray & C. Schunn (Eds.), *Proceedings of the twenty-fourth annual conference of the cognitive science society* (pp. 970–975). Mahwah, NJ: Lawrence Erlbaum Associates.

Table 8.2 Results of multiple regression analyses predicting both error orientations from team characteristics

	Problem-solving approach	Blaming approach
	β	β
Boundedness/stability	.15	−.23*
Task interdependence	.03	.07
Team autonomy	.30**	−.07
R^2 (adjusted)	.11	.04
F test	*F*(3.87) 4.853**	*F*(3.87) 2.37#

N=91 teams
**$p<.01$; *$p<.05$; #$p<.10$

of innovation. ($r=-.16$, n.s.). Interestingly, the team member and the manager ratings of innovation correlate only mildly ($r=.25$, $p<.05$), which suggests that team members and managers have a different perception of what innovative team behavior entails. We can also see that both control variables (i.e. gender and age) are not significantly related to any of the error orientations or to the ratings of innovation. We therefore decided not to include these variables in our subsequent regression analyses.

Table 8.2 shows the results of the regression analyses of team boundedness and stability, task interdependence, and team autonomy on the problem-solving approach and the blaming approach. The analyses show that team autonomy is positively related to the problem-solving approach ($\beta=.30$, $p<.01$) (hypothesis 3a corroborated), but is unrelated to the blaming approach ($\beta=-.07$, n.s.) (hypothesis 3b not confirmed). Furthermore, team boundedness/ stability is negatively related to the blaming approach ($\beta=-.23$, $p<.05$) (hypothesis 1b corroborated), but not to the problem-solving approach ($\beta=.15$, n.s.) (hypothesis 1a not confirmed). Task interdependence appears not to be related to the blaming approach and the problem-solving approach (respectively $\beta=.03$, n.s. and $\beta=.07$, n.s.), meaning that we cannot confirm hypotheses 2a and 2b.

Hypothesis 4 concerns the relationship between the problem-solving and blaming approach, on the one hand, and team innovation, on the other hand. Table 8.3 shows the results of the multiple regression analyses predicting perceived team innovation from team characteristics, mediated by both error orientations. In step 1, the independent variables are included as predictors of team innovation, whereas in step 2, the error orientations are included as predictors of team innovation, in addition to the independent variables.

The analyses (see Table 8.3, step 2) show that the problem-solving approach is positively related to the team member rating of team innovation ($\beta=.36$, $p<.001$), but not to the team manager rating of innovation ($\beta=-.19$, n.s.). Surprisingly, the blaming approach is unrelated to the team member ratings of innovation ($\beta=-.02$, n.s.), although it is negatively related to the manager rating of innovation ($\beta=-.26$, $p<.05$). This means that we can partly confirm hypotheses 4a and 4b.

In the fifth hypothesis, we propose that both error orientations have a mediating effect in the relationship between team characteristics (boundedness/ stability

Table 8.3 Results of multiple regression analyses predicting perceived team innovation from team characteristics, mediated by both error orientations

	Team innovation (team member rating)		Team innovation (manager rating)	
	Step 1	Step 2	Step 1	Step 2
	β	β	β	β
Boundedness/stability	.27**	.21*	.16	.13
Task interdependency	.03	.02	.00	.03
Team autonomy	.36***	.25*	.05	.08
Problem-solving approach		.36***		–.19
Blaming approach		–.02		–.26*
$R^{2\ (\text{adjusted})}$	.24	.34	.00	.07
ΔR^2		.10		.07
F test	*F(3,87)* 10.51***	*F(5,85)* 10.28***	*F(3,84)* .96	*F(5,82)* 2.25#

$N=91$ teams
*** $p<.001$; ** $p<.01$; * $p<.05$; # $p<.10$

(H5a), task interdependency (H5b), team autonomy (H5c) and team innovation). To test for the hypothesized mediation effect, we applied the procedure suggested by MacKinnon et al. (2007). These researchers argue that a mediation exists if (1) the independent variable (team boundedness/ stability, task interdependency and team autonomy) has a significant effect on the mediating variable (problem-solving and blaming approach), and (2) the mediating variable has a significant effect on the dependent variable (team performance and innovation) in a regression analysis of the independent and mediating variable on the dependent variable. Should the independent variable have no significant effect on the dependent variable in such an analysis, we have a case of pure mediation. If the independent variable (in addition to the mediating variable) does have a significant effect on the dependent variable, we have a case of partial mediation.

Since team autonomy was the only variable that was significantly related to a problem-solving approach, the problem-solving approach can potentially only mediate the relationship between autonomy and team innovation. As can be seen in Table 8.3 (step 2), the problem-solving approach is positively related to the team member rating of team innovation ($\beta=.36$, $p<.001$), and team autonomy is also directly related to the team member rating of team innovation ($\beta=.25$, $p<.05$), meaning that the problem-solving approach is indeed a partial mediator in the relationship between team autonomy and team innovation, as is also evidenced by the Sobel test for mediation ($Z=2.28^*$) (H5c partly corroborated). Furthermore, the blaming approach is negatively related to manager ratings of team innovation ($\beta=-.26$, $p<.05$), whereas boundedness/stability is unrelated to the manager ratings of innovation ($\beta=.13$, n.s.), meaning that the blaming approach may be a full mediator in the relationship between boundedness/ stability and team innovation. However, the Sobel test for mediation did not reach significance in this case ($Z=.15$, n.s.) (H5a rejected).

Discussion

Since teams can be seen as the fundamental learning blocks in organisations (Chan, Pearson, & Entrekin, 2003; Senge, 1990), managers and teams need to know about the optimal conditions for team learning and team innovation (Dunphy & Bryant, 1996; Edmondson, 1999). This study shows that a team's error orientation is indeed related to team innovation. Teams with a problem-solving approach to errors are evaluated as more innovative by team members, whereas the blaming approach had no effect on team member's evaluation of team innovation. Teams with a blaming approach to errors are evaluated as less innovative by the manager, whereas the problem-solving approach had no effect on the managers' evaluation of team innovation.

It is striking that the predictors of team member ratings of team innovation are not the same as the predictors of manager ratings of team innovation. This finding is in line with several studies of group performance that show differences between team-member performance ratings and managerial performance ratings (Ancona, 1990; Ancona & Caldwell, 1992; Gladstein, 1984). An explanation for this is that managers and team members have different interests and refer to different data. Whereas team members are interested in creating a productive and pleasant atmosphere, managers are mostly interested in the output. Team members possess detailed information about team interaction and tend to have representations that link internal processes to performance (Ancona, 1990; Gladstein, 1984). Managers are more removed from the internal team processes and will base their performance evaluations more on the concrete, visible output of the team. An explanation for our findings might be that managers will not really notice a team's problem-solving approach to errors, as they will associate this approach with healthy and normal team processes. Moreover, especially in the case of self-managing teams, managers might only interfere with a team when something is going wrong and when team processes have become problematic, while teams that are able to solve their own problems might be left alone by the manager. When a team scores high on a blaming approach, conflicts and negative emotions are more likely to arise and managers are more likely to hear about it as team members are more likely to complain about it.

Team members can be expected to appreciate a team atmosphere in which mistakes can be discussed in an open and constructive way. They are likely to feel more comfortable in such an atmosphere and may confuse these affective outcomes of teamwork with task-related outcomes. On the one hand, team members in such a team might have a clearer picture of what is going on in the team and might therefore give a more realistic evaluation of team innovation than managers who are more removed from the team. On the other hand, managers might have a more business-oriented evaluation of team innovation and are less likely to confuse affective outcomes of teamwork with task-related outcomes. In any case, although there is a difference between the predictors of manager and team member ratings of team innovation, when we combine our results, we can conclude that a problem-solving approach is favorable, whereas a blaming approach is unfavorable, for team innovation. Apparently, a constructive way of dealing with mistakes leads to product and process improvement in the eyes of team members, whereas a blaming approach towards mistakes leads to conservative behavior in the eyes of managers. This finding points to the relevance of getting to know more about the conditions in a team that lead to one or the other orientation towards errors.

Our results show that bounded and stable teams tend to make less use of a blaming approach. When team members are able to develop long-term working relations with each other and are able to develop a certain kind of group feeling and team identity, they will more likely develop a feeling of trust and psychological safety (Edmondson, 1999) and will therefore be less likely to blame and punish each other when mistakes are made. Furthermore, team members in bounded and stable teams are more likely to develop closer working relationships involving more exchange of information. In such a context, mistakes are simply less likely to occur, making a blaming approach less relevant. This means that, if organisations want to prevent a blaming approach in teams, they should create teams with clear team boundaries and with stable team members. Stable teams are sometimes thought to become slaves to routine and to become less responsive to changing conditions (Edmondson, Bohmer, & Pisano, 2001). Our results show no negative direct relationship between a team's stability and team innovation, which suggests that the advantages of keeping a team together may be greater than the possible disadvantages.

Our results also show that teams with autonomy in their work, methods, scheduling, team objectives, etc., are more likely to develop a problem-solving orientation and are more likely to be innovative (at least in the eyes of the team members). When a team has a low degree of autonomy, a problem-solving approach to errors may not be rewarding because the team has little leeway to experiment with the alternative approaches that they may develop as a result of the problem-solving process. Having freedom to develop new methods or activities may make team members feel more motivated and responsible for finding new solutions for errors.

Surprisingly, task interdependence was not related to any of the error orientations. It is possible that task interdependence has effects on both error orientations that cancel each other out. On the one hand, more task interdependency can lead to a problem-solving approach within the team because there is more communication and interaction among team members, making the open discussion of mistakes more likely, and causing team members to be more motivated to find a solution for mistakes of their colleagues, as they will feel more responsible for the team accomplishment. However, on the other hand, a high degree of task interdependency may bring about a blaming approach when team members feel they are negatively affected by the mistakes made by another team member. It is possible that these opposite effects of task interdependency compensate for each other. Other team characteristics, task characteristics, or personal characteristics should be considered in future research to help explain this dynamic.

References

Ancona, D. G. (1990). Outward bound: Strategies for team survival in the organisation. *Academy of Management Journal, 33*, 334–365.

Ancona, D. G., & Caldwell, D. F. (1992). Demography and design: Predictors of new product team performance. *Organization Science, 3*, 321–341.

Anderson, N., & West, M. A. (1996). The team climate inventory: Development of the TCI and its applications in teambuilding for innovativeness. *European Journal of Work and Organizational Psychology, 5*(1), 53–66.

Andriessen, J. H. E. (1999). Samenwerken op afstand en kwaliteit van de arbeid. *Gedrag en Organisatie, 12*, 445–459.

Arenas, A., Tabernero, C., & Briones, E. (2006). Effects of goal orientation, error orientation and self-efficacy on performance in an uncertain situation. *Social Behavior and Personality, 34*(5), 569–586.

Argyris, C., & Schön, D. A. (1996). *Organisational learning II: Theory, method and practice.* Reading, MA: Addison-Wesley Publishing company.

Bliese, P. D. (Ed.). (2000). *Within-group agreement, non-independence, and reliability: Implications for data aggregation and analyses.* San Francisco: Jossey-Bass.

Bradley, J., White, B. J., & Mennecke, B. E. (2003). Teams and tasks. A temporal framework for the effects of interpersonal interventions on team performance. *Small Group Research, 34*, 353–387.

Campion, M. A., Medsker, G. J., & Higgs, A. C. (1993). Relations between work group characteristics and effectiveness: Implications for designing effective work groups. *Personnel Psychology, 46*, 823–847.

Campion, M. A., Papper, E. M., & Medsker, G. J. (1996). Relations between work team characteristics and effectiveness: A replication and extension. *Personnel Psychology, 49*, 429–452.

Cannon, M. D., & Edmondson, A. C. (2001). Confronting failure: Antecedents and consequences of shared beliefs about failure in organisational work groups. *Journal of Organizational Behavior, 22*, 161–177.

Chan, C. C. A., Pearson, C., & Entrekin, L. (2003). Examining the effects of internal and external team learning on team performance. *Team Performance Management, 9*(7/8), 174–181.

Dunphy, D., & Bryant, B. (1996). Teams: Panaceas or prescriptions for improved performance? *Human Relations, 49*, 677–699.

Edmondson, A. (1999). Psychological safety and learning behavior in work teams. *Administrative Science Quarterly, 44*(2), 350–383.

Edmondson, A. C. (2004). Learning from failure in health care: Frequent opportunities, pervasive barriers. *Quality & Safety in Health Care, 13*, 3–9.

Edmondson, A., Bohmer, R. M., & Pisano, G. P. (2001). Disrupted routines: Team learning and new technology implementation in hospitals. *Administrative Science Quarterly, 46*, 685–716.

Ellström, P. E. (2001). Integrating learning and work: Problems and prospects. *Human Resource Development Quarterly, 12*(4), 421–435.

Gartmeier, M., Hetzner, S., Gruber, H., & Heid, H. (2009). Fehlerorientierung und Eigeninitiative im Bankensektor. *Zeitschrift für Arbeits- und Organisationspsychologie, 53*, 149–162.

Gibson, C. B., & Vermeulen, F. (2003). A healthy divide: Subgroups as a stimulus for team learning behavior. *Administrative Science Quarterly, 48*, 202–239.

Gladstein, D. (1984). Groups in context: A model of task group effectiveness. *Administrative Science Quarterly, 29*, 499–517.

Heimbeck, D., Frese, M., Sonnnentag, S., & Keith, N. (2003). Integrating errors into the training process: The function of error management instructions and the role of goal orientation. *Personnel Psychology, 2003*(56), 333–361.

Hofmann, D. A., & Mark, B. (2006). An investigation of the relationship between safety climate and medication. *Personnel Psychology, 59*, 847–869.

Janz, B. D., Colquitt, J. A., & Noe, R. A. (1997). Knowledge worker team effectiveness: The role of autonomy, interdependence, team development and contextual support variables. *Personnel Psychology, 50*, 877–904.

Keith, N., & Frese, M. (2005). Self-regulation in error management training: Emotion control and metacognition as mediators of performance effects. *Journal of Applied Psychology, 90*(4), 677–691.

Kirkman, B. L., & Rosen, B. (1999). Beyond self-management: Antecedents and consequences of team empowerment. *The Academy of Management Journal, 42*, 58–74.

Kriegesmann, B., Kley, T., & Schwering, M. G. (2005). Creative errors and heroic failures: Capturing their innovative potential. *The Journal of Business Strategy, 26*(3), 57–64.

Langfred, C. W. (2005). Autonomy and performance in teams: The multilevel moderating effect of task interdependence. *Journal of Management, 31*, 513–529.

Langfred, C. W., & Moye, N. A. (2004). Effects of task autonomy on performance: An extended model considering motivational, informational, and structural mechanisms. *Journal of Applied Psychology, 89*, 934–945.

Leach, D. J., Wall, T. D., Rogelberg, S. G., & Jackson, P. R. (2005). Team autonomy, performance and member job strain: Uncovering the teamwork KSA link. *Applied Psychology: An International Review, 54*, 1–24.

MacKinnon, D. P., Fairchild, A. J., & Fritz, M. (2007). Mediation Analysis. *Annual Review of Psychology, 58*, 593–614.

Molleman, E. (2000). Modalities of self-managing teams: The 'must', 'may', 'can' and 'will' of local decision making. *International Journal of Operations & Production Management, 20*, 889–910.

Molleman, E., Nauta, A., & Jehn, K. A. (2004). Person-job fit applied to teamwork: A multilevel approach. *Small Group Research, 35*, 515–539.

Saavedra, R., Earley, P. C., & Van Dyne, L. (1993). Complex interdependence in task-performing groups. *Journal of Applied Psychology, 78*, 61–72.

Senge, P. M. (1990). *The fifth discipline: The art and practice of the learning organisation*. London: Doubleday.

Stewart, G. L., & Barrick, M. R. (2000). Team structure and performance: Assessing the mediating role of intrateam process and the moderating role of task type. *Academy of Management Journal, 43*, 135–148.

Tjosvold, D., Sun, H. F., & Wan, P. (2005). Effects of openness, problem solving, and blaming on learning: An experiment in China. *The Journal of Social Psychology, 6*, 629–644.

Tjosvold, D., Yu, Z. Y., & Hui, C. (2004). Team learning from mistakes: The contribution of cooperative goals and problem solving. *Journal of Management Studies, 41*, 1223–1245.

Van Dyck, C. (2000). *Putting error to good use: Error management culture in organizations*. Amsterdam: Vrije Universiteit.

Van Dyck, C., Frese, M., & Sonnentag, S. (1998). *Organizational error management climate: On enhanced error handling and organizational performance*. Paper presented at the Academy of Management Conference, San Diego, CA.

Van Woerkom, M. (2003). *Critical reflection at work. Bridging individual and organizational learning*. Doctoral dissertation, University of Twente, Enschede.

Van Woerkom, M., & Croon, M. (2009). The relationship between team learning activities and team performance. *Personnel Review, 38*, 560–577.

Wageman, R., Hackman, J. R., & Lehman, E. (2005). Team diagnostic survey: Development of an instrument. *The Journal of Applied Behavioral Science, 41*, 373–398.

Wang, G., & Netemeyer, R. G. (2002). The effects of job autonomy, customer demandingness and trait competitiveness on salesperson learning, self-efficacy and performance. *Journal of the Academy of Marketing Science, 30*, 217–228.

Chapter 9
Error Orientation in the Context of Intuitive and Competent Behaviour: Results of an Exploratory Study in the Domain of Emergency Medicine

Christian Harteis and Franziska Frost

A huge body of educational research exists, which analyses both the main issues of this article, i.e., the individual attitude towards errors and the intuition as an important component of high level professional performances. Several theoretical approaches claim processes of intuitive behaviour and its advantages to cope with confusing and challenging situations. Usually, authors claim that implicit knowledge stocks, which are acquired through rich experiences during a professional career, are the basis of intuitive behaviour. These approaches of expertise will be explained in the following paragraphs. A perspective, which is widely neglected, concerns the role of individual attitudes for professional behaviour. Confidence or trust to keep in control of a situation can be seen as crucial prerequisites, which allow individuals to follow their intuitions when dealing with challenging situations. Error orientation can be considered as a special form of confidence to keep control of an erroneous situation. This contribution extends available research on professional competence by connecting two quite well-established issues of professional behaviour and by exploring the role of error orientation for intuitive and competent behaviour.

C. Harteis, Ph.D. (✉)
Fakultät für Kulturwissenschaften, University of Paderborn, Paderborn, Germany
e-mail: Christian.harteis@upb.de

F. Frost, Dipl.-Päd.
TUM School of Education, Technische Universität München, Munich, Germany
e-mail: franziska.frost@tum.de

J. Bauer and C. Harteis (eds.), *Human Fallibility: The Ambiguity of Errors for Work and Learning*, Professional and Practice-based Learning 6,
DOI 10.1007/978-90-481-3941-5_9, © Springer Science+Business Media Dordrecht 2012

Expertise Research as an Approach to Explaining Professional Behaviour

Research on expertise can be considered as one of the most popular scientific approaches which explain the stable capability for high performances. It claims that knowledge structures are the explanation of individual capabilities and tries to analyse the development and change of knowledge from being a novice to becoming an expert (Boshuizen, Bromme, & Gruber, 2004). The most common research perspective focuses on knowledge and mental processes during problem-solving processes. By contrasting subjects of varying performance levels, research on expertise tries to gain insight into the form of advanced knowledge and the acquisition of competence (Gruber & Rehrl, 2003). There is strong evidence that outstanding problem-solving capabilities do not only result from quantitative disparities in the amount of knowledge between experts and novices but that in particular there are qualitative differences in their thought processes (Gruber & Renkl, 2000). This means that experts' knowledge base is not only broader but also better embedded, easily accessible, and applicable in a more flexible way (Chase & Simon, 1973; Ericsson, 1985), which finally allows experts to perform consistently at a high level (Gruber & Rehrl, 2003).

It is particularly in the domain of emergency medicine in which expertise implies a holistic, fast and precise recognition of patterns (Patel, Arocha, & Kaufman, 1999). Schmidt, Norman, and Boshuizen (1990) describe the development of expertise in the clinical context of physicians by means of a four-stage model. The experiences physicians gain in the clinical field within these stages transform their theoretical knowledge qualitatively and, thus, enable them to behave competently and efficiently. With increasing expertise, explicit knowledge structures become less important and are restructured and integrated in more implicit knowledge forms. This kind of knowledge finally provides the basis of intuitive acting (Myers, 2002). Hence, this theoretical approach induces the expectation that experienced emergency physicians behave as more competent and intuitive than less-experienced ones.

Perspectives on Intuition

Several approaches of research on intuition can also be found in psychology literature. Current research reflects different definitions and perspectives on intuitive behaviour (Easen & Wilcockson, 1996). Intuition as used here in this chapter is based on an implicit knowledge base, which is acquired through years of knowledge acquisition and practical experience (Myers, 2002). Although intuition is considered to be a mainly spontaneous and non-conscious phenomenon (Easen & Wilcockson, 1996), it is instead recognized as a reliable characteristic of professional competence rather than as being an arbitrary moment of problem solving.

> "Intuition usually is defined as the capability to act or decide appropriately without deliberately and consciously balancing alternatives, without following a certain rule or routine, and possibly without awareness (Gigerenzer, 2007; Hogarth, 2001; Klein, 2003; Myers,

2002). It allows action which is quick (e.g. reaction to a challenging situation) and surprising, in the sense that it is extraordinary in performance level or shape (Harteis, Koch, & Morgenthaler, 2008, p. 68)."

Biederman and Shiffar (1987) provided empirical evidence for the professional capability of intuitive performances: They revealed that trained employees of a chicken farm can distinguish the gender of chickens intuitively within seconds and with an accuracy of 98%, but the employees are not able to explicitly describe decision criteria for their work. When studying the behaviour of firemen in emergency cases, Klein (2003) also concluded that decisions in emergency cases are not based on rational pondering of different alternatives, but on mental models based on professional experience, which allow intuitive and quick solutions.

It is the comprehensive stock of domain-specific knowledge on the one hand and the rich experience of the professional career on the other hand which allow experts to integrate numerous facts, certain rules or principles and to cope with incomplete and inconsistent information on a challenging situation in order to come up with a well-founded and appropriate decision. Myers (2002) describes intuitive acting as the unconscious use of implicit knowledge. In contrast, novices do not possess such a complex and implicit fundament for their decision making. Hence, even though they are of course able to behave intuitively, their intuition does not reliably result in as appropriate decisions as does experts' intuitive behaviour. Such an approach applies a developmental view on intuition as a component of professional competence, since all the necessary knowledge is the result of explicit and implicit learning processes during the career.

Dreyfus and Dreyfus (1986) developed a well-received model of expertise, which identifies intuition as a characteristic of the highest level of expertise. The authors refute the tradition of a solely rational and analytic perspective on expert achievement. Instead, they detected the prominent role of intuition for extraordinary performance through observations in different domains (e.g. pilots and chess players). They created their model of expertise development on the basis of these observations, in which novices gradually acquire and develop domain-specific practical knowledge that becomes increasingly implicit the more they develop their routines. During the development of expertise, these implicit knowledge stocks gain increasing impact on the behaviour. It is an important facet of expertise, particularly in ill-structured domains, in which a high standard of performance is reliably determined by intuitive mental processes, just as Dreyfus and Dreyfus characterised the highest level of expertise by the spontaneous application of flexible behaviour patterns instead of reactive application of fixed routines and rules.

> "It seems that a beginner makes inferences using rules and facts like a heuristically programmed computer, but that with talent and a great deal of involved experience the beginner develops into an expert who intuitively sees what to do without applying rules (Dreyfus, 1997, p. 23)."

Implicit knowledge and intuition are therefore the fundamental sources of professional competence. Schmidt et al.'s (1990) model of the development of clinical expertise reflects the same idea, although they chose lower stages of skill development. An enrichment of declarative knowledge with domain-specific experiences and recurrences of knowledge demands are crucial qualitative influences on the experts' knowledge. Thus, a dense network of implicit knowledge develops, which enables individuals to acquire flexible knowledge applications and professional expertise. The better this implicit knowledge base is developed, the more the individuals can include various aspects within their intuitive behaviour in challenging problem situations when quick decisions are necessary.

Hence, it is plausible to expect that the quality of emergency physicians' intuitive decisions improves with increasing work experience. However, it is important to consider that it is not the simple quantitative amount of experience that shapes an individual's expertise but rather the quality of reflected, meaningful experiences. It is, thus, indispensable that an individual reflects on his or her own behaviour, own knowledge and own experiences, and uses metacognitive strategies in order to permanently improve their own practices so as to develop and maintain expertise and the capability to decide intuitively in an appropriate way. These reflective and evaluative processes shape mental models of professional behaviour, which provide patterns for a deeper understanding of professional practices. For Klein (2003), such mental models shape the fundament for intuitive behaviour. He establishes a theoretical model, which claims an interplay between intuition and metacognition – the latter as a conscious reflection upon practice and experiences. Accordingly, individuals reflect experiences and conduct mental simulations of alternatives which – in the event that they end up successful – then enlarge behavioural patterns for challenging situations, which can guide future intuitive behaviour. The transition in consciousness between intuition and metacognition is not abrupt but instead smooth (Hogarth, 2001; Sloman, 2002). Cognitive researchers claim two parallel mental systems of information processing: An intuitive, unconscious system and a rational, conscious system. Both are supposed to operate permanently and in parallel – and both influence each decision or mental activity. Each mental activity can thus be located on a continuum between absolutely intuitive and absolutely rational (Sloman, 2002). Both methods of information processing are inseparable and their relationship is determined by mutual completion and improvement. Intuition enables valuable experiences, which constitute the raw material for rational thinking. Retrospective reflection of intuitive thoughts sharpens unconscious thoughts and enhances intuition (Easen & Wilcockson, 1996; Greenhalgh, 2002; Quirk, 2006). The interplay of intuitive insights and rational analysis is the most important element of medical expertise (Quirk, 2006). Finally, intuition is an important component of professional behaviour particularly in the domain of emergency medicine, as most of the professional tasks are shaped by complex, unclear situations with extreme time constraints (Greenhalgh, 2002; Quirk, 2006).

The Role of Error Orientation for Intuitive Behaviour and Decision Making

Error orientation as individual attitude towards errors has a two-fold relevance for intuition: First, studies on intuition describe intuitive behaviour as subjective perception of an agreement between situational demands and own capabilities (e.g. flow experience; Csikszentmihalyi, 1990) and of confidence to control situational developments (Klein, 2003). That means that intuitive behaviour obviously goes along with the subjective trust to remain in control of the situation, i.e. errors are not perceived as a danger. Thus, intuitive behaviour is considered not to be related to a hostile attitude towards errors. Second, error orientation is relevant for processes of professional learning. When gaining new experience in the professional field, errors can hardly be avoided. However, if and to what extent subjects learn from their mistakes particularly depends on their attitude towards errors (Oser, 1999). As mentioned above, reflection on experiences (of errors) initiate crucial learning processes to establish patterns of intuitive behaviour. Hence, error orientation influences the development of expertise. The construct error orientation includes different aspects (cf. Rybowiak, Garst, Frese & Batinic, 1999) among which are the facets of emotional and strategic handling of errors, which are the most important ones.

Strategic Handling of Errors

Strategic handling of errors comprises goal-oriented, reflective efforts intentionally applied in order to learn from errors. This includes for example conscious thinking about errors, analysis of failure causes, and active efforts to correct errors. Reflection about errors is seen as a crucial requirement to learn from errors as well as to develop professional competence (Kolodner, 1993; Oser, 1999). In Ericsson's (2006) well-known "deliberate practice" model, the well-directed correction of errors is an essential moment of the development of expertise. An empirical study in the banking sector revealed positive correlations between the extent and the quality of error reflection on the one hand and thc employees' professional competence on the other hand (Kipfmüller, Gartmeier, Heid, & Gruber, 2007).

The application of strategies for the purpose of learning from errors can be seen as a metacognitive activity. Hence, strategic handling of errors is considered to support the development of a professional intuition. Reflection and analysis about errors enlarge implicit and explicit knowledge structures and support their development. Therefore, professional practices incorporating reflective and evaluative processes should improve expertise and the reliability of experts' intuition. Greenhalgh (2002) provides the following explanation:

> "In particular, critical reflection on past intuitive judgments highlights areas of ambiguity in complex decision making, sharpens perceptual awareness, exposes the role of emotions in driving "hunches" (perhaps also demonstrating the fallibility of relying on feelings alone), encourages a holistic view of the patient's predicament, identifies specific educational needs, and may serve to "kick-start" a more analytical chain of thought on particular problems (p. 399)."

Emotional Handling of Errors

Aside from the cognitive aspects of error orientation, emotional factors of error orientation can also be identified. Errors are often associated with negative emotions like fear, shame, burden and anger, especially in social settings in which individuals feel unsafe. However, recent research about errors suggests that negative emotions concerning errors constrains zest for action and impede learning processes: Those subjects who showed positive attitude towards errors proved to grapple with their weaknesses, to search for their reasons and, finally, to overcome them in a constructive way (Cannon & Edmondson, 2005; Keith & Frese, 2005). Politis and Gabrielsson (2007) found similar empirical evidence in the domain of entrepreneurs. People who acknowledge that errors comprise potential for development are able to utilise these as an opportunity to establish new knowledge structures (Oser, 1999).

The study reported in this article tests assumptions similar to the considerations explained above. A positive attitude towards errors is expected to have positive effects on competence development and intuitive behaviour, whereas a negative error orientation establishes constraints in the learning processes and flows of action. An unstressed approach to errors stimulates new ideas and creativity. Contrarily, McGrath (1999) claims: "An antifailure bias can, in short, have counterintuitive negative effects. It can interfere significantly with people's ability to make sense out of experience" (p. 21). It is particularly in unfamiliar and uncertain situations with looming serious consequences in which emotions play a key role for intuitive decision making processes (Sayegh, Anthony, & Perrewé, 2004). Perceiving fear of failures and their severe consequences, emergency physicians often feel urged to affirm their treatment rationally (Mannebach, 2001). However, to a certain extent, emergencies are always shaped by uncertainty that has to be dealt with. Quirk (2006) emphasises that particularly those emergencies demand intuitive behaviour, whose feelings are dominated by fear and panic. Since intuitive behaviour utilises a rich knowledge base and many years of experiences, it allows adequate decisions in time-limited and problematic situations.

Research Questions

The theoretical considerations explained in the paragraphs above induce a research model placing error orientation as a moderating variable between professional experience and professional performance and intuitive behaviour. The main research interests focus the analysis of effects of emergency physicians' work experience on their competence and their intuitive behaviour. It is assumed that the error orientation facets of strategic and emotional handling of errors affect these interrelations significantly. The hypotheses to be empirically tested are:

(I) Emergency physicians with many years of work experience are more competent than less-experienced physicians.
(II) Emergency physicians with many years of work experience act more intuitively than less-experienced physicians.
(III) There is a positive interrelation between the degree of intuitive decision making and the emergency physicians' quality of treatment.

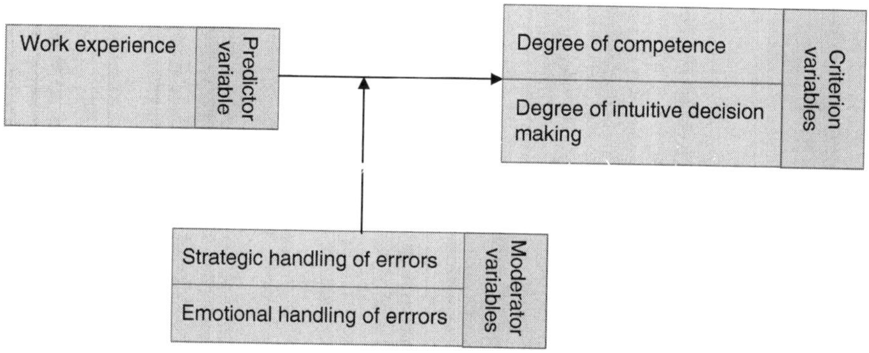

Fig. 9.1 Causal connections of the moderated research model

(IV) The positive interrelations in (I) and (II) are moderated by the variable strategic handling of errors.
(V) The positive interrelations in (I) and (II) are moderated by the variable emotional handling of errors.

According to Baron and Kenney (1986), the effect of moderating variables can be described as the follows:

> "In general terms, a moderator is a qualitative (e.g. sex, race, class) or quantitative (e.g. level of reward) variable that affects the direction and/or strength of the relation between an independent or predictor variable and a dependent or criterion variable (p. 1174)."

Hence, it is assumed that the error orientation facets affect the interdependencies described in hypotheses (I) and (II). Figure 9.1 sketches this model of causal connection.

Method

Sample

The sample consists of $N = 30$ participants who volunteered for this study. They all work in the field of emergency medicine at the university hospital in Regensburg (Germany). The collected data were used anonymously. The participants' ages ranged from min = 24 to max = 48 years, with the average of M = 31.20 (STD = 6.316) years. The sample comprises subjects of different levels of educational and practical experiences. The years of work experience ranged from min = 0 to max = 18 years. As emergency medicine is a domain dominated by males, the gender distribution does not reproduce equal distribution. There are $n_1 = 12$ females and $n_2 = 18$ males who participated in the study.

Procedure

In order to test hypotheses I–V, a laboratory setting with a cross-sectional design was developed. Data were collected in the period between September and November 2008. A medical emergency case was simulated on the basis of computer-steered patient mannequins, which induces intuitive behaviour. Each participant had to medicate a simulated life-threatening situation whereby usual equipment is available. Hence, the situation demanded acting under extreme time pressure, which was supposed to initiate intuitive behaviour. The emergency case was designed in such a way that mere routine activities were not appropriate for success, since they shaped extraordinary disease patterns with hidden challenges. Instead, creative and intuitive capabilities were necessary to solve the situation. Additionally, the support of a medical assistant who reacted only on the participant's instructions was provided – as is usual in real emergency cases. The patient simulation mannequins reacted realistically on the physicians' treatments.

The entire situation was video recorded. Additionally, two observers followed the event and monitored on a checklist if the participant executed all the steps that are needed to be taken for a successful diagnosis and a treatment according to official medical guidelines. Furthermore, an experienced senior physician evaluated the participants' behaviour according to different scales. The duration of an adequate patient treatment was estimated at about 10 min. The actual duration the participants needed for the right diagnosis was recorded, but after 20 min, the treatment was stopped. Each participant's *degree of competence (criterion variable)* is composed of a mean value of the three measures: score on checklist, expert evaluation, and duration of treatment.

Immediately after the casework, we interviewed each participant which included the analysis of the video recording of his or her casework. The "stimulated recall" technique (Bloom, 1954) was applied to find out which steps the participant could consciously recognise. Therefore, the subject was requested to comment on each single decision he or she identified in the video. All utterances were recorded and transcribed afterwards. Deviations from the standard solution implemented in the checklist and the amount of decisions the subjects realised when watching the video tape constitute the *degree of intuitive decision making (criterion variable)*.

Finally, the participants were asked to complete a questionnaire which covered personal data (age, gender, years of work experience, amount of experienced emergency cases) and the two error orientation scales originally created by Rybowiak et al. (1999). The number of medicated emergency cases was used to define the subjects' *work experience (predictor variable)*. The mean values of the error orientation scales *strategic handling of errors* and *emotional handling of errors* shaped the two *moderating variables*. The complete data acquisition (including transcription) took an average of 390 min per participant.

Results

Descriptive Data Analysis

The amount of experienced emergency cases ranged from min = 0 to max = 2,000 with a mean value of M = 246 (SD = 463). The checklist (degree of competence) allowed a maximum score of 30, the participants achieved between min = 8 and max = 26. The mean was M = 14.63 (SD = 4.13). Subjects' degrees of intuitive decision making ranged from min = 4.00 to max = 16.00 with a mean of M = 9.00 (SD = 3.55). Both error orientation facets were gathered on rating scales from 1 (does not apply to me at all) until 7 (applies very well to me). The facet strategic handling of errors yielded a mean of M = 5.76 (SD = 0.80; min = 3.75; max = 6.75), whereas the facet emotional handling of errors has a mean of M = 3.93 (SD = 1.12; min = 2.25; max = 6.25). Both scales can be judged as reliable (strategic handling of errors $\alpha = .77$ (three items); emotional handling of errors $\alpha = .72$ (four items); α = Cronbach's alpha).

Inferential Data Analysis

Main effects. In order to test hypotheses I and II simple regression analyses were conducted. Data were used in *z*-standardized form. The predictor *working experience* accounts significantly for 23.7% ($R^2 = .237$; $p < .01$) of the dependent variable *degree of competence*. Thereby the criterion's sub-categories show fairly different data: The significant explanation of variance through *working experience* reaches 24.7% ($R^2 = .247$; $p < .01$) for the sub-category expert evaluation. For both remaining sub-categories, no share of variance could be explained significantly (duration of treatment $R^2 = .102$; $p < .09$; checklist score $R^2 = .123$; $p < .06$). Consequently, hypothesis I was only partly confirmed.

As the regression analysis revealed a significant variance explanation of 20.9% ($R^2 = .209$; $p < .05$) between the variables *work experience* and *degree of intuitive decision making*, hypothesis II was supported. However, Urban and Mayerl (2008) state that regression coefficients of more than $R^2 = .60$ are recognized as a very good outcome. Hence, the interdependency found here is considerably low.

The test of a positive interrelation between the *degree of intuitive decision making* and the emergency physician's *degree of competence* was conducted by a Bravais–Pearson correlation analysis. This decision reflects that the theoretical pattern developed above does not allow assumptions about the direction of a possible interrelation. The correlation coefficient between the *degree of intuitive decision making* and the *degree of competence* is $r = .70$ ($p < .01$) and can thus be classified as strong correlation. Concerning the sub-categories of different results, *intuitive decision making* correlates moderately with the duration of treatment ($r = .53$; $p < .01$) and the expert evaluation ($r = .55$; $p < .01$), whereas there is a very strong correlation related to the

Table 9.1 Comparison of simple and multiple regression models with the moderator variable strategic handling of errors

Predictor: working experience	Simple regression model	Multiple regression model	
Criterion:	R^2	R^2	ΔR^2
Degree of intuitive decision making	.222*	.222	.000
Degree of competence	.275*	.352**	.077
Expert evaluation	.297**	.385**	.088
Checklist score	.139	.183	.044
Duration of treatment	.168	.186	.018

R^2 squared stability index, ΔR^2 additional variance explanation through moderator
*$p<.05$; **$p<.01$

Table 9.2 Comparison of simple and multiple regression models with the moderator variable emotional handling of errors

Predictor: working experience	Simple regression model	Multiple regression model	
Criterion:	R^2	R^2	ΔR^2
Degree of intuitive decision making	.233*	.388**	.155*
Degree of competence	.237**	.557**	.319**
Expert evaluation	.279*	.497**	.219**
Checklist score	.123	.345*	.222**
Duration of treatment	.105	.325*	.220**

R^2 squared stability index, ΔR^2 additional variance explanation through moderator
*$p<.05$; **$p<.01$

category checklist score ($r=.82$; $p<.01$). Hence, hypothesis III can very clearly be considered as confirmed.

Moderated effects. In order to test the moderating effects framed in hypothesis IV and V, multiple regression analyses were calculated, which followed the procedure recommended by Aiken, West, and Reno (1991). Thereby the following two different coherencies were compared: (a) the interrelation between *work experience* and *error orientation*, which were included as predictors simultaneously, and the respective criterion variable; and (b) the interrelationship between the product of *work experience* and *error orientation* (calculated in form of z-standardized data) and the respective criterion variable. In case the coherence in (b) is significantly higher than in (a), the moderating effect of the respective error orientation facet can be considered as confirmed. The F distribution with one degree of freedom serves as the appropriate reference for significance testing here. The following tables show the test values (R^2) of both model calculations. These values reflect the percentage of variance that can be explained by including all variables into the regression in relation to the total variance. The value ΔR^2 in the last column indicates the difference in the amount of explained variance between both models.

Table 9.1 indicates that the multiple regression models (which include the moderator variable *strategic handling of errors*) do not explain significantly more variance than the simple regression models without interaction terms. Therefore, hypothesis IV needs to be rejected. However, the multiple regression models comprising the moderator "emotional handling of errors" explain significantly more variance in case of all criterion variables, as shown in Table 9.2. Thus, hypothesis V is supported clearly by the data.

Discussion

This empirical study provides evidence for the assumption that emergency physicians use their intuition during emergency cases. It also reveals that their degree of intuitive decision making, as an indicator for intuitive behaviour, is positively correlated with their overall degree of competence. As the Dreyfus and Dreyfus (1986) model suggests, intuition can be considered as an important characteristic of professional competence and expertise. The more experienced the emergency physicians were, the more they relied on their intuitive thoughts and the better were their performances as indicated by their treatment qualities. However, as the coherences between work experience and degree of competence with respect to intuitive decision making were rather low, the number of medicated emergency cases is not a sufficient predictor. It seems instead plausible that the additional consideration of the moderator variable emotional handling of errors describes human behaviour much more precisely. It can be concluded that it is not just the quantitative amount of work experience that accounts for the development of qualified and intuitive behaviour. Peoples' attitudes toward errors also determine to what extent they learn from their experiences (cf. Cannon & Edmondson, 2005; Oser, 1999). This study showed that emergency physicians, who do not mainly associate errors with feelings of anxiety, anger and shame, but do have a rather positive attitude towards errors, are able to learn more from their experiences, since they performed better. Obviously, there is a qualitative difference in the learning outcomes depending on the learners' individual attitude towards errors. In addition, the findings indicate that people who have the courage to learn by discovery, and whose creative mind is not occupied by the fear of potentially making errors, can obviously better use the great potential of their intuition.

Remarkably, the empirical findings do not support the hypothesis that physicians who consciously use strategies to learn from errors perform better and more intuitively than physicians sharing less meta-cognitive activities. Since there no negative correlations were found, our findings do not contradict the view of many popular and well-received authors who claim that the conscious reflection of errors and goal-oriented improvement positively influence the development of competence (e.g. Ericsson, 2006; Kolodner, 1993; Oser, 1999) with respect to the improvement of intuitive behaviour (Greenhalgh, 2002; Quirk, 2006). However, the statistical values of the analyses are too weak to provide support for these authors' theses. The application of a broader and more widespread moderating construct, like general reflection, could probably attain more definite results.

Conclusions

This study shows empirically, firstly, that intuition is part of professional competence. It also shows, secondly, not only quantitative but also qualitative differences in learning through experience: Peoples' attitudes towards errors proved to be a determining factor for learning activities and the improvement of intuitive behaviour. As errors are often associated with negative feelings, which drastically constrain learning success and the usage of intuitive behaviour, it is important to provide learners as well as professionals with a work environment which supports the development of error-friendly attitudes. Further research should investigate a broader range of factors which influence the development of such attitudes and their effect on professional performance and intuitive behaviour. Plausibly, feedback loops in experiential learning environments and goal-oriented repetitions of appropriate behavioural patterns appear promising for teaching a positive error orientation simultaneously with important components of expertise. The domain of this study represents an explicit orientation towards rational decision making and low error tolerance. In this regard, emergency medicine is similar to other domains (e.g. aviation, construction engineering, and food production). Hence, the insights of this study are not necessarily limited to the area of emergency medicine and may eventually also shed light on other domains.

References

Aiken, L. S., West, S. G., & Reno, R. R. (1991). *Multiple regression: Testing and interpreting interactions*. Newbury Park, CA: Sage Publications.

Baron, R. M., & Kenney, D. A. (1986). The moderator-mediator variable distinction in social psychological research: Conceptual, strategic, and statistical considerations. *Journal of Personality and Social Psychology, 51*(6), 1173–1182.

Biederman, I., & Shiffar, M. M. (1987). Sexing day-old chicks. *Journal of Experimental Psychology. Learning, Memory, and Cognition, 13*, 640–645.

Bloom, B. (1954). The thought process of students in discussion. In S. J. French (Ed.), *Accent on teaching: Experiments in general education* (pp. 23–46). New York: Harper.

Boshuizen, H. P. A., Bromme, R., & Gruber, H. (2004). *Professional learning: Gaps and transitions on the way from novice to expert*. Dordrecht, the Netherlands: Kluwer Academic Publishing.

Cannon, M. D., & Edmondson, A. C. (2005). Failing to learn and learning to fail (intelligently). How great organisations put failure to work to improve and innovate. *Long Range Planning, 38*, 299–319.

Chase, W. G., & Simon, H. A. (1973). Perception in chess. *Cognitive Psychology, 4*, 55–81.

Csikszentmihalyi, M. (1990). *Flow. The psychology of optimal experience*. New York: Harper and Row.

Dreyfus, H. L. (1997). Intuitive, deliberative, and calculative models of expert performance. In C. E. Zsambok & G. Klein (Eds.), *Naturalistic decision making* (pp. 17–28). Mahwah, NJ: Lawrence Erlbaum Associates.

Dreyfus, H. L., & Dreyfus, S. E. (1986). *Mind over machine*. New York: Macmillan, Free Press.

Easen, P., & Wilcockson, J. (1996). Intuition and rational decision-making in professional thinking: A false dichotomy? *Journal of Advanced Nursing, 24*, 667–673.

Ericsson, K. A. (1985). Memory skill. *Canadian Journal of Psychology, 39*, 188–231.

Ericsson, K. A. (2006). The influence of experience and deliberate practice on the development of superior expert performance. In K. A. Ericsson, N. Charness, P. J. Feltovich, & R. R. Hofman (Eds.), *The Cambridge handbook of expertise and expert performance* (pp. 683–703). Cambridge, UK: Cambridge University Press.

Gigerenzer, G. (2007). *Gut feelings, the intelligence of the unconscious and the power of intuition*. New York: Viking.

Greenhalgh, T. (2002). Intuition and evidence – Uneasy bedfellows? *British Journal of General Practice, 52*, 395–400.

Gruber, H., & Rehrl, M. (2003). Bedingungen zur Stimulation von Kompetenzentwicklung [Conditions for stimulating competence development]. In Bundesinstitut für Berufsbildung (Ed.), *Berufsbildung für eine globale Gesellschaft. Perspektiven im 21. Jahrhundert, Dokumentation 4. BIBB-Fachkongress 2002* (pp. 1–12). Berlin: Bundesinstitut für Berufsbildung.

Gruber, H., & Renkl, A. (2000). Die Kluft zwischen Wissen und Handeln. Das Problem des trägen Wissens [The gap between knowing and acting. The problem of inert knowledge]. In G. H. Neuweg (Ed.), *Wissen – Können – Reflexion. Ausgewählte Verhältnisbestimmungen* (pp. 155–174). Innsbruck, Austria: Studienverlag.

Harteis, C., Koch, T., & Morgenthaler, B. (2008). How intuition contributes to high performance: An educational perspective. *US-China Education Review, 5*(1), 68–80.

Hogarth, R. M. (2001). *Educating intuition*. Chicago/London: The University of Chicago Press.

Keith, N., & Frese, M. (2005). Self-regulation in error management training: Emotion control and metacognition as mediators of performance effects. *Journal of Applied Psychology, 90*, 677–691.

Kipfmüller, S., Gartmeier, M., Heid, H., & Gruber, H. (2007). *Reflection on mistakes in the workplace*. Conference paper presented at the annual meeting of the American Educational Research Association (AERA), Chicago, IL.

Klein, G. (2003). *Intuition at work. Why developing your gut instincts will make you better at what you do*. New York: Doubleday.

Kolodner, J. (1993). *Case-based reasoning*. San Mateo, CA: Kaufmann.

Mannebach, H. (2001). Reflexionen über den "Guten Arzt" [Reflections on the good physician]. *Zeitschrift für Gesundheitswissenschaften, 9*(1), 85–94.

McGrath, R. G. (1999). Falling forward: Real options reasoning and entrepreneurial failure. *Academy of Management Review, 24*(1), 13–30.

Myers, D. G. (2002). *Intuition. Its powers and perils*. New Haven, CT: Yale University Press.

Oser, F. (1999). *Fehlerwelten: vom Fehlermachen und Lernen aus Fehlern* [Error-worlds: About making errors and learning from errors]. Leverkusen, Germany: Leske+Budrich.

Patel, V. L., Arocha, J. F., & Kaufman, D. R. (1999). Expertise and tacit knowledge in medicine. In R. J. Sternberg & J. A. Horvath (Eds.), *Tacit knowledge in professional practice – Researcher and practitioner perspectives* (pp. 75–99). London: Lawrence Erlbaum Associates.

Politis, D., & Gabrielsson, J. (2007). *Entrepreneurs' attitudes towards failure – An experiential learning approach. Frontiers of Entrepreneurship Research 2007*. Wellesley, MA: Babson College.

Quirk, M. (2006). *Intuition and metacognition in medical education: Keys to developing expertise*. New York: Springer.

Rybowiak, V., Garst, H., Frese, M., & Batinic, B. (1999). Error orientation questionnaire (EOQ): Reliability, validity, and different language equivalence. *Journal of Organisational Behavior, 20*, 527–547.

Sayegh, L., Anthony, W. P., & Perrewé, P. L. (2004). Managerial decision-making under crisis: The role of emotion in an intuitive decision process. *Human Resource Management Review, 14*(2), 179–199.

Schmidt, H. G., Norman, G. R., & Boshuizen, H. P. A. (1990). A cognitive perspective on medical expertise: Theory and implications. *Academic Medicine, 65*, 611–621.

Sloman, S. A. (2002). Two systems of reasoning. In T. Gilovich, D. Griffin, & D. Kahneman (Eds.), *Heuristics and biases* (pp. 379–396). Cambridge, UK: Cambridge University Press.

Urban, D., & Mayerl, J. (2008). *Regressionsanalyse: Theorie, Technik und Anwendung* [Regression analysis: Theory, technique and application]. Wiesbaden, Germany: Verlag für Sozialwissenschaften.

Chapter 10
Human Fallibility and Learning from Errors at Work

Johannes Bauer, Martin Gartmeier, and Christian Harteis

Human fallibility and learning from errors are issues that are receiving increasing attention in the field of professional learning and development. Ten years ago, however, there were virtually no studies on learning from errors in this field, though there is a long tradition of research on human fallibility and errors, as well as safety and error management (Frese & Zapf, 1994; Glendon, Clarke, & McKenna, 2006; Perrow, 1984; Rasmussen, 1987; Reason, 1990; Senders & Moray, 1991). More recent developments in this area focus, for example, on critical incident reporting (Barach & Small, 2000; Zhao & Olivera, 2006; cf. also Chap. 14 in this volume) or organizational learning (Argote & Todocara, 2007; Argyris & Schön, 1996; Sitkin, 1992; van Dyck, Baer, Frese, & Sonnentag, 2005). Whereas these lines of inquiry focus primarily on the organizational level, studies on individual learning from errors and its contribution to individual workers' professional development are still rare (Bauer & Mulder, 2008). So far, there is only limited evidence explaining *under which conditions* individuals can *learn what* from *which kind of errors* at work. One reason for this lack of knowledge about error-related learning processes is the huge variability of the types of errors and situations in which errors may occur (Bauer, 2008a; Bauer & Mulder, 2008).

Notes This chapter is an extended version of the article: Bauer, J., Gartmeier, M., & Harteis, C. (2010). Lernen aus Fehlern im Arbeitskontext: Lernprozesse, Lernergebnisse und förderliche Rahmenbedingungen. *Wirtschaftspsychologie, 12*, 7–16.

J. Bauer, Ph.D. (✉) • M. Gartmeier, Ph.D.
TUM School of Education, Technische Universität München, Schellingstr. 33, D-80799 Munich, Germany
e-mail: jbauer@tum.de; martin.gartmeier@tum.de

C. Harteis, Ph.D.
Institute of Educational Science, University of Paderborn, Paderborn, Germany
e-mail: Christian.harteis@upb.de

J. Bauer and C. Harteis (eds.), *Human Fallibility: The Ambiguity of Errors for Work and Learning*, Professional and Practice-based Learning 6,
DOI 10.1007/978-90-481-3941-5_10,

The goal of this chapter is to provide an overview of several studies on the questions raised above that have been conducted since 2002 at the University of Regensburg (Germany).[1] On the basis of current approaches of professional learning (Boshuizen, Bromme, & Gruber, 2004) and workplace learning (Bauer & Gruber, 2007; Billett, 2004; Tynjälä, 2008), the studies investigated individual learning from errors and its relationship to the development of professional knowledge, skills, and expertise. In this respect, our studies differ from the other lines of inquiry mentioned above, which focus on organizational safety and error management as well as organizational learning. Nevertheless, our findings contribute to these fields of research, because organizational development strategies cannot be implemented without considering individual processes of learning and competence development (Edmondson, 2004).

More specifically, the present chapter addresses the following questions concerning human fallibility and learning from errors at work:

1. How can errors at work be conceptualized from a scientific point of view? How do practitioners in work organizations interpret errors?
2. How can the *process* of learning from errors be conceptualized and empirically investigated?
3. How can the *outcomes* of learning from errors be conceptualized and empirically investigated?
4. What are the individual and contextual conditions for learning from errors at work?

By integrating theoretical frameworks and findings from several studies on these issues, this chapter contributes to advancing our understanding of learning from errors in the workplace and provides a basis for continuing studies on this emerging issue in research on professional learning. The remainder of the chapter is organized along the four stated questions. In the conclusion, we discuss consequences for organizational practice.

Errors at Work

Drawing upon cognitive and action-oriented approaches to human error, errors can be conceptualized and understood as individual actions or decisions that result in a deficient deviation from a desired goal and that endanger the attainment of dependent goals (Bauer, 2004, 2008b; Frese & Zapf, 1994; Rasmussen, 1987; Reason, 1990; Senders & Moray, 1991; Zhao & Olivera, 2006). This definition, firstly, implies a hierarchical theory of human action. Action theory proposes that yielding complex

[1] The present studies were part of a series of research projects funded by the German Research Foundation (DFG) and lead by Prof. Dr. Helmut Heid and Prof. Dr. Hans Gruber (He 1158/4-2; Gr 1384/11-1; Gr 1384/11-2) as well as of the Ph.D. projects of Martin Gartmeier and Johannes Bauer.

goals – such as healing a patient – depends on the attainment of a hierarchical network of related goals and sub-goals (Frese & Zapf, 1994; Leontiev, 1978). Secondly, deviation from such a goal is attributed to the actions of an actor who is assumed to have sufficient skill and knowledge to perform the task, and it occurs contrary to his or her expectations and intentions (Senders & Moray, 1991). Errors can thereby be distinguished from failure caused by a simple lack of knowledge, from accidents and from deliberate violations (Wehner, Mehl, & Diekmann, 2010). Finally, judging an action to be an error is performed by referring to normative criteria that relate to the desired goal (Heid, 1999; Hughes, 1951; Rasmussen, 1987; Senders & Moray, 1991). Therefore, 'error' is not an objective characteristic describing an action or its result. 'Error' is an evaluative term of language that is used by a beholder on the basis of a comparison between an observed state and a normative anticipation, in order to express a deficient discrepancy between the two (cf. Billett in this volume).

The norm-dependency of error judgments described above is the reason some authors believe that the concept of error is ambiguous and hard to operationalize for empirical research (Weingart, 2008). However, norm-dependency is no unique problem of the concept of error, but a general problem of concepts that specify a quality of human action, such as 'creativity' (Csikszentmihalyi, 1999) or 'superior expert performance' (Ericsson, Charness, Feltovich, & Hoffman, 2006). Bauer (2008a) argued, in analogy to a systems-perspective on creativity (Csikszentmihalyi, 1999), that an action can be evaluated to be an error if (1) it is judged as a deficient deviation from an expected standard, (2) by knowledgeable and central members of a given occupation, organization, or local community of practice (Wenger, 1998), (3) at a given point of time. This perspective can be referred to as a social negotiation perspective on error judgments.

Taking the described social negotiation perspective allows analyses of different understandings of errors as well as of social discourses and power in error judgments (Heid, 1999). In an interview study that we conducted in several industrial and service enterprises, we found that the understandings of errors and the criteria for error judgments vary heavily, even within a single company (Harteis, Bauer, & Gruber, 2008; Harteis, Bauer, & Haltia, 2007; Harteis, Bauer, & Heid, 2006). In a first step of the study, we asked managers and staff members ($N=28$) to provide examples of non-trivial errors that occurred in their daily work. Content analysis revealed a large heterogeneity in the described error situations (Harteis et al., 2007). Secondly, we prompted error situations and asked the participants whether the respective situation would count as an error in their organization. We observed high agreement (79–93%) for situations that concerned production and sales as well as for situations that potentially resulted in a risk for employees' health (Harteis et al., 2008). In contrast, there was considerable lower agreement for other situations that, for example, concerned social relationships at work (39–67%). We found no differences between managers and staff members in this respect.

These findings illustrate that a high level of agreement concerning criteria for error judgments should not be taken for granted. This has consequences for organizational practice as well as for research on errors and learning from errors. Firstly, organizations should aim at the development of clear, socially agreed, and shared criteria for what constitutes an error in the context of specific tasks. Secondly, researchers should be aware that the understanding of error can vary strongly between them and study participants as well as among the participants. Just like organizations, researchers should not assume that participants have comparable notions of errors in mind, for example, when answering a questionnaire or interview questions. Therefore, a situated approach that anchors questions on errors in concrete error episodes seems to be advantageous to enhancing validity (Bauer, 2008b; Bauer & Mulder, 2011; Gartmeier, Bauer, Gruber, & Heid, 2010; Oser & Spychiger, 2005; Wehner & Mehl, 2008). Moreover, for studies on learning from errors, it seems particularly important to focus on errors that are arguably relevant to learning. Several scholars have argued that different types of errors vary in the learning potential they provide and that learning from them requires different types of activities (Bauer & Mulder, 2007; Glendon et al., 2006; Keith & Frese, 2005; Rybowiak, Garst, Frese, & Batinic, 1999). Typically, errors based on a higher level of cognitive action–regulation (Frese & Zapf, 1994; Rasmussen, 1987) are assumed to contain a higher potential for learning in terms of constructing knowledge from a cognitive re-evaluation of the experience. The rationale for this is that these errors potentially enable individuals to deliberately revise their knowledge and practice through the engagement in learning activities (Keith & Frese, 2005).

The Process of Learning from Errors: Engagement in Learning Activities

The concept of individual learning from errors implies the notion of an experience-based construction of knowledge that emerges from experiencing an error situation (Bauer & Gruber, 2007). Therefore, we contextualize our theoretical framework of learning from errors in theories of experiential learning and informal workplace learning (Billett, 2004; Boshuizen et al., 2004; Kolb, 1984; Kolodner, 1983; Tynjälä, 2008). Different perspectives of experiential learning theory are relevant here. We distinguish between a cognitive and an activity perspective, which serve different but complementary purposes for conceptualizing learning through errors at work. The cognitive perspective explains learning as the acquisition and improvement of knowledge and focuses on the memory and knowledge structures involved. Theories of case-based reasoning and the modification of scripts in dynamic memory (Kolodner, 1983; Schank, 1999) have provided models of how schematic, action-oriented knowledge structures (i.e., scripts) are extended and modified through reflecting on the experience of deviant episodes. Furthermore, this line of inquiry explains how the experience of errors may lead to improved performance and – in the long run – cognitive flexibility through the drawing of analogies to newly encountered episodes (i.e., case-based reasoning). As will be argued in the following section, the cognitive perspective is particularly relevant to the analysis of the outcomes of learning from errors. In contrast, the activity perspective offers opportunities for understanding the process of learning from errors and for making it accessible for empirical research. This perspective will be elaborated in this section.

The activity perspective views learning as a self-organised effort to improve performance (Boshuizen et al., 2004). This perspective is useful in determining which activities are relevant in order to learn from an error. The theoretical basis of the activity perspective lies, firstly, in theories of experiential learning cycles (Gruber, 2001; Kolb, 1984) that model experiential learning as action–reflection–action cycles. These models have also been acknowledged in more recent work on organizational learning and management (Boshuizen et al., 2004; Glendon et al., 2006). Applied to learning from errors at work, an experiential learning cycle can be modeled to involve the engagement in learning activities regarding (1) reflection on the causes of an error, (2) the development of new or revised action strategies that aim to avoid the error in the future, and (3) experimenting with and implementing the new or revised strategies (Bauer & Mulder, 2007). Each of these activities can be performed individually or in social cooperation with others at work. There is some evidence to suggest that learning activities performed during social interactions with others at work (i.e., joint analysis of causes and the development of new action strategies) are particularly relevant to learning from errors (Edmondson, 2004). This appraisal is consistent with the emphasis on the role of social exchange in recent research on workplace learning (Billett, 2004; Eraut et al., 1998). Communication and exchange can foster the development of shared knowledge and understanding of errors, as well as of solutions and strategies with which to handle them (Cannon & Edmondson, 2001; van Dyck et al., 2005).

Modeling learning from errors by the described learning cycle has the advantage of addressing concrete learning behavior that can be measured in empirical studies. In contrast, asking workers about their learning seems disadvantageous, because people tend to respond using the notion of formal learning if they are asked about "learning" at work (Simons & Ruijters, 2004). A problem with the model is, however, that it is quite generic and needs to be contextualized to the requirements of a specific field. That is, the question of what concrete learning activities are relevant within a particular field of work has to be answered. We have addressed this question in several studies.

In the interview study discussed in the previous section, the participants were asked to describe the reactions to the error situation that they had previously described (Harteis et al., 2008). They also provided information on whether something was done to prevent similar errors in future and whether the error was documented in any way. Indeed, the majority of the participants described activities regarding reflection on the causes of the error (79%). In most of the cases, the error was documented (70%). In another, open-ended question, the subjects were asked to describe in more detail how the error was dealt with. Most of the answers fell into three categories. Firstly, the error was discussed with colleagues in order to analyze its probable causes and to derive conclusions for future acting. Secondly, new agreements, rules or work processes, which were supposed to be less prone to this type of error, were negotiated. Finally, new control and prevention mechanisms were considered. Answers beyond these three categories concerned, for example, sensitizing co-workers to the error.

In interpreting these findings, it has to be acknowledged that the subjects referred to various error situations that are difficult to compare. It is reasonable to assume that the described error situations differ in their learning relevance. Nevertheless, the findings indicate that, as claimed in the model of error-related learning activities, reflection on potential causes of an error as well as the consideration of new strategies for future action could seem important for learning from errors in work practice. Moreover, these activities seem to be performed primarily through social interaction with colleagues. For organizational development initiatives, it can be concluded that the development of an organizational culture that supports a learning-oriented handling of errors is a major task (cf. Edmondson, 2004).

The findings discussed above could be corroborated in two more interview studies that were conducted in different contexts. In expert interviews in the domain of nursing, Bauer and Mulder (2007) elicited typical examples of knowledge- and rule-based errors, as well as relevant learning activities, for this field of work. In contrast to the earlier study (Harteis et al., 2008), the interviews focused on a specific type of error and related learning activities. The participants ($N=10$) were identified as experts, based on their long professional experience, their supervisory position and peer-assessment as being highly qualified. Consistent with the model of learning activities and with the earlier findings, the study indicated the relevance of the engagement in systematic reflection on causes of an error as well as the development of new action strategies. Again, the role of social exchange was stressed as crucial for these learning activities.

Another interview study was conducted in cooperation with our colleague Petri Haltia from University of Turku in Finland (Harteis et al., 2007). The focus was on workers in a Finnish shipyard. As in the other studies, the participants emphasized the role of joint reflection and discussion of errors. However, the participants also described constraints for learning from errors through engagement in these learning activities. In particular, they indicated that (team) discussions about errors as well as the use of error reporting tools sometimes had only a superficial function and did not lead to learning. These statements illustrate that in order to learn from errors, in-depth reflection on root causes, results, and ways of prevention should be performed with the intention of changing the underlying causes of an error, rather than merely seeking a quick fix to an error situation (Edmondson, 2004).

Outcomes of Learning from Errors

This section addresses the question of how potential outcomes of learning from errors at work can be conceptualized theoretically and operationalized for empirical research. Above, the case has been made that the cognitive perspective on experiential learning is helpful for this purpose (Bauer, 2008b). This cognitive perspective explains learning as the acquisition and improvement of knowledge through experiencing personally relevant episodes and focuses on the memory and knowledge structures involved. Therefore, this perspective allows for the modeling of cognitive processes and the representation of the outcomes of learning from errors (Bauer, 2008b; Bauer & Gruber, 2007; Gruber, 2001). In particular, theories of case-based reasoning and the modification of scripts in dynamic memory (Kolodner, 1983; Schank, 1999; Schank & Abelson, 1977) have provided models of how schematic, action-oriented knowledge structures (i.e., scripts) are extended and modified through reflecting on the experience of deviant episodes, including errors. Through reflecting on the causes of an error episode, an underlying script can be enriched by an additional part (i.e., an *index*) that distinguishes the deviant parts from the expected ones. The index assists the actor to remember the deviant episode in recurrences of similar situations and to choose alternative action strategies (i.e., case-based reasoning). Hence, the cognitive perspective explains how the experience of errors may lead to improved performance and – in the long run – cognitive flexibility through drawing analogies to newly encountered episodes.

Gartmeier, Bauer, Gruber, and Heid (2008) elaborated on parallels between the model of indicated scripts (Kolodner, 1983) and the theory of *negative knowledge* (Oser & Spychiger, 2005; cf. Minsky, 1994), which comes from an educational–didactical background. The term 'negative knowledge' denotes knowledge about conditions for errors in specific action sequences (procedural aspect) as well as inadequate assumptions concerning a specific context (declarative aspect). Oser and Spychiger (2005) assume that negative knowledge is acquired through learning from errors and helps to avoid similar errors in similar situations. Hence, as in Kolodner's (1983) model, knowledge about relevant errors in specific task episodes is considered helpful for avoiding errors and choosing a promising course of action.

One relevant yet open question is: how is it possible to empirically assess the described knowledge resulting from error-related learning? To address this question, we conducted a study in the context of elder care nursing. Employees ($N=37$) working in this field with a professional experience of between 0 and 30 years were confronted with 20 nursing and medical diagnoses of varying typicality (e.g., dementia, diabetes, social isolation, parental role conflict). With every diagnosis, two questions were posed: *What do you think you should pay special attention to in interaction with elderly people with the following diagnosis? What should be avoided?* The verbal protocols resulting from the subjects' reflection upon the questions posed were content analyzed (Gartmeier, Gruber, & Heid, 2010). The aim of this study was to identify the elder care nurses' knowledge about error-enabling conditions and situations in which errors typically occur. Drawing upon the theoretical differentiation between declarative and procedural negative knowledge (Oser & Spychiger, 2005), we investigated the question of whether these facets of negative knowledge could be traced and illustrated in a context-specific way. Moreover, the explorative task of identifying hitherto undescribed forms of negative knowledge was also pursued.

The results showed facets of declarative as well as procedural negative knowledge, while self-reflective as well as vicarious negative knowledge could be identified.

In the latter facet, the care expressed their knowledge about limitations the older people they work with possess on various levels (Gartmeier, Gruber, et al. 2010). The latter two forms of negative knowledge are particularly interesting in the context of elder care nursing. In their statements of self-reflective negative knowledge, the elder care nurses described limitations on the level of their own professional competence and professional role in the provision of care. For instance, they described their limited influence on the progression of certain diseases as well as the limitations of their own area of responsibility for certain work tasks (in delineation of, e.g., the responsibilities of physicians). This category additionally comprises statements in which the study participants described deficient aspects or lack of their own professional knowledge or skills (Parviainen & Eriksson, 2006).

As was already foreshadowed, the study subjects took the perspectives of the older persons they worked with in their statements of vicarious negative knowledge. They described limitations on the level of their abilities (knowledge about what somebody is not able to do, e.g., activities which are inappropriate for certain persons) and recognition (knowledge about what somebody does not recognize or understand, e.g., nursing home residents suffering from dementia and wrongly perceiving certain aspects of reality and "live in their own world").

In addition to the description and categorization of these facets of negative knowledge, Gartmeier, Gruber, et al. (2010) investigated relationships between these facets and different error types as described in the relevant literature. The elder care nurses benefit from their vicarious negative knowledge in their ability to avoid errors on the level of interpersonal relationships to the nursing home residents. Here, the category of *errors on the level of interpersonal relationships* described by Bauer (2008b), such as not confusing or causing nursing home residents to be taken aback, is relevant.

In another analysis of the same data, Gartmeier, Lehtinen, Gruber, and Heid (2010) investigated various degrees of specificity in the elder care nurses' negative knowledge. This research perspective was focused on due to the assumption that a person's ability to avoid errors based on negative knowledge improves along with the specificity with which negative knowledge can be applied to situations at work. Global statements of negative knowledge ("no two persons are the same") were differentiated from diagnosis specific ("don't over-challenge persons suffering from dementia") and further specified statements ("if you bathe persons with cardiac insufficiency, take care that the water in the tub is only lukewarm"), which often had a strongly situational focus. The comparison of different groups of professional experience (0–3, 4–9, and 10 and more years) showed a superiority of the group with the highest professional experience concerning the degree to which highly specified negative knowledge was expressed (Gartmeier, Lehtinen, et al. 2010). This result supports the assumption that error-specific experiential knowledge emerges through the encountering of relevant episodes at work and is further differentiated in the course of increased professional experience. In this process, it also becomes relevant for a wider range of situations. Furthermore, the results of this study underline that a focus upon specific error-cases and situations is a promising perspective for research on (learning from) errors at work.

Conditions for Learning from Errors

In the previous sections, we have conceptualized learning from errors as the engagement in error-related learning activities. The engagement in these activities is assumed to lead to the learning outcomes in terms of the modification of scripts in dynamic memory. The conditions under which individual workers engage in these activities have, however, so far been neglected. There are many open questions regarding individual differences in learning from errors as well as the predictors for the engagement in error-related learning activities. Like any other form of learning that takes place within a work context, engagement in learning after errors has to be understood as being dependent on characteristics of both the individual learner and the work context (Billett, 2004). In particular, engagement in social learning activities after an error cannot be taken for granted because it involves admitting the error to others (Edmondson, 1999). Therefore, studies on how individual workers interpret errors, how they can constructively use errors at work for learning, and what role the social environment of the workplace plays in supporting or inhibiting learning are required. Such studies could improve our understanding of how learning from errors contributes to the development of skilled performance within professional contexts. Furthermore, they are of practical relevance to, for example, the development of organizational programs that aim at fostering learning from errors (Aspden, Corrigan, Wolcott, & Erickson, 2004; Glendon et al., 2006).

Bauer and Mulder (2011) investigated conditions for the engagement in social learning activities after errors in the nursing profession. The study aimed at analyzing the role of variables that have been hypothesized to have an impact on learning from errors, namely the cognitive, emotional, and motivational interpretations of an error situation, as well as the perception of a trustful and psychologically-safe social climate among colleagues (Arndt, 1996; Bauer & Mulder, 2008; Edmondson, 1996; Meurier, Vincent, & Parmar, 1997; Tjosvold, Yu, & Hui, 2004; Tucker & Edmondson, 2003). The type of error focused on was the misinterpretation of a nursing situation and the subsequent making of a wrong decision. In the study, a sample of nurses ($N=276$) completed a questionnaire. The questionnaire started by presenting three vignettes of error cases that related to the above-mentioned type of error and had been developed from an expert interview study on typical errors in nursing (Bauer & Mulder, 2007). The vignettes concerned (1) the misinterpretation of values on a medical instrument, (2) the misjudgment of complications, and (3) the misjudgment of the risk of bedsores. The nurses were asked to choose one of the vignettes and imagine the situation vividly, and to then rate whether they would engage in joint reflection with colleagues on potential causes of the error and the development of strategies to avoid similar errors in future (i.e., *engagement in social learning activities*). In the analyses, the hypotheses tested were that the engagement in social learning activities depends on the nurses' cognitive, motivational, and emotional interpretation of the error situation (Edmondson, 2004; Rybowiak et al., 1999; Zhao & Olivera, 2006). More precisely, this involves the estimation of the error situation as relevant to learning, the emotional strain evoked by the error, and the motivational tendency to cover up the error. Furthermore, it was hypothesized that the engagement in social learning activities depends on the perception of a safe team climate, as measured by the perceived level of trust among the team members and the experience of a non-punitive handling of critical situations and errors within the team (Cannon & Edmondson, 2001; Edmondson, 1999; Harteis et al., 2007; Tjosvold, Yu, & Hui, 2004). These hypotheses were tested in a structural equation model that contained the mentioned variables as (correlated) predictors for the engagement in social learning activities.

As expected, the results indicated that the estimation of an error as relevant to learning ($\beta=.28$) and the tendency to cover up an error ($\beta=-.33$) are significant predictors for the engagement in social learning activities ($R^2=.29$). In contrast, the expected relationships could not be found for emotional strain because of the error and for the perception of a safe team climate. However, there were large correlations between (1) the estimation of an error as relevant to learning and error strain, and (2) the tendency to cover the error and a safe team climate. That is, the errors were estimated as more relevant to learning when the participants perceived the situations as emotionally straining ($r=.51$). Moreover, the reported tendency to cover up an error was low if the participants rated their team climate as being trustful and safe ($r=-.44$).

The overall pattern of findings described indicates a potential mediation model as a hypothesis for further research that was tested in an exploratory analysis. The findings indicated, firstly, a significant indirect effect of emotional strain on the engagement in social learning activities ($\beta=.18$) that is mediated completely by the subjective learning relevance of the error situation. Secondly, an indirect effect of the perception of a safe team climate on the engagement in social learning activities could be found ($\beta=.18$) that is mediated completely by the tendency to cover up an error. These exploratory findings require cross-validation in an independent sample and, therefore, should be interpreted cautiously. However, they inspire the assumption that the emotional strain suffered as a consequence of having committed an error creates a subjective need to change the underlying causes and is, thus, indirectly related to engagement in social learning activities (Gruber, 2001; Oser & Spychiger, 2005). Furthermore, it may be hypothesized that a safe team climate reduces the tendency to cover up an error by mitigating perceived disadvantages that may prevent a nurse from communicating an error to colleagues (Edmondson, 1999).

The analyses described above can be considered *variable-centered* because they describe what variables potentially influence the engagement in social learning activities after errors at work. In a second step, these analyses were complemented by *person-centered* analysis that aimed at answering questions regarding how individuals differ in their interpretations of error situations and their engagement in learning activities after errors at work (Bauer & Mulder, 2011). In a latent profile analysis, four qualitatively different latent classes of nurses could be identified in respect to the investigated variables. Of these classes, only Class 1, comprising 58.8% of the sample, showed a clear orientation towards joint reflection and learning after errors. The mean values of this class on the engagement in social learning activities were highest in the sample. Moreover, these nurses rated their team climate as safe.

In contrast, the other latent classes were characterized by answer profiles that seem dysfunctional for learning from errors. The answer profile of the second-largest class (Class 2, 23.7%) indicated indifference regarding the error situation. Nurses in this class report the lowest mean values for all social learning activities as well as for the subjective learning relevance in the sample. Class 3 (13.8%) was characterized by a strong tendency to self-focus and emotional strain, and had the most negative team climate in the sample. This answer profile can be considered an at-risk profile, because it combines a psychologically unhealthy reaction to errors with insufficient social resources (Nolen-Hoeksema, Wisco, & Lyubomirsky, 2008). This combination may lead to a passive state of negative 'brooding' (i.e., *rumination*) rather than an orientation towards problem-solving, action, and learning after errors (Bauer & Mulder, 2007; Rybowiak et al., 1999). Finally, there was a small latent class of nurses (Class 4, 3.7%) who tended to seek social exchange with colleagues after errors, but without a clear learning-orientation. Presumably, talking with others about an error serves primarily as a form of social relief for these nurses, not as a catalyst for learning purposes. This finding is consistent with the results presented above, which indicate that discussions about errors only lead to learning when they are performed with an orientation towards critical inquiry (cf. Edmondson, 2004; Harteis et al., 2007).

In summary, the results of the study support the assumption that the interpretation of an error situation as a learning opportunity is important for the engagement in social learning activities after errors (Edmondson, 2004; Rybowiak et al., 1999; Zhao & Olivera, 2006). In contrast, as can be expected, the tendency to cover up errors because of feared repercussions seems to be an inhibiting factor. This pattern of findings is consistent with the assumption that communication about errors depends on a subjective cost–benefit balance (Zhao & Olivera, 2006). Moreover, the findings from the latent profile analysis provide support for the hypothesis that employees – nurses in the present case – have qualitatively different ways of interpreting and reacting to errors (Arndt, 1996; Harteis et al., 2008).

Conclusion

In this chapter, we have addressed four central questions concerning errors as a catalyst for learning, error-related learning activities and learning outcomes, as well as conditions for learning from errors at work. From our perspective, research on these four questions is crucial to advancing our understanding of how and under what conditions errors at work may contribute to improving knowledge, skills, and practice. From a practical perspective, our findings are largely consistent with current conceptions that aim at establishing a learning-oriented *error culture* in organizations (Glendon et al., 2006). They indicate that establishing such a culture requires a participatory strategy in which staff and management jointly negotiate common values and goals regarding errors, and common strategies for error prevention, error management, and learning from errors. However, as the results of the person-centered analyses show, there seem to be different individual ways of reacting to errors that organizational development programs have to take into account.

We acknowledge the limited conclusiveness of many of our studies and findings due to their qualitative and exploratory nature. Therefore, their validity and generalizability should be scrutinized in further research. Particularly, the question concerning under what conditions the engagement in error-related learning leads to improvements in knowledge and practice is still open. Nevertheless, our studies can provide potentially useful theoretical conceptualizations and empirical approaches for future research on learning from errors in work contexts.

From our perspective, a great challenge for future research lies in the conducting of intervention studies that aim at fostering learning from errors in the contexts of professional education and work. Many of the existing studies have followed either descriptive approaches (aimed at providing descriptions of how errors are used for learning) or correlational ones (with the purpose of finding correlates regarding individual and contextual conditions for learning errors) (cf. Bauer, Mehl, & Wehner, 2010). More evidence is needed, however, on how learning from errors can be supported in various contexts. For this purpose, we suggest, firstly, that future studies focus on how learning the typical errors in one's field of work as well as elaboration on authentic error-cases can be included in professional education. This demand is consistent with studies showing the didactic value of including errors in training (Dick & Jacob, 2010; Große & Renkl, 2007; Keith & Frese, 2005). In some fields of work, training simulations that provide explicit opportunities to make errors in a safe context constitute a major element of professional learning (e.g., aviation; Helmreich, 2000). More evidence is needed regarding whether and how these approaches can be transferred to other fields of professional training and work.

Secondly, future studies should investigate how both educators and students can be supported to adequately manage occurring errors as well as to define and use them as learning opportunities (Keith & Frese, 2005). The focus on teachers, trainers, or mentors is crucial, because they are responsible for scaffolding error-related learning processes by, for example, guiding learners' reflection on the causes of errors and providing opportunities for deliberate practice that aims at improving learners' individual performance (Ericsson, Whyte, & Ward, 2007). So far, we have insufficient knowledge about how teachers are prepared to fulfill these tasks. Promising initial steps are currently being taken to assess and trainerror-related competencies of (vocational) teachers (Seifried & Wuttke, 2010).

References

Argyris, C., & Schön, D. (1996). *Organizational learning II: Theory, method, and practice.* Reading, MA: Addison-Wesley.

Argote, L., & Todocara, G. (2007). Organizational learning. In G. P. Hodgkinson & J. K. Ford (Eds.), *International review of industrial and organizational psychology* (Vol. 22, pp. 193–234). Chichester, UK/New York: Wiley.

Arndt, M. (1996). Aus Fehlern lernen [Learning from errors]. *Pflege, 9*, 12–18.

Aspden, P., Corrigan, J. M., Wolcott, J., & Erickson, S. M. (2004). *Patient safety*. Washington, DC: National Academies Press.

Barach, P., & Small, S. D. (2000). Reporting and preventing medical mishaps: Lessons from non-medical near miss reporting systems. *British Medical Journal, 320*, 759–765.

Bauer, J. (2004). Fehlerkultur und epistemische Überzeugungen als Einflussfaktoren individuellen Kompetenzerwerbs am Arbeitsplatz. In H. Gruber, C. Harteis, H. Heid, & B. Meier (Eds.), *Kapital und Kompetenz* [Capital and competence] (pp. 59–75). Wiesbaden, Germany: VS Verlag.

Bauer, J. (2008a). Fehler und Lernen aus Fehlern. Die Notwendigkeit deskriptiver und kumulativer empirischer Forschung [Errors and learning from errors. A plea for descriptive and cumulative empirical research]. *Erwägen, Wissen, Ethik, 19*, 306–310.

Bauer, J. (2008b). *Learning from errors at work. Studies on nurses' engagement in error related learning activities*. Doctoral dissertation, University of Regensburg, Regensburg.

Bauer, J., & Gruber, H. (2007). Workplace changes and workplace learning: Advantages of an educational micro perspective. *International Journal of Lifelong Education, 26*, 675–688.

Bauer, J., Mehl, K., & Wehner, T. (2010). Aus Fehlern lernen [Editorial: Learning from errors]. *Wirtschaftspsychologie, 12*, 3–6.

Bauer, J., & Mulder, R. H. (2007). Modelling learning from errors in daily work. *Learning in Health and Social Care, 6*, 121–133.

Bauer, J., & Mulder, R. H. (2008). Conceptualisation of learning through errors at work – A literature review. In S. Billett, C. Harteis, & A. Eteläpelto (Eds.), *Emerging perspectives on learning through work* (pp. 115–128). Rotterdam, the Netherlands: Sense.

Bauer, J., & Mulder, R. H. (2011). Engagement in learning after errors at work. Enabling conditions and types of engagement. *Journal of Education and Work*. doi:10.1080/13639080.2011.573776. Advance online publication.

Billett, S. (2004). Workplace participatory practices. Conceptualising workplaces as learning environments. *Journal of Workplace Learning, 16*, 312–324.

Boshuizen, H. P. A., Bromme, R., & Gruber, H. (Eds.). (2004). *Professional learning: Gaps and transitions on the way from novice to expert*. Dordrecht, the Netherlands: Kluwer.

Cannon, M. D., & Edmondson, A. C. (2001). Confronting failure: Antecedents and consequences of shared beliefs about failure in organisational work groups. *Journal of Organisational Behavior, 22*, 161–177.

Csikszentmihalyi, M. (1999). Implications of a systems perspective for the study of creativity. In R. J. Sternberg (Ed.), *Handbook of creativity* (pp. 313–335). Cambridge, UK: Cambridge University Press.

Dick, M., & Jacob, M. (2010). Vom Misserfolg jenseits des Fehlers: Das entdeckende Potential des Triadengesprächs [On failure beyond errors: The potential of discovering new insights within the triad conversation]. *Wirtschaftspsychologie, 12*, 67–77.

Edmondson, A. C. (1996). Learning from mistakes is easier said than done: Group and organisational influences on the detection and correction of human error. *Journal of Applied Behavioral Science, 32*, 5–28.

Edmondson, A. C. (1999). Psychological safety and working behaviour in work teams. *Administrative Science Quarterly, 44*, 350–383.

Edmondson, A. C. (2004). Learning from errors in health care: Frequent opportunities, pervasive barriers. *Quality & Safety in Health Care, 13*, 3–9.

Eraut, M., Alderton, J., Cole, G., & Senker, P. (1998). *Development of knowledge and skills in employment*. Sussex: University of Sussex.

Ericsson, K. A., Charness, N., Feltovich, P. J., & Hoffman, R. R. (Eds.). (2006). *The Cambridge handbook on expertise and expert performance*. Cambridge, UK: Cambridge University Press.

Ericsson, K. A., Whyte, J., & Ward, P. (2007). Expert performance in nursing. Reviewing research on expertise in nursing within the framework of the expert-performance approach. *Advances in Nursing Science, 30*(1), E58–E71.

Frese, M., & Zapf, D. (1994). Action as the core of work psychology: A German approach. In H. C. Triandis, M. D. Dunette, & L. M. Hough (Eds.), *Handbook of industrial and organizational psychology* (2nd ed., pp. 271–340). Palo Alto, CA: Consulting Psychologists Press.

Gartmeier, M., Bauer, J., Gruber, H., & Heid, H. (2008). Negative knowledge: Understanding professional learning and expertise. *Vocations and Learning: Studies in Vocational and Professional Education, 1*, 87–103.

Gartmeier, M., Bauer, J., Gruber, H., & Heid, H. (2010). Workplace errors and negative knowledge in elder care nursing. *Human Resource Development International, 13*, 5–25.

Gartmeier, M., Gruber, H., & Heid, H. (2010). Tracing error-related knowledge in interview data: Negative knowledge in elder care nursing. *Educational Gerontology, 36*, 733–752.

Gartmeier, M., Lehtinen, E., Gruber, H., & Heid, H. (2010). Negative expertise: Comparing differently experienced elder care nurses' negative knowledge. *European Journal of Psychology of Education, 26*, 273–300.

Glendon, I., Clarke, S. G., & McKenna, E. F. (2006). *Human safety and risk management*. Boca Raton, FL: Taylor & Francis.

Große, C. S., & Renkl, A. (2007). Finding and fixing errors in worked examples: Can this foster learning outcomes? *Learning and Instruction, 17*, 612–634.

Gruber, H. (2001). Acquisition of expertise. In J. J. Smelser & P. B. Baltes (Eds.), *International encyclopedia of the social & behavioral sciences* (pp. 5145–5150). Oxford, UK: Elsevier.

Harteis, C., Bauer, J., & Gruber, H. (2008). The culture of learning from mistakes: How employees handle mistakes in everyday work. *International Journal of Educational Research, 47*, 223–231.

Harteis, C., Bauer, J., & Haltia, P. (2007). Learning from errors at the workplace – Insights from two studies in Germany and Finland. In H. Gruber & T. Palonen (Eds.), *Learning at the workplace – New developments* (pp. 119–138). Turku, Finland: Finnish Educational Research Association.

Harteis, C., Bauer, J., & Heid, H. (2006). Der Umgang mit Fehlern als Merkmal betrieblicher Fehlerkultur und Voraussetzung für Professional Learning [Handling mistakes in daily working life as an attribute of an inner-firm mistake culture and precondition for professional learning]. *Schweizerische Zeitschrift für Bildungswissenschaften, 28*, 111–129.

Heid, H. (1999). Autorität. Über die Verwandlung von Fehlern in Verfehlungen. In W. Althof (Ed.), *Fehlerwelten. Vom Fehlermachen und Lernen aus Fehlern* [Error worlds: On errors and learning from errors] (pp. 129–136). Leverkusen, Germany: Leske+Budrich.

Helmreich, R. L. (2000). On error management. *British Medical Journal, 320*, 781–785.

Hughes, E. C. (1951). Mistakes at work. *The Canadian Journal of Economics and Political Science, 17*, 320–327.

Keith, N., & Frese, M. (2005). Self-regulation in error management training: Emotion control and metacognition as mediators of performance effects. *Journal of Applied Psychology, 90*, 677–691.

Kolb, D. A. (1984). *Experiential learning*. Englewood Cliffs, NJ: Prentice Hall.

Kolodner, J. (1983). Towards an understanding of the role of experience in the evolution from novice to expert. *International Journal of Man-Machine Studies, 19*, 497–518.

Leontiev, A. (1978). *Activity, consciousness, and personality*. Englewood Cliffs, CA: Prentice-Hall.

Meurier, C. E., Vincent, C. A., & Parmar, D. G. (1997). Learning from errors in nursing practice. *Journal of Advanced Nursing, 26*, 111–119.

Minsky, M. (1994). Negative expertise. *International Journal of Expert Systems, 7*, 13–19.

Nolen-Hoeksema, S., Wisco, B. E., & Lyubomirsky, S. (2008). Rethinking rumination. *Perspectives on Psychological Science, 3*, 400–424.

Oser, F., & Spychiger, M. (2005). *Lernen ist schmerzhaft* [Learning is painful]. Weinheim, Germany: Beltz.

Parviainen, J., & Eriksson, M. (2006). Negative knowledge, expertise and organizations. *International Journal of Management Concepts and Philosophy, 2*, 140–153.

Perrow, C. (1984). *Normal accidents: Living with high risk technologies*. Princeton, NJ: Princeton University Press.

Rasmussen, J. (1987). The definition of human error and a taxonomy for technical system design. In J. Rasmussen, K. Duncan, & J. Leplat (Eds.), *New technology and human error* (pp. 23–30). Chichester, UK/New York: Wiley.

Reason, J. T. (1990). *Human error*. Cambridge, UK: Cambridge University Press.

Rybowiak, V., Garst, H., Frese, M., & Batinic, B. (1999). Error orientation questionnaire (EOQ): Reliability, validity, and different language equivalence. *Journal of Organizational Behavior, 20*, 527–547.

Schank, R. C. (1999). *Dynamic memory revisited*. Cambridge, UK: Cambridge University Press.

Schank, R. C., & Abelson, R. (1977). *Scripts, plans, goals, and understanding*. Hillsdale, NJ: Erlbaum.

Seifried, J., & Wuttke, E. (2010). "Professionelle Fehlerkompetenz" – Operationalisierung einer vernachlässigten Kompetenzfacette von (angehenden) Lehrkräften ["Professional error competence" – How to operationalize a neglected competence of (future) teachers]. *Wirtschaftspsychologie, 12*, 17–28.

Senders, J. W., & Moray, N. P. (1991). *Human error. Cause, prediction, and reduction*. Hillsdale, NJ: LEA.

Simons, P. R.-J., & Ruijters, M. C. P. (2004). Learning professionals: Towards an integrated model. In H. P. A. Boshuizen, R. Bromme, & H. Gruber (Eds.), *Professional learning: Gaps and transitions on the way from novice to expert* (pp. 207–229). Dordrecht: Kluwer.

Sitkin, S. B. (1992). Learning through failure: The strategy of small losses. *Research in Organizational Behavior, 14*, 231–266.

Tjosvold, D., Yu, Z. Y., & Hui, C. (2004). Team learning from mistakes: The contribution of cooperative goals and problem solving. *Journal of Management Studies, 41*, 1223–1245.

Tucker, A. L., & Edmondson, A. C. (2003). Why hospitals don't learn from failures: Organizational and psychological dynamics that inhibit system change. *California Management Review, 45*, 55–72.

Tynjälä, P. (2008). Perspectives into learning at the workplace. *Educational Research Review, 3*, 130–154.

Van Dyck, C., Frese, M., Baer, M., & Sonnentag, S. (2005). Organizational error management culture and its impact on performance: A two-study replication. *Journal of Applied Psychology, 90*, 1228–1240.

Wehner, T., & Mehl, K. (2008). Über die Schwierigkeiten, aus Fehlern zu lernen [On difficulties of learning from errors]. *Erwägen, Wissen, Ethik, 19*, 265–273.

Wehner, T., Mehl, K., & Dieckmann, P. (2010). Handlungsfehler und Fehlerprävention. In U. Kleinbeck & K.-H. Schmidt (Eds.), *Enzyklopädie der Psychologie: Arbeitspsychologie* [Encyclopedia of psychology: Work psychology] (Theme D, Series. 3, Vol. 1, pp. 785–820). Göttingen, Germany: Hogrefe.

Weingart, P. (2008). Fehlerparadoxon. Transdisziplinäre Grundlagen zur Theorie und Produktivität des Fehler [The paradox of errors. A transdisciplinary framework on the productivity of errors]. *Erwägen, Wissen, Ethik, 19*, 283–290.

Wenger, E. (1998). *Communities of practice. Learning, meaning, and identity*. Cambridge, UK: Cambridge University Press.

Zhao, B., & Olivera, F. (2006). Error reporting in organizations. *Academy of Management Review, 31*, 1012–1030.

Part IV
Enabling Learning from Errors

Chapter 11
Managing Errors During Training

Nina Keith

Errors are a fact of life. We make errors every day and every hour – as we speak, as we interact with people, and as we pursue our everyday work activities. Errors can occur in many types of tasks of various levels of difficulty. However, new and challenging tasks, for which we lack the necessary knowledge and skills, seem to be particularly error prone. Training is a situation in which errors are bound to happen, because training – by definition – aims at improving knowledge and skills that still need to be developed (Aguinis & Kraiger, 2009). Against this background, it is somewhat surprising that, until recently, relatively few approaches to training and learning have explicitly dealt with the issue of errors. Traditionally, errors are implicitly or explicitly ascribed a negative role in the learning process. A prominent example is behaviorism sensu Skinner (1953): Errors are equated with punishment that inhibits behavior but that does not contribute to learning. Similarly, Bandura's (1986) social cognitive theory states that learners should be "spared the costs and pain of faulty effort" (p. 47). Consequently, an error-free learning environment is advocated.

The present chapter deals with an approach that explicitly acknowledges errors as a natural part of learning and training and promotes a positive attitude toward errors during the learning process. The basic idea is that errors can be beneficial for learning under some circumstances because they provide negative but informative feedback about where knowledge and skills need further improvement (Frese et al., 1991; Ivancic & Hesketh, 1995/1996). This approach further argues that errors may occur when new skills are required to master a novel task or when work requirements change and, as a consequence, established routines become obsolete (Bauer & Mulder, 2007). Therefore, approaches that explicitly incorporate errors during

N. Keith, Ph.D. (✉)
Department of Psychology, Organizational and Business Psychology,
Technische Universität Darmstadt, Darmstadt, Germany
e-mail: keith@psychologie.tu-darmstadt.de

J. Bauer and C. Harteis (eds.), *Human Fallibility: The Ambiguity of Errors for Work and Learning*, Professional and Practice-based Learning 6,
DOI 10.1007/978-90-481-3941-5_11,

training may better prepare employees to cope with changes than approaches that attempt to avoid errors during training (Heimbeck, Frese, Sonnentag, & Keith, 2003; cf. Smith, Ford, & Kozlowski, 1997). One such training method, which has been labeled error training (e.g., Dormann & Frese, 1994; Heimbeck et al., 2003), error management training (e.g., Frese et al., 1991; Keith & Frese, 2005, 2008; Nordstrom, Wendland, & Williams, 1998), error-filled training (Ivancic & Hesketh, 1995/1996), or error-based training (Smith et al., 1997), will be the focus of this chapter.

The chapter is organized as follows. I will begin by describing the conceptual background and the typical design of error management training in contrast to conventional training methods. The subsequent sections will deal with the effectiveness of error management training, the psychological processes that may account for this effectiveness, and the role of individual differences in error management training. Finally, I will discuss the implications of existing research on error management training for training theory and practice and provide suggestions for future research.

Conceptual Background and Design of Error Management Training

In general, *errors* are defined as acts that involve an unintentional deviation from truth or accuracy (Gove, 1993). In the context of organizational training, we are primarily concerned with *action errors*, that is, with human errors that occur in goal-oriented behavior (Frese & Zapf, 1994). Action errors involve (1) unintended deviations from plans or goals that were (2) potentially avoidable (Keith & Frese, 2011; Reason, 1990; van Dyck, Frese, Baer, & Sonnentag, 2005; Zapf, Brodbeck, Frese, Peters, & Prümper, 1992; Zhao & Olivera, 2006). When dealing with the issue of errors in organizations and errors during training, there are two broad approaches which one may adopt. These two approaches can be illustrated when considering the trajectory of action → error → consequences (cf. Keith & Frese, 2011). The first approach, which may be called *error prevention*, aims at erecting a barrier between the action and the error, that is, errors are eliminated before they occur. A typical means to protect trainees from making errors during training is to provide a tight structure and step-by-step guidance through the training material, as is done in conventional tutorials. The focus of such *error-avoidance training* is on teaching correct procedures (i.e., correct actions that do not lead to errors) to trainees. Indeed, error-avoidance training seems to be useful in some training domains and for some populations. For example, for rehabilitation of memory impairment in some clinical populations, error-avoidance training is an effective technique (Kessels & de Haan, 2003). In the domain of computer skills, some studies showed training time to be shorter for training methods that prevented trainees from making errors during training; for example, by blocking some functions of the computer program (Carroll & Carrithers, 1984).

The second approach, which may be called *error management*, does not aim at preventing errors per se but attempts to erect a barrier between errors and their potential negative consequences (Frese, 1995). This approach argues that it makes sense to distinguish errors from error consequences because not every error necessarily has negative consequences. For example, an error that is detected correctly and immediately may not produce any detrimental effects. An error management approach also accounts for the finding that, despite all efforts, errors are ubiquitous and will inevitably occur, even among experts (Prümper, Zapf, Brodbeck, & Frese, 1992; Reason, 1990). It is therefore worthwhile not to focus solely on error prevention but to enable trainees to effectively deal with errors after they have occurred (i.e., error management). In addition, an error management approach acknowledges the potentially positive effects of errors, such as learning and innovation (Sitkin, 1992; van Dyck et al., 2005). For this purpose, errors should not be avoided but explicitly incorporated in training; trainees should be given ample opportunities to make errors during training and to learn from them (Heimbeck et al., 2003; Ivancic & Hesketh, 1995/1996).

In *error management training*, these ideas are implemented by providing only minimal task information to trainees and by reducing direct instructions to a minimum. The design of error management training is best illustrated using the example of computer software training. While conventional error-avoidance training uses direct instruction and provides correct solutions for training tasks (e.g., step-by-step instructions on how to create and format a table), trainees of error management training would receive only minimal information on the functions of the computer program. For example, they would receive a list of commands (Frese et al., 1991) or general information on the available toolbars and menus as well as thc undo and delete functions (e.g., Keith & Frese, 2005). Apart from that, they would be encouraged to independently explore the system and work on relatively complex training tasks (e.g., complex formatting of a table) without guidance and close feedback by the trainer – a procedure inevitably leading to many errors. These errors would not be immediately corrected by the trainer. Instead, trainees would be encouraged to try to find solutions for themselves. In other words, error management training is an active learning approach which views learners as active participants in training rather than passive recipients of instruction (Bell & Kozlowski, 2008, 2010). This principle is also in line with action theory, which assumes that knowledge and skills are best acquired through action-oriented mental models and through actively executing actions (Frese & Zapf, 1994; Hacker, 1998; cf. Frese, Beimel, & Schoenborn, 2003). The aspect of active exploration in error management training is similar to exploratory or discovery learning which stresses the importance of allowing the learner to actively explore and test ideas (Bruner, 1966). Unlike pure discovery methods, error management training gives explicit training tasks as learning objectives, thereby providing a minimum of structure during training (cf. Mayer, 2004). In addition, there is a greater emphasis on errors in error management training than in pure discovery learning (Keith & Frese, 2005).

A second characteristic of error management training are the so-called error management instructions (Frese et al., 1991; also called error-encouragement framing,

Bell & Kozlowski, 2008). These are short written or verbal instructions that positively frame errors and problems during training and encourage exploring, making and learning from errors during training. These instructions are designed to counter participants' negative emotional reactions in the face of errors made during training (Heimbeck et al., 2003). Without such instructions, many trainees would probably experience negative reactions to their errors (cf. Hajcak & Foti, 2008). Many applications of error management training provide these instructions at the beginning of training and throughout the practice phase whenever participants encounter problems or errors. Instructions are also prominently displayed during training (e.g., on a notice or sign) in brief statements such as the following:

- Whenever you make an error, remember that errors are a natural part of the learning process!
- Errors are helpful because they show you what you still can learn!
- Say to yourself: Great! I have made an error! I will find a way to solve this problem and I will learn something new! (e.g., Debowski, Wood, & Bandura, 2001; Frese et al., 1991; Heimbeck et al., 2003; Keith & Frese, 2005)

In sum, the two main principles of many applications of error management training are (1) active exploration based on minimal guidance and complex training tasks and (2) explicit positive framing of errors and encouragement during training – seemingly simple principles which have proven to be effective, as we shall see in the next section.

Effectiveness of Error Management Training

Training effectiveness involves the extent to which training results in improved performance or other favorable outcomes that are considered to be antecedents of job performance (Aguinis & Kraiger, 2009). To evaluate training effectiveness, effect sizes are often derived from comparisons between the focal training method and no-training or pre-training states (i.e., absolute effect size). A large meta-analysis of organizational training interventions (summarizing data from 165 sources) found training to be associated with medium to large effect sizes (average Cohen's $d=0.62$; Arthur, Bennett, Edens, & Bell, 2003). Studies investigating effectiveness of error management training did not compare error management training with no training at all but with a comparison training method, such as error-avoidance training (i.e., relative effect size) and used skill-based learning criteria (e.g., number of tasks solved on a transfer test). Several studies were conducted in the domain of computer software skills and found error management training to lead to better skill acquisition than comparison training methods (e.g., Chillarege, Nordstrom, & Williams, 2003; Dormann & Frese, 1994; Frese et al., 1991). Effects were also found for domains such as driving simulator training (Ivancic & Hesketh, 2000), decision making (Gully, Payne, Koles, & Whiteman, 2002), surgical skills training (Rogers, Regehr, & MacDonald, 2002), and firefighting (Joung, Hesketh, & Neal, 2006).

A meta-analysis that compiled results from 24 studies comparing error management training with alternative training methods found a positive and significant effect (Cohen's d) of 0.44. This result implies that, on average, error management training led to better outcomes than a training method that did not involve active exploration and encouragement of errors (Keith & Frese, 2008). It should be noted, however, that not all studies that were summarized in the meta-analysis supported error management training. Some studies did not find a significant difference between training methods (e.g., Lazar & Norcio, 2003) and still others found a difference in favor of the alternative training method (Debowski et al., 2001; Gully et al., 2002). The effect sizes ranged from −0.73 (Debowski et al., 2001) to larger than 1 (e.g., Chillarege et al., 2003).Theoretically, some degree of variation can be expected as error management training cannot necessarily be effective across all kinds of tasks and outcomes. Accordingly, Keith and Frese (2008) identified several aspects that affected the magnitude of the effect size (i.e., moderators). In the following, I will review three major results of their meta-analysis because they inform us of the situations in which error management training can be expected to be useful or, conversely, in what situations alternative error-avoidance training methods may work just as well as or even better than error management training.

Finding 1: Error Management Training Affects Post-Training Transfer Rather Than Within-Training Performance

When evaluating training effectiveness, it is important to distinguish between immediate within-training performance and post-training transfer performance because training interventions that benefit the former do not necessarily benefit the latter and vice versa (Goodman & Wood, 2004; Hesketh, 1997; Keith & Frese, 2005, 2008; Schmidt & Bjork, 1992). For example, providing trainees with close guidance and timely feedback during training will probably improve immediate performance during training (e.g., faster learning rate than without guidance and feedback) but does not necessarily benefit long-term performance. The classic study by Shea and Morgan (1979) demonstrates this point. Participants learned several movements either in blocked practice or randomized order. During training, the blocked-practice group outperformed the randomized-order group. On a post-training transfer task, however, the pattern was reversed, particularly if the transfer tasks were given in randomized order. This result (and similar ones that were found in different task domains; cf. Schmidt & Bjork, 1992) implies that introducing difficulties during training may impede immediate training performance while at the same time boosting long-term post-training transfer, at least if the psychological processes induced by these difficulties are similar to the processes needed for solving the transfer tasks (Hesketh, 1997; Salas & Cannon-Bowers, 2001). This issue is also captured in the principle of transfer-appropriate processing which postulates that processes required for solving transfer tasks should be practiced during training (Morris, Bransford, & Franks, 1977; cf. Keith & Frese, 2005).

Error management training is an example for a training method that introduces difficulties during training but which may benefit performance in the long run (Keith & Frese, 2008): During training, participants receive only minimal guidance and otherwise work independently without much assistance from the trainer. As a result, participants make many errors and immediate training performance may be worse compared to participants who receive error-avoidance training with close guidance and detailed instructions. The transfer situation, however, is no longer as safe and structured as the training situation and opens up the chance to make errors. In this situation, participants of error management training, who have learned to effectively deal with errors during training, have an advantage. In other words, error management training resembles the transfer situation more than well-structured and guided error-avoidance training (Heimbeck et al., 2003). In line with this reasoning, Keith and Frese (2008) found type of outcome to moderate effectiveness of error management training: Only studies that used post-training transfer tasks (as opposed to studies that used within-training performance) to evaluate training effectiveness yielded significant effect sizes in favor of error management training. This result implies that error management training cannot be expected to positively affect immediate training performance but that its benefits are expected to unfold on post-training transfer tasks. This result suggests that conclusions about training effectiveness can be misleading if they are based on within-training performance. Evaluations of training effectiveness should generally be based on transfer tasks that are separate from training tasks (cf. Schmidt & Bjork, 1992).

Finding 2: Effectiveness of Error Management Training Is More Pronounced for Transfer Tasks That Are Dissimilar from Training Tasks (i.e., Adaptive Transfer)

The previous discussion focused on the general distinction between within-training and post-training transfer performance. When discussing the issue of transfer, however, an additional distinction that pertains to types of transfer tasks can be useful. One such distinction is based on the similarity between training and transfer tasks (Ivancic & Hesketh, 2000). According to this distinction, *analogical transfer* refers to situations in which transfer tasks are similar to training tasks and can be solved by using procedures that are analogous to those learned during training. *Adaptive transfer*, in contrast, implies "using one's existing knowledge base to change a learned procedure, or to generate a solution to a completely new problem" (Ivancic & Hesketh, 2000, p. 1968; a similar distinction pertains to near and far transfer; e.g., Barnett & Ceci, 2002). In other words, rote application of procedures learned during training is not sufficient for solving adaptive transfer tasks.

Organizational training programs may differ as to whether the goal is to promote analogical or adaptive transfer. For example, analogical transfer is required in situations in which a particular procedure or a manageable number of clearly identifiable procedures need to be performed on the job. In this case, it makes sense to directly teach these particular procedures during training, without taking the time-consuming detour of independent exploration and error encouragement as is done in error management training. Adaptive transfer, in contrast, becomes essential in situations in which not all potential work-related problems and their solutions can be taught during training and in which, therefore, the goal is to enable trainees to independently develop solutions to completely new problems. To promote adaptive transfer, training methods that encourage errors during training, such as error management training, may be particularly useful because errors and setbacks, which participants have learned to deal with during training, occur particularly often on adaptive transfer tasks (cf. Ivancic & Hesketh, 1995/1996; Smith et al., 1997). For analogical transfer, it may likewise be argued that error management training is useful because errors attract attention which in turn facilitates retrieval of similar problems and their solutions as participants work on new but similar tasks (Ivancic & Hesketh, 1995/1996, 2000). On the other hand, other training methods that do not utilize exploration and errors but directly teach the required skills may be equally effective for such tasks. A comparison of error management training with alternative training methods may yield smaller or even no differences. In line with this proposition, Keith and Frese (2008) found type of transfer task to moderate effectiveness of error management training: Studies that used analogical transfer task to evaluate training effectiveness yielded a significant but small average effect size whereas studies that used adaptive transfer tasks yielded a large average effect. This result implies that error management training may be particularly well suited in promoting adaptive transfer.

Finding 3: Task-Generated Feedback Is Important for Error Management Training to Be Effective

Feedback can serve as a motivator (Ilgen, Fisher, & Taylor, 1979) and also has an informational function (Ivancic & Hesketh, 1995/1996). Feedback informs an individual about the extent to which the standard or goal has been reached (Carver & Scheier, 1998; Frese & Zapf, 1994; Goodman & Wood, 2004; Hacker, 1998; Latham & Locke, 1991; Sonnentag, 1998). Errors constitute a particular type of feedback – negative feedback that indicates a deviation between the current state and the goal or standard. Errors convey that one's task strategies have not been effective (i.e., the goal is not reached) and that they need to be adjusted, for example, by trying different solutions until the tasks is solved (i.e., until the goal is reached). In order for errors to be used in this way, however, errors must be recognizable. For example, if a computer program generates a complex output in response to a participant's command and the participant is not able to interpret the output appropriately, he or she cannot judge the extent to which the goal or standard is reached – or whether he or she has made an error. Many common office applications, in contrast, which are based on WYSIWYG (what you see is what you get), provide readily interpretable feedback. For example, if the goal of the participant is to generate and format a table, he or she can track visual changes on the screen in response to his or her actions and judge the extent to which the goal is reached.

It is conceivable that a minimum of task-generated feedback is necessary for error management training to be effective. In guided training, the trainer can provide external feedback and help interpret task-generated feedback (Debowski et al., 2001). In error management training, however, where participants work independently, no such assistance is provided and participants depend solely on the feedback that is generated by the task. In line with this reasoning, Keith and Frese (2008) found error management to be more effective than alternative training methods only on tasks that provided clearly interpretable feedback (it should be noted that the corresponding moderator analysis was significant only at the 10%-level, which was probably due to restricted range; that is, most of the included primary studies used tasks which provided more or less clear feedback). This result implies that error management training may not be suitable for tasks that provide unclear feedback or that participants may need some additional instructions on interpreting task-generated feedback (e.g., how to interpret an output file generated by the computer program).

Taken together, the results of the meta-analysis suggest that error management training (1) may not positively affect or even suppress immediate training performance, (2) is most beneficial for performance on tasks that go beyond what was taught during training (i.e., adaptive transfer), and (3) requires an appropriate level of task-generated feedback that can be interpreted by participants as they work independently on the tasks. These results help us understand the conditions (e.g., type of tasks to be trained) under which error management training may be a good choice as a training method – or under which alternative training methods may work equally well. The following sections will discuss psychological processes that underlie the effectiveness of error management training. That is, what are the processes that are instigated in error management training – but not or to a lesser extent in conventional guided training – which account for its effectiveness?

Processes in Error Management Training That Account for Its Effectiveness

In training research and practice, it is essential not only to determine whether a particular training method is effective but also to identify the processes that explain *why* it is effective. With regard to error management training, several processes have been proposed although few studies have directly tested the proposed mechanism. Most of these approaches either focus on cognitive or on emotional/motivational processes during training. A third perspective attempts to integrate both perspectives by examining self-regulation of cognitions and emotions. In the following, I will review the three perspectives

Emotional and Motivational Processes as Effective Mechanisms of Error Management Training

As outlined above, a distinct feature of error management training are so-called error management instructions – simple instructions that emphasize the positive function errors have in learning, and which are designed to encourage trainees to make and learn from errors. It seems plausible that participants of error management training who read such instructions experience less demotivation and fewer negative emotions (e.g., frustration, anxiety, or anger) in the face of errors compared to participants of alternative training methods. In line with this reasoning, empirical evidence suggests error management instructions to be an effective element of error management training (Bell & Kozlowski, 2008; Heimbeck et al., 2003; Keith & Frese, 2008).

Studies that attempt to measure motivational or emotional processes directly yield inconsistent results. For example, Wood, Kakebeeke, Debowski, and Frese (2000) expected intrinsic motivation to mediate effects of error management training in an electronic search task. Contrary to expectations, they found intrinsic motivation to be unrelated to performance. A study by Nordstrom et al. (1998) investigated changes in participants' levels of frustration in the course of the training and post-training transfer phases. In line with predictions, frustration decreased in participants of error management training whereas it increased in participants of an alternative training method (this study also found group differences in performance but did not test for a mediation effect by frustration). A similar study, however, could not replicate this effect (Chillarege et al., 2003).

In sum, together with a study that will be described in more detail below (Keith & Frese, 2005; see also Bell & Kozlowski, 2008), the available evidence suggests that the positive framing of errors in error management instructions affects emotional processes of participants (e.g., reduced anger and frustration in the face of errors) which in turn benefits transfer performance. This is in line with a resource allocation perspective that assumes off-task activities such as negative emotions impede learning because they divert attention away from the task at hand (Kanfer & Ackerman, 1989). Yet, mere absence of disturbing negative emotions does not ensure learning. Rather, the free attentional resources need to be devoted to cognitive processes that maximize learning (Kanfer & Ackerman, 1989; Keith & Frese, 2005). The next section will review cognitive processes that may account for performance effects of error management training.

Cognitive Processes as Effective Mechanism of Error Management Training

Error management training is an exploratory training method that uses rather difficult tasks during training which are expected to elicit errors. Both aspects – exploration and errors made during training – may contribute to learning. For example, it has been suggested that errors help to develop an appropriate mental model of the training subject because errors pinpoint incorrect assumptions and motivate participants to correct those assumptions (Frese, 1995; Heimbeck et al., 2003; Ivancic & Hesketh, 1995/1996, 2000). This proposition is in line with the finding that error-related events are associated with richer mental models than those of successful events (Ellis & Davidi, 2005). Errors also interrupt task completion and thereby attract attention which is then devoted to understanding the causes of and a solution for the problem (Ivancic & Hesketh, 1995/1996).

Action theory implies that actively exploring task solutions in error management training may lead to better mental models than passively receiving and following instructions as is done in conventional training methods (Frese & Zapf, 1994; Hacker, 1998). In addition, during exploration, participants' attention is constantly triggered. In order to solve the tasks, they need to constantly reflect on what they are doing and whether their strategies are successful – at least much more than participants of conventional guided training. In other words, exploration in error management training more likely triggers conscious and deeper-level processing than merely following instructions in conventional training. This deeper-level processing in turn contributes to learning and performance (Heimbeck et al., 2003; Ivancic & Hesketh, 1995/1996).

In line with this reasoning, Dormann and Frese (1994) found the extent of exploration during training to be related to post-training performance (the design of this study did not allow testing for mediation effects of amount of exploration). In addition, a study by Bell and Kozlowski (2008), testing effects of several elements of active training approaches, found exploration during training (vs. step-by-step guidance) to benefit performance.

Effective Mechanisms of Error Management Training: A Self-regulatory Perspective

The previous sections have described emotional/motivational and cognitive processes that may mediate the effectiveness of error management training. There is probably no single mechanism but rather several that together account for the effectiveness of error management training. In an attempt to integrate emotional/motivational and cognitive approaches, Keith and Frese (2005) introduced a self-regulatory perspective that stresses both emotional and cognitive paths (see also Bell & Kozlowski, 2008). Self-regulation involves processes "that enable an individual to guide his or her goal-directed activities over time" (Karoly, 1993, p. 25) and serves to reduce discrepancies between goals and performance (Sitzmann & Ely, 2010). Keith and Frese (2005) argued that self-regulation is particularly important for participants in error management training because they work independently and do not receive much guidance during training (cf. Bell & Kozlowksi, 2008; Ford, Smith, Weissbein, Gully, & Salas, 1998). They also argued that the very same

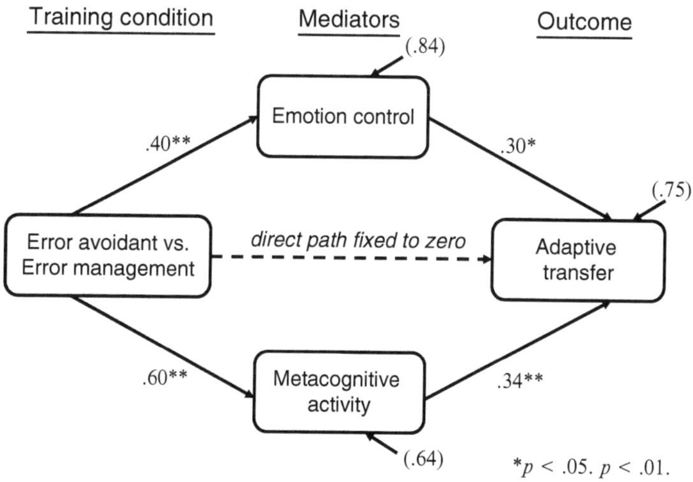

Fig. 11.1 Emotion control and metacognitive activity mediating effects of training condition on adaptive transfer (standardized parameter estimates from LISREL analysis) (Adapted from Keith & Frese, 2005, Fig. 1. With kind permission from the American Psychological Association)

self-regulatory skills that participants exert during training are useful when they are confronted with novel tasks that were not introduced during training (i.e., adaptive transfer). Self-regulation can be directed at the "modulation of thought, affect, behavior, or attention" (Karoly, 1993, p. 25). The two self-regulatory skills investigated by Keith and Frese (2005) were emotion control (i.e., self-regulation of emotions or affect) and metacognition (i.e., self-regulation of cognitions). *Emotion control* is aimed at reducing negative emotional reactions to setbacks and errors (Kanfer, Ackerman, & Heggestad, 1996). Error management training may encourage emotion control through positive error framing instructions. *Metacognition* includes planning, monitoring, evaluation, and revision of task strategies during task completion (Brown, Bransford, Ferrara, & Campione, 1983). Because "errors prompt learners to stop and think about the causes of the error" (Ivancic & Hesketh, 2000, p. 1968) and to come up with and test potential solutions to the problem, error management training may be conducive to the development of such activities. In short, Keith and Frese (2005) expected emotion control and metacognitive activities to be stimulated in error management training but not or to a lesser extent in conventional guided training. They further expected these two self-regulatory skills to benefit performance on adaptive transfer tasks and to explain effectiveness of error management training.

The model and results of the study are depicted in Fig. 11.1. In line with expectations, emotion control and metacognitive activity during training fully and independently mediated the effect of training method (i.e., error management vs. conventional guided training) on adaptive transfer performance. These results highlight the importance of both emotional and cognitive processes for the effectiveness of error management training. They are also in line with the principle of transfer appropriate processing (Morris et al., 1977) which states that processes that are needed during transfer should be practiced during training. Error management training is more similar to the transfer situation – in which no trainer is available who provides structure and guidance – than conventional guided training. Participants in error management training learn to exert self-regulatory skills of emotion control and metacognition during training as they work independently on tasks – skills that prove useful when confronted with novel adaptive transfer tasks that need to be solved without external guidance.

Individual Differences in Error Management Training

One major goal of organizational training research is to identify and develop training methods that optimize learning (Kraiger, 2002). At same time, it is generally acknowledged that one training method may not benefit all participants alike. Training effects may differ depending on participants' interests, abilities, and motivation (Gully & Chen, 2010). This notion is described by the term aptitude–treatment interaction (ATI; sometimes called *attribute*–treatment interaction) which was coined by Cronbach and Snow (1977). With regard to error management training, it may be argued that not all participants benefit alike from exploration and low training structure. In particular, exploration and making errors may provoke anxiety or be too demanding cognitively in some participants, as argued by proponents of cognitive load theory (e.g., Kirschner, Sweller, & Clark, 2006). In addition, not all participants may engage in effective exploration spontaneously; some participants may use less efficient strategies, such as trial-and-error, when left without guidance (Van der Linden, Sonnentag, Frese, & Van Dyck, 2001). Finally, the same training instructions (i.e., to work independently and to make errors and learn from them) may impact differently on participants' behavior depending on individual differences (e.g., Schmidt & Ford, 2003). Major findings in research related to error management training that explicitly addresses such questions will be discussed later.

Heimbeck et al. (2003) suggested the effect of error management training to depend on participants' goal orientation. Goal orientations describe an individual's tendency to adopt particular goals in situations related to learning and achievement (Dweck & Leggett, 1988). In particular, three relatively independent goal orientations are distinguished in the literature (e.g., VandeWalle, 1997): A learning goal orientation describes the tendency to adopt goals of competence improvement and mastery; prove goal orientation is the tendency to adopt the goal of demonstrating competence to others; and avoidance goal orientation is the tendency to avoid appearing incompetent to others. Heimbeck et al. (2003) argued that error management training may best fit with a learning goal orientation whereas participants high in prove goal and avoidance goal orientation may benefit more from a structured and guided training method. Results deviated from the predicted pattern in that all trainees benefited equally well from error management training (performance was generally best in error management training), but performance in the alternative training method depended on prove goal and avoidance goal orientations.

With regard to cognitive abilities, Gully et al. (2002) found that trainees with higher cognitive ability benefited more from error management instructions than those with lower cognitive ability. The same pattern emerged for the Big Five factor of openness to experience. However, it should be noted that this study did not include a separate transfer phase but used late training performance as a criterion. Another study found that trainees with higher cognitive ability showed more metacognitive activity after receiving an exploratory than a guided training whereas for trainees of lower ability, metacognitive activity did not differ between training methods (Bell & Kozlowski, 2008). This study also found that error management instructions lead to higher state learning orientation only among trainees with lower dispositional learning orientation.

Studies investigating interactions of individual difference variables with training methods are not only useful in determining the best fit between trainee and training method but they also have the potential to advance theoretical understanding of psychological processes stimulated during training. An explicit attempt to draw on existing theory to describe ATI patterns in error management training was made by Keith, Richter, and Naumann (2010). They also aimed at describing motivational and cognitive processes in an integrated model. This research did *not* expect to find one training method to be better suited for some trainees than others; rather it was predicted (and found) that all participants benefit from exploratory error management training, whereas the effectiveness of guided training depends on trainees' motivational and cognitive characteristics (i.e., the same pattern that Heimbeck et al. found for prove goal and avoidance goal orientation). In other words, error management training was expected to vitiate the effects of motivational and cognitive personal characteristics on training effectiveness.

Keith et al. (2010) based their predictions on resource allocation theory (Kanfer & Ackerman, 1989) which in turn builds on cognitive theories of skill acquisition. According to these theories, every task draws on a limited pool of attentional resources (e.g., Kahnemann, 1973). Resource dependency of a task (i.e., the degree to which devoting resources to tasks leads to performance improvement) is a function of task characteristics (e.g., task difficulty) and practice. Specifically, in the beginning of skill acquisition, many tasks are resource dependent; after some practice, however, resource dependence is reduced (Norman & Bobrow, 1975). This effect is also known as routinization, automatization, or proceduralization (e.g., Anderson, 1982; Hacker, 1998). For example, many everyday tasks (e.g., driving) draw on attentional resources when performed for the first time, and performance depends on the degree of attention devoted to the task (i.e., resource dependency). After a while, however, the task becomes routinized and can be performed well irrespective of the attentional resources devoted – the task has become resource insensitive. This practice effect is illustrated in the change of slope of the performance–resource function (Norman & Bobrow, 1975). In early phases of skill acquisition, the slope is steep (i.e., the more resources are devoted to the task, the better task performance). After several trials, the slope becomes flat (i.e., performance is substantially improved regardless of amount of resources devoted to the task).

The theory by Kanfer and Ackerman (1989) relates individual differences in motivation and ability to the concept of attentional resources. An individual's motivation affects attentional resources as he or she decides how much effort (i.e., attentional resources) to spend on a task. For example, if a trainee perceives the training content to be useful, then he or she will work harder during training than a participant who judges the training content not to be useful for him or her. For cognitive ability, Kanfer and Ackerman (1989) assume a direct correspondence with attentional resources: The higher an individual's cognitive ability, the more attentional resources are available to him or her. Applied to the effects of practice and the performance–resource function, it follows that individual differences in motivation and cognitive ability may affect performance in early phases of skill acquisitions but that this effect declines over time (i.e., reduced or no effect in late phases of skill acquisition). In line with this prediction, research found a decline of correlations between cognitive ability and performance in the course of practice in consistent and moderately complex tasks (e.g., Ackerman, 1988).

Based on resource allocation theory, Keith et al. (2010) predicted an interaction between training method and individual differences in motivation and cognitive ability. They argued that, in a way, the transfer phase in error management training corresponds to a later phase of skill acquisition for trainees. During training, they have worked independently on tasks and used self-regulatory skills such as metacognition – the same processes that are essential for solving the transfer tasks. For them, there is a high degree of overlap between training and transfer tasks. As a consequence, the transfer tasks become more resource insensitive and the effect of individual differences on transfer performance is reduced. In contrast, in guided training, the transfer situation imposes new and challenging demands on attentional resources as trainees work independently and without the external guidance received during training. For them, the transfer task is resource dependent, that is, motivational and cognitive individual differences predict performance differences. Results for cognitive ability are depicted in Fig. 11.2 (similar results were found for motivation). As predicted, training method interacted with cognitive ability. Cognitive ability had a substantial effect on adaptive transfer performance for participants of guided training ($\beta = .52$, $p < .01$). However, in exploratory error management training, this effect was significantly smaller ($\beta = .24$, $p < .05$). Note that this pattern does *not* imply that one training method fits better to some trainees while another fits better to others. Instead, all participants, in particular those with lower cognitive ability, benefited from exploratory error management training. Higher ability participants benefited from both training methods.

These results contribute to a better understanding of the moderating effects of cognitive ability and motivation during training. It should be noted that, although the results of the Keith et al. (2010) study are consistent with resource allocation theory, the theory's predictions were not tested directly. It would be desirable to include several training and transfer phases to capture a more complete picture of the processes involved. Such an approach would also account for the finding that

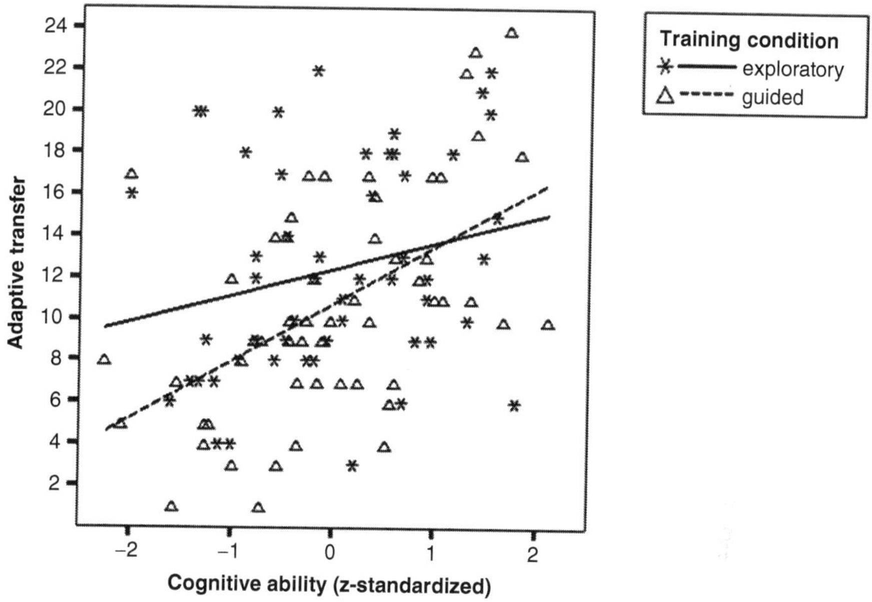

Fig. 11.2 Interaction effect of training condition (exploratory error management training vs. traditional guided training) and cognitive ability on adaptive transfer performance (Adapted from Keith et al., 2010, Fig. 2b. With kind permission from John Wiley & Sons)

self-regulatory activities can be expected to gradually develop and affect performance over time (e.g., Sitzmann, Bell, Kraiger, & Kanar, 2009; Sitzmann & Ely, 2010). Also, attentional resources and metacognitive self-regulation may be measured more directly in future research (cf. Keith et al., 2010). Finally, all studies that tested interaction effects of individual differences and error management versus alternative training methods used samples of university students. Generalizations need to be drawn with caution to the extent to which students differ from the general population in the investigated individual differences variables (e.g., higher cognitive ability).

Practical Implications for Organizational Training and Open Research Questions

Error management training is an active training approach that explicitly incorporates errors in training by asking participants to explore the task and by encouraging them to make errors and learn from them. This approach is different from conventional training methods that focus on teaching correct solutions by providing detailed guiding instructions which are – at least implicitly – designed to avoid errors during training.

As described in this chapter, research has demonstrated error management training to be effective and suggests that its effectiveness is due to emotional and cognitive processes (such as emotion control and metacognition). These processes are stimulated in error management training (but not or to a lesser extent in conventional guided training) and they are useful when solving transfer tasks. Research on interactions of training method and inter-individual difference variables further suggests error management training to reduce negative effects of low motivation and cognitive ability. The research reviewed in this chapter has several practical implications for the delivery of training in organizations.

First, the finding on the effectiveness of error management training is in contrast to traditional approaches to learning and training that deny that errors have any positive function in the learning process (e.g., Bandura, 1986; Skinner, 1953). Incorporating active exploration and errors during training is beneficial for learning and performance, and trainers may consider designing training methods accordingly. For example, trainers could give trainees the opportunity to actively explore their learning material and refrain from providing immediate help in response to errors. Participants should be given the opportunity to deal with errors and impasses independently because this approach gives them the opportunity to develop self-regulatory skills helpful in solving transfer problems. To prevent participants from reacting negatively to errors, trainers may repeatedly emphasize positive aspects of errors in the course of the training, as is done in error management instructions. Such instructions are inexpensive and easy to administer and therefore could be included in virtually any training, verbally or on notices that are prominently placed.

Second, trainers may keep in mind that performance during training is not necessarily indicative of learning. Rather, training methods that initially impede performance may be better for learning in the long run than methods that lead to better immediate performance. This claim has been made by several training researchers (e.g., Hesketh, 1997; Schmidt & Bjork, 1992), and research on error management training supports this claim: Training performance in error management training may be low in comparison with participants who receive detailed guiding instructions on correct task solutions. In the transfer phase, however, when all participants are required to work independently without the help of a trainer, the pattern is reversed. Trainers may keep this in mind when motivating trainees to work independently. Subjective reactions by some trainees may be negative towards working independently; that is, some trainees may prefer to receive more help and instruction from the trainer (cf. Schmidt & Bjork, 1992).

Some qualifications need to be made concerning the scope of error management training application. Research has shown error management training to be particularly effective for adaptive transfer tasks in which the development of novel solutions that have not been practiced during training is required. For analogical transfer tasks (i.e., transfer tasks that are similar to training tasks and that merely require the application of practiced strategies), error management training effects are small in comparison with alternative training methods (e.g., Keith & Frese, 2008). This result implies that trainers may consider the training goal when making the decision to use error management training or traditional guided training methods. If the training goal is to learn a few clear-cut skills or procedures that need to be applied on the job in exactly the same manner, it may be more suitable to teach these very skills or procedures directly through guided instruction and subsequent practice. If, however, the tasks on the job require a wide range of skills and adaptations which cannot be covered completely during training, using error management training rather than guided approaches seems most appropriate (Bell & Kozlowski, 2010; Debowski et al., 2001; Ivancic & Hesketh, 1995/1996; Keith & Frese, 2005, 2008). Another aspect that needs to be considered is the degree of task-inherent feedback. In order to learn from active exploration and errors, the task must provide feedback that can be readily interpreted by participants. On tasks that provide only ambiguous feedback, trainers may consider including modules that explicitly deal with the interpretation of feedback before engaging trainees in active exploration. They may even decide against using error management training.

This chapter introduced one training method that explicitly incorporated errors in training – error management training – which entails active exploration and positive framing of errors. There may be several other ways to integrate errors in training. For example, Joung et al. (2006) trained fire-fighters for incident command by providing them with stories that described incidents either with or without errors which led to severe consequences. In line with predictions, participants who had heard the error stories performed better then those who had heard stories in which no errors had occurred when confronted with new scenarios following their training. The authors conclude that, in situations where the prospect of making errors oneself is too threatening or in which there is no safe environment available for making errors (e.g., high-resolution simulator training), this type of vicarious error management training may be useful (see also Lorenzet, Salas, & Tannenbaum, 2005). On the other hand, as mentioned above, action regulation theory assumes that people learn from actions (Frese & Zapf, 1994; Hacker, 1998). In line with this assumption, some studies have found that training in which participants were only informed of potential errors but were prevented from making errors themselves is not very effective (see Frese, 1995). Similarly, a driving simulator training that involved actively making errors was effective but not guided training that involved watching videos of drivers making errors (Ivancic & Hesketh, 2000, Studies 1 and 2). Future research may investigate the conditions under which making errors oneself is necessary for learning as opposed to learning from errors made by others.

Future research may also include job performance measures to evaluate effectiveness of error management training. Many existing studies have used post-training performance as a proxy for performance on the job (cf. Ghodsian, Bjork, & Benjamin, 1997). Both from a theoretical perspective and, based on the research reviewed in this chapter, it makes sense to expect error management training to be effective for promoting performance on the job – more so than guided training methods. Participants of error management training learn to work independently and deal with errors they make early on during training. Back on the job, errors will inevitably occur despite all efforts to avoid them. Participants of error management training may be better prepared for this situation than those of guided training who were protected from making errors during training (cf. Frese, 1995; Ivancic & Hesketh, 1995/1996).

A considerable amount of research on error management training has been conducted using tasks that involved the computer (e.g., learning new computer software or a decision-making task delivered on the computer). Notwithstanding the relevance of computer tasks for many of today's jobs and in everyday life, it would be desirable to apply error management training in other skill domains. An interesting domain may be social skills. From a theoretical perspective, there is reason to expect error management training to be particularly well suited for the acquisition of social skills: Social situations tend to be unstructured and unpredictable. Not every potential social situation (e.g., interactions between a supervisor and his or her subordinate or interactions with clients) can be covered during training. Rather, trainees need to adapt flexibly to new social situations. Given that error management training has been shown to be particularly well suited for adaptive transfer, social skills may be a fruitful domain to apply error management training. On the other hand, social situations may involve unclear feedback (e.g., a supervisor does not immediately know whether the interaction with his or her subordinate was successful). It may be argued that error management training is not an appropriate training method because no trainer is present to interpret social feedback.

A well-established training method for teaching social skills (e.g., supervisory skills) is behavior modeling training. Behavior modeling training is derived from social-cognitive theory (Bandura, 1986) and emphasizes guidance and error avoidance. Typically, behavior modeling trainees watch correct behavior that is demonstrated by a model, subsequently practice this behavior, and receive feedback and social reinforcement by the trainer and fellow participants (e.g., Latham & Saari, 1979). This training method has been shown to be highly effective (for meta-analytical results, see Taylor, Russ-Eft, & Chan, 2005). It should be noted, however, that many applications of behavior modeling training have integrated errors in training "based on trainer intuition" (Baldwin, 1992, p. 152), although Bandura's theory originally promotes correct behavior and error avoidance. These applications included what is called negative models; that is, models who demonstrate undesired behavior in addition to positive models who demonstrate desired behavior. A study that compared positive-only modeling with both positive and negative modeling showed the former to lead to better analogical transfer and the latter to lead to better adaptive transfer. Also, the above mentioned meta-analysis found larger effect sizes in favor of positive-only modeling for declarative knowledge criteria whereas, for job behavior criteria, the combination of positive and negative modeling yielded larger effect sizes. These results are in line with the present view that guided training methods (such as behavior modeling) may be well suited for promoting analogical transfer but that training methods that incorporate errors in training are better suited for adaptive transfer.

In one study that taught the social skill of charismatic communication, we have compared error management training (i.e., a training condition in which participants did not watch a model but performed the skill based on minimal information and were subsequently directed to learn from errors they made) and behavior modeling training (i.e., a training condition in which participants watched a model demonstrating correct behavior). Results were in line with previous research in that both training methods improved analogical transfer performance but only error management training led to better adaptive transfer performance (Frese, Muelhausen, Wiegel, & Keith, 2010). Future research may continue to investigate the effectiveness of error management training for diverse social skills as compared to existing training methods. Also, research may explore ways in which existing training methods can be fruitfully combined. For example, depending on task difficulty or a trainee's pre-training experience, it may be useful to combine guided and error management training. In the beginning, when the goal is to develop a routine, guided methods may be used, whereas in later stages, when adaptation to new situations is the goal, modules of error management training may be included.

Future research may also continue to investigate interaction effects between training method and participant characteristics. As reviewed above, research indicates error management training to attenuate effects of cognitive and motivational participant characteristics. This research suggests that error management training is appropriate for all trainees irrespective of their cognitive and motivational characteristics, whereas such personal characteristics influence performance in guided training. As a limitation, it should be noted that this research is based on university students and that generalizability of these findings needs to be viewed with caution.

On a final note, this chapter has focused on how errors can be fruitfully integrated within formal training. However, a considerable part of job knowledge and skills is acquired through informal learning activities that occur on the job (Kraiger, 2002; Tannenbaum, Beard, McNall, & Salas, 2010). It may be interesting to investigate whether individuals in organizations informally learn from errors on the job. Indeed, research has shown individuals to differ in the extent to which they engage in so-called deliberate practice activities while pursuing their everyday work activities, and these differences in turn predict performance (e.g., Keith & Ericsson, 2007; Sonnentag & Kleine, 2000; Unger, Keith, Hilling, Gielnik, & Frese, 2009). Deliberate practice involves systematic practice with the goal of performance improvement and has been shown to relate to expert performance in domains such as chess, music, or sports (Ericcson, Krampe, & Tesch-Römer, 1993). Research may continue to investigate how errors that occur on the job can be used by individuals and organizations to promote learning (e.g., Bauer & Mulder, 2007; Keith & Frese, 2011; Van Dyck et al., 2005).

References

Ackerman, P. L. (1988). Determinants of individual differences during skill acquisition: Cognitive abilities and information processing. *Journal of Experimental Psychology: General, 117*, 288–318.

Aguinis, H., & Kraiger, K. (2009). Benefits of training and development for individuals and teams, organizations, and society. *Annual Review of Psychology, 60*, 451–474.

Anderson, J. R. (1982). Acquisition of cognitive skill. *Psychological Review, 89*, 369–406.

Arthur, W., Jr., Bennett, W., Jr., Edens, P. S., & Bell, S. T. (2003). Effectiveness of training in organizations: A meta-analysis of design and evaluation features. *Journal of Applied Psychology, 88*, 234–245.

Baldwin, T. T. (1992). Effects of alternative modeling strategies on outcomes of interpersonal-skills training. *Journal of Applied Psychology, 77*, 147–154.

Bandura, A. (1986). *Social foundations of thought and action: A social cognitive theory*. Englewood Cliffs, NJ: Prentice Hall.

Barnett, S. M., & Ceci, S. J. (2002). When and where do we apply what we learn? A taxonomy for far transfer. *Psychological Bulletin, 128*, 612–637.

Bauer, J., & Mulder, R. H. (2007). Modelling learning from errors in daily work. *Learning in Health and Social Care, 6*, 121–133.

Bell, B. S., & Kozlowski, S. W. J. (2008). Active learning: Effects of core training design elements on self-regulatory processes, learning, and adaptability. *Journal of Applied Psychology, 93*, 296–316.

Bell, B. S., & Kozlowski, S. W. J. (2010). Toward a theory of learner-centered training design: An integrative framework of active learning. In S. W. J. Kozlowski & E. Salas (Eds.), *Learning, training, and development in organizations* (pp. 263–300). New York: Taylor & Francis.

Brown, A. L., Bransford, J. D., Ferrara, R. A., & Campione, J. C. (1983). Learning, remembering, and understanding. In J. H. Flavell & E. M. Markman (Eds.), *Handbook of child psychology* (Vol. 3, pp. 77–166). New York: Wiley.

Bruner, J. S. (1966). *Toward a theory of instruction*. Cambridge, MA: Harvard University Press.

Carroll, J. M., & Carrithers, C. (1984). Blocking learner error states in a training-wheels system. *Human Factors, 26*, 377–389.

Carver, C. S., & Scheier, M. F. (1998). *On the self-regulation of behavior*. New York: Cambridge University Press.

Chillarege, K. A., Nordstrom, C. R., & Williams, K. B. (2003). Learning from our mistakes: Error management training for mature learners. *Journal of Business and Psychology, 17*, 369–385.

Cronbach, L. J., & Snow, R. E. (1977). *Aptitudes and instructional methods: A handbook for research on interactions*. New York: Irvington.

Debowski, S., Wood, R. E., & Bandura, A. (2001). Impact of guided exploration on self-regulatory mechanisms and information acquisition through electronic search. *Journal of Applied Psychology, 86*, 1129–1141.

Dormann, T., & Frese, M. (1994). Error management training: Replication and the function of exploratory behavior. *International Journal of Human Computer Interaction, 6*, 365–372.

Dweck, C. S., & Leggett, E. L. (1988). A social-cognitive approach to motivation and personality. *Psychological Review, 95*, 256–273.

Ellis, S., & Davidi, I. (2005). After-event reviews: Drawing lessons from successful and failed experience. *Journal of Applied Psychology, 90*, 857–871.

Ericsson, K. A., Krampe, R. Th., & Tesch-Römer, C. (1993). The role of deliberate practice in the acquisition of expert performance. *Psychological Review, 100*, 363–406.

Ford, J. K., Smith, E. M., Weissbein, D. A., Gully, S. M., & Salas, E. (1998). Relationships of goal orientation, metacognitive activity, and practice strategies with learning outcomes and transfer. *Journal of Applied Psychology, 83*, 218–233.

Frese, M. (1995). Error management in training: Conceptual and empirical results. In C. Zucchermaglio, S. Bagnara, & S. U. Stucky (Eds.), *Organizational learning and technological change, series F: Computer and systems sciences* (Vol. 141, pp. 112–124). Berlin, Germany: Springer.

Frese, M., Beimel, S., & Schoenborn, S. (2003). Action training for charismatic leadership: Two evaluations of studies of a commercial training module on inspirational communication of a vision. *Personnel Psychology, 56*, 671–697.

Frese, M., Brodbeck, F. C., Heinbokel, T., Mooser, C., Schleiffenbaum, E., & Thiemann, P. (1991). Errors in training computer skills: On the positive function of errors. *Human Computer Interaction, 6*, 77–93.

Frese, M., Muelhausen, S., Wiegel, J., & Keith, N. (2010). *Comparing two training approaches to charismatic communication: Social learning versus error management*. Manuscript submitted for publication.

Frese, M., & Zapf, D. (1994). Action as the core of work psychology: A German approach. In H. C. Triandis, M. D. Dunette, & L. M. Hough (Eds.), *Handbook of industrial and organizational psychology* (Vol. 4, pp. 271–340). Palo Alto, CA: Consulting Psychologists Press.

Ghodsian, D., Bjork, R. A., & Benjamin, A. S. (1997). Evaluating training *during* training: Obstacles and opportunities. In M. A. Quinones & A. Ehrenstein (Eds.), *Training for a rapidly changing workplace* (pp. 63–88). Washington, DC: American Psychological Association.

Goodman, J., & Wood, R. E. (2004). Feedback specificity, learning opportunities, and learning. *Journal of Applied Psychology, 89*, 809–821.

Gove, P. B. (Ed.). (1993). *Webster's third new international dictionary of the English language unabridged*. Köln, Germany: Könemann.

Gully, S. M., & Chen, G. (2010). Individual differences, attribute-treatment interactions, and training outcomes. In S. W. J. Kozlowski & E. Salas (Eds.), *Learning, training, and development in organisations* (pp. 3–64). New York: Taylor & Francis.

Gully, S. M., Payne, S. C., Koles, K. L. K., & Whiteman, J. A. K. (2002). The impact of error management training and individual differences on training outcomes: An attribute-treatment interaction perspective. *Journal of Applied Psychology, 87*, 143–155.

Hacker, W. (1998). *Allgemeine Arbeitspsychologie: Psychische Regulation von Arbeitstätigkeiten* [General industrial psychology: Mental regulation of working activities]. Bern, Switzerland: Huber.

Hajcak, G., & Foti, D. (2008). Errors are aversive: Defensive motivation and the error-related negativity. *Psychological Science, 19*, 103–108.

Heimbeck, D., Frese, M., Sonnentag, S., & Keith, N. (2003). Integrating errors into the training process: The function of error management instructions and the role of goal orientation. *Personnel Psychology, 56*, 333–361.

Hesketh, B. (1997). Dilemmas in training for transfer and retention. *Applied Psychology: An International Review, 46*, 317–339.

Ilgen, D. R., Fisher, C. D., & Taylor, M. S. (1979). Consequences of individual feedback on behavior in organizations. *Journal of Applied Psychology, 64*, 359–371.

Ivancic, K., & Hesketh, B. (1995/1996). Making the best of errors during training. *Training Research Journal, 1*, 103–125.

Ivancic, K., & Hesketh, B. (2000). Learning from error in a driving simulation: Effects on driving skill and self-confidence. *Ergonomics, 43*, 1966–1984.

Joung, W., Hesketh, B., & Neal, A. (2006). Using "War Stories" to train for adaptive performance: Is it better to learn from error or success? *Applied Psychology: An International Review, 55*, 282–302.

Kahneman, D. (1973). *Attention and effort*. Englewood Cliffs, NJ: Prentice Hall.

Kanfer, R., & Ackerman, P. L. (1989). Motivation and cognitive abilities: An integrative/aptitude-treatment interaction approach to skill acquisition [monograph]. *Journal of Applied Psychology, 74*, 657–690.

Kanfer, R., Ackerman, P. L., & Heggestad, E. D. (1996). Motivational skills and self-regulation for learning: A trait perspective. *Learning and Individual Differences, 8*, 185–209.

Karoly, P. (1993). Mechanisms of self-regulation: A systems view. *Annual Review of Psychology, 44*, 23–52.

Keith, N., & Ericsson, K. A. (2007). A deliberate practice account of typing proficiency in everyday typists. *Journal of Experimental Psychology: Applied, 13*, 135–145.

Keith, N., & Frese, M. (2005). Self-regulation in error management training: Emotion control and metacognition as mediators of performance effects. *Journal of Applied Psychology, 90*, 677–691.

Keith, N., & Frese, M. (2008). Effectiveness of error management training: A meta-analysis. *Journal of Applied Psychology, 93*, 59–69.

Keith, N., & Frese, M. (2011). Enhancing firm performance and innovativeness through error management culture. In N. M. Ashkanasy, C. P. M. Wilderom, & M. F. Peterson (Eds.), *Handbook of organizational culture and climate* (2nd ed., pp. 137–157). Thousand Oaks, CA: Sage Publications.

Keith, N., Richter, T., & Naumann, J. (2010). Active/exploratory training promotes transfer even in learners with low motivation and cognitive ability. *Applied Psychology: An International Review, 59*, 97–123.

Kessels, R. P., & de Haan, E. H. (2003). Implicit learning in memory rehabilitation: A meta-analysis on errorless learning and vanishing cues methods. *Journal of Clinical and Experimental Neuropsychology, 25*, 805–814.

Kirschner, P. A., Sweller, J., & Clark, R. E. (2006). Why minimal guidance during instruction does not work: An analysis of the failure of constructivist, discovery, problem-based, experiential, and inquiry-based teaching. *Educational Psychologist, 41*, 75–86.

Kraiger, K. (ed.) (2002). *Creating, implementing, and managing effective training and development*. San Francisco, CA: Jossey-Bass.

Latham, G. P., & Locke, E. A. (1991). Self-regulation through goal setting. *Organizational Behavior and Human Decision Processes, 50*, 212–247.

Latham, G. P., & Saari, L. M. (1979). Application of social-learning theory to training supervisors through behavioral modeling. *Journal of Applied Psychology, 64*, 239–246.

Lazar, J., & Norcio, A. (2003). Training novice users in developing strategies for responding to errors when browsing the web. *International Journal of Human Computer Interaction, 15*, 361–377.

Lorenzet, S. J., Salas, E., & Tannenbaum, S. I. (2005). Benefiting from mistakes: The impact of guided errors on learning, performance, and self-efficacy. *Human Resource Development Quarterly, 16*, 301–322.

Mayer, R. E. (2004). Should there be a three-strikes rule against pure discovery learning? The case for guided methods of instruction. *American Psychologist, 59*, 1–14.

Morris, C. D., Bransford, J. D., & Franks, J. J. (1977). Levels of processing versus transfer appropriate processing. *Journal of Verbal Learning and Verbal Behavior, 16*, 519–533.

Nordstrom, C. R., Wendland, D., & Williams, K. B. (1998). "To err is human": An examination of the effectiveness of error management training. *Journal of Business and Psychology, 12*, 269–282.

Norman, D. A., & Bobrow, D. G. (1975). On data-limited and resource-limited processes. *Cognitive Psychology, 7*, 44–64.

Prümper, J., Zapf, D., Bordbeck, F. C., & Frese, M. (1992). Errors of novices and experts: Some surprising differences in computerized office work. *Behaviour and Information Technology, 11*, 319–328.

Reason, J. (1990). *Human error*. Cambridge, UK: Cambridge University Press.

Rogers, D. A., Regehr, G., & MacDonald, J. (2002). A role for error training in surgical technical skill instruction and evaluation. *The American Journal of Surgery, 183*, 242–245.

Salas, E., & Cannon-Bowers, J. A. (2001). The science of training: A decade of progress. *Annual Review of Psychology, 52*, 471–499.

Schmidt, R. A., & Bjork, R. A. (1992). New conceptualizations of practice: Common principles in three paradigms suggest new concepts for training. *Psychological Science, 3*, 207–217.

Schmidt, A. M., & Ford, J. K. (2003). Learning within a learner control environment: The interactive effects of goal orientation and metacognitive instruction on learning outcomes. *Personnel Psychology, 56*, 405–429.

Shea, J. B., & Morgan, R. L. (1979). Contextual interference effects on the acquisition, retention, and transfer of a motor skill. *Journal of Experimental Psychology: Human Learning and Memory, 5*, 179–187.

Sitkin, S. B. (1992). Learning through failure. *Research in Organizational Behavior, 14*, 231–266.

Sitzmann, T., Bell, B. S., Kraiger, K., & Kanar, A. M. (2009). A multilevel analysis of the effect of prompting self-regulation in technology-delivered instruction. *Personnel Psychology, 62*, 697–734.

Sitzmann, T., & Ely, K. (2010). Sometimes you need a reminder: The effects of prompting self-regulation on regulatory processes, learning, and attrition. *Journal of Applied Psychology, 95*, 132–144.

Skinner, B. F. (1953). *Science and human behavior*. New York: The Free Press.

Smith, E. M., Ford, J. K., & Kozlowski, S. W. J. (1997). Building adaptive expertise: Implications for training design strategies. In M. A. Quinones & A. Ehrenstein (Eds.), *Training for a rapidly changing workplace* (pp. 89–118). Washington, DC: American Psychological Association.

Sonnentag, S. (1998). Expertise in professional software design: A process study. *Journal of Applied Psychology, 83*, 703–715.

Sonnentag, S., & Kleine, B. M. (2000). Deliberate practice at work: A study with insurance agents. *Journal of Occupational and Organizational Psychology, 73*, 87–102.

Tannenbaum, S. I., Beard, R. L., McNall, L. A., & Salas, E. (2010). Informal learning and development in organizations. In S. W. J. Kozlowski & E. Salas (Eds.), *Learning, training, and development in organizations* (pp. 303–331). New York: Taylor & Francis.

Taylor, P. J., Russ-Eft, D. F., & Chan, D. W. L. (2005). A meta-analytic review of behavior modeling training. *Journal of Applied Psychology, 90*, 692–709.

Unger, J. M., Keith, N., Hilling, C., Gielnik, M. M., & Frese, M. (2009). Deliberate practice among South African small business owners: Relationships with education, cognitive ability, knowledge, and success. *Journal of Occupational and Organizational Psychology, 82*, 21–44.

van der Linden, D., Sonnentag, S., Frese, M., & van Dyck, C. (2001). Exploration strategies, performance, and error consequences when learning a complex computer task. *Behavior and Information Technology, 20*, 189–198.

van Dyck, C., Frese, M., Baer, M., & Sonnentag, S. (2005). Organizational error management culture and its impact on performance: A two-study replication. *Journal of Applied Psychology, 90*, 1228–1240.

VandeWalle, D. (1997). Development and validation of a work domain goal orientation instrument. *Educational and Psychological Measurement, 57*, 995–1015.

Wood, R. E., Kakebeeke, B. M., Debowski, S., & Frese, M. (2000). The impact of enactive exploration on intrinsic motivation, strategy, and performance in electronic search. *Applied Psychology: An International Review, 49*, 263–283.

Zapf, D., Brodbeck, F. C., Frese, M., Peters, H., & Prümper, J. (1992). Errors in working with computers: A first validation of a taxonomy for observed errors in a field setting. *International Journal of Human Computer Interaction, 4*, 311–339.

Zhao, B., & Olivera, F. (2006). Error reporting in organizations. *Academy of Management Review, 31*, 1012–1030.

Chapter 12
Reflecting on Learning from Errors in School Instruction: Findings and Suggestions from a Swiss-German Video Study

Inger Marie Dalehefte, Tina Seidel, and Manfred Prenzel

Introduction

Errors are important in learning situations, but remain a very sensitive topic in instruction. Although the consequences of errors appear more existential in certain other professions, there can be no doubt that errors and mistakes that occur during instruction have to be handled with care because of their relevance for teaching and learning processes. Therefore, establishing a climate that enables students to reflect on and learn from errors should be one of teachers' professional tasks. How errors are treated in the classroom seems to depend on culturally specific beliefs and practices. Video studies of mathematics instruction have shown that the potential of learning from errors is probably weighted differently in other cultures. For instance, the Japanese, U.S. and German videos published in the TIMSS 1995 Video Study (Stigler, Gonzales, Kawanaka, Knoll, & Serrano, 1999) gave the impression that enforcing learning processes from errors was a typical feature in Japanese instruction. A further comparison between Italian and U.S. mathematics lessons revealed country-specific differences in handling mistakes (Santagata, 2005). This chapter presents findings from a video study in physics instruction conducted in Germany and the German-speaking parts of Switzerland. The aim of the Swiss–German video

I.M. Dalehefte, Ph.D. (✉)
Leibniz Institute for Science and Mathematics Education (IPN),
Christian Albrechts University, Kiel, Germany
e-mail: dalehefte@ipn.uni-kiel.de

T. Seidel, Ph.D. • M. Prenzel, Ph.D.
TUM School of Education, Munich, Germany
e-mail: tina.seidel@tum.de; manfred.prenzel@tum.de

J. Bauer and C. Harteis (eds.), *Human Fallibility: The Ambiguity of Errors for Work and Learning*, Professional and Practice-based Learning 6,
DOI 10.1007/978-90-481-3941-5_12,

study was to investigate and compare the conditions in physics instruction which seem to play an important role in students' learning. In this chapter, we present findings on conditions that can help students to learn from errors. We will also discuss briefly how teachers can learn from video studies about conditions for learning from errors and handling mistakes.

Errors in School Instruction

The consequences of errors are more obvious and dramatic in certain professions compared to school instruction. And so the simulation and training of routines and critical incidences forms part of the technical training of airplane pilots or neurosurgeons. However, such aggravating consequences do not appear in the case of "human failure" in school instruction, yet teachers also bear important responsibilities. They account for the learning processes of their students and are responsible for providing a cognitively stimulating and motivating learning environment. How teachers interpret such situations and how they act is important for learning processes. Indeed, teachers themselves can make errors in lessons. In this chapter, though, we will consider more closely the role of students' errors and misconceptions of their learning. Errors – or at least some of them – can be very important for learning processes in instruction. Within this chapter, we aim to show that how students' errors are handled contributes to learning opportunities and therefore can be very valuable for students' learning processes. We consider the classroom climate to play an important role for errors and mistakes to occur. We will, therefore, take a closer look at the role which errors play in instruction from the perspective of external observers and the students.

Making errors in instructional settings leads to positive and negative consequences. Thus, this chapter is not meant to "apotheosize" error making (cf. Oser, 2007). This chapter deals with the fact that errors and error making often play a problematical role in instruction, which may also vary from one country to another. For instance, in traditional German classrooms, there does not seem to be much room for dealing productively with errors in instructional routines, although it is well known that errors provide a unique opportunity to learn. Recently, and triggered by findings from comparative studies, the desire to profit from this opportunity is strong (BLK, 1997; Ostermeier, Prenzel & Duit, 2010). In the IPN Video Study "Teaching and learning in physics instruction – a video study" conducted in Germany from 2002 to 2004 (Prenzel, Duit, Euler & Lehrke, 1999), this problem area was focused upon and some specific characteristics relevant for error making were identified (Meyer, Seidel & Prenzel, 2006; Schulmeiß, 2004). In this chapter, we go one step further and present findings from a cooperative project between the German IPN Video Study in physics instruction and the Swiss Project "Teaching and learning cultures in physics instruction – a video study" (Labudde, 2002). We thereby establish a connection between different learning cultures and also elaborate on how to establish a better classroom climate in instruction, in which errors can be dealt with well and turned into fruitful instruments of instruction.

Role of Errors and Handling Mistakes in Mathematics and Science Instruction: An International View

International video studies have shown that instructional routines provide different amounts of opportunities for making errors. For example, the Japanese videos released in the TIMSS 1995 Video Study (Stigler et al., 1999) gave the impression that provoking errors is an accepted and widely used method in Japanese mathematics instruction. Moreover, a comparative video study of Italian and U.S. mathematics lessons (Santagata, 2004, 2005) showed that Italian and U.S. students experience the occurrence of their mistakes differently and that this largely depends on how teachers organize instructional activities and determine the roles of classroom participants. Mistakes are discussed twice as often in Italy as in the United States. Also, differences in handling mistakes were obvious: U.S. teachers mitigate students' responses; Italian teachers aggravate them. These two examples of comparative video studies highlight cultural differences in handling errors and mistakes in mathematics instruction.

A comparison of geographically, culturally, and linguistically similar countries makes it easier to rule out certain interpretation biases often associated with international comparative studies (Dalehefte et al., 2009). The neighboring countries, Switzerland and Germany, meet these requirements to a high degree. Despite many similarities, these countries display remarkable differences with regard to their former achievements in international achievement tests, such as, for instance, in the Third International Mathematics and Science Study (Beaton et al., 1996) and in the Programme for International Student Assessment (OECD, 2000, 2004). In general, the Swiss students achieved better results than their German colleagues in the TIMSS and PISA surveys up to 2006, especially in mathematics and to some extent also in science. This fact makes a comparison between German and Swiss instruction especially attractive. The reasons for achievement differences between Swiss and German students in international comparative studies might, amongst others, have their origins in country-specific distinctions due to teacher education, curricula, (Labudde, 1999, 2003) and pedagogical attitudes and traditions (Klieme & Reusser, 2003).

In the following comparative video study in physics instruction presented here, differences have been found regarding important instructional conditions (Dalehefte et al., 2009). For example, Swiss physics lessons tend to show more clarity and coherence as well as a larger range of process-oriented teaching conditions than do German lessons. The extent to which conditions related to error making are provided in the two countries will be part of this chapter. Given the previous research findings and experts' reports, we expect to reveal better conditions for learning from errors in the Swiss sample. One reason for this expectation is the fact that learning from errors is considered to be a desideratum for the German mathematics and science classroom (BLK, 1997). However, several studies show the surprising fact that students hardly make any observable errors in German mathematics and science instruction (Heinze, 2004; Meyer et al., 2006). There may be several practical and emotional reasons for this. For instance, the typical teacher-centered style of developing questions in a narrowly-focused teacher–student interaction has been accused of offering little room for error making in mathematics and science instruction (BLK, 1997; Heinze, 2006). This narrowly-focused classroom talk was also referred to in the IPN Video Study in physics instruction (Seidel et al., 2007). One essential assumption typical for German instruction remains that situations which are meant to foster learning processes (*learning situations*) are blended with situations in which the students are supposed to present their abilities and knowledge (*achievement situations*). This presents a very difficult problem concerning the occurence and use of errors as learning opportunities (BLK, 1997) because blending learning and evaluation situations influences the extent to which students dare to admit their weaknesses and misconceptions (Meyer et al., 2006).

A further reason to assume better learning conditions from errors in the Swiss sample is that research indicates a better learning climate for error making in Switzerland than in Germany. For instance, in a comparative study, Heinze (2006) draws attention to noticeable differences between the positive perception of Swiss students with regard to the supportive behavior of the teacher and their possibilities to learn from their own errors in mathematics instruction and that of German students. In the German sample, the students reported that they received less cognitive than emotional support from the teacher. No differences were found between Swiss and German students' anxiety about making errors (Heinze, 2006).

Learning from errors has indeed been a subject of discussions among Swiss researchers for several years. Above all, the Swiss research group of Fritz Oser and colleagues has contributed relevant work in highlighting the importance of error making in Swiss instruction. Their findings show that students report in questionnaires and interviews about a positive climate for error making and that teachers handle errors in an appropriate way. However, individual errors have not been taken into much consideration (Spychiger, Oser, Hascher, & Mahler, 1999).

These studies indicate that Swiss instruction in one way or another provides a better climate for learning from errors. Nevertheless, these findings refer to the questionnaire data of students' subjective perceptions. In order to investigate the extent to which a supportive learning climate for error making occurs, using video analyses can be of advantage to get one step closer to actual instruction in classrooms. Video analyses offer the possibility of identifying concrete situations which may play a role in handling errors and mistakes in instruction. For example; under what circumstances are errors allowed to occur and to what extent are they taken up on and discussed.

Prerequisites for Errors to "Enter the Stage"

In school lessons, teaching and learning is the focal point and enduring activity of teachers and students. Thus, where learning takes place, internal (within individuals) and external (observable) errors will always occur (Oser, 2007). Errors can force the learning of "negative" knowledge (Oser, Hascher, & Spychiger , 1999), which means the acquisition of knowledge about how and why things go wrong, in comparison to "positive" knowledge about how and why things are right. These aspects are, according to Oser, "two sides of the same coin" because they complement each other in the acquisition of knowledge. From this viewpoint, error making, error checking, and error correction should be a normal situation to be expected in an instructional learning environment. Errors have the potential to draw attention to gaps in knowledge, misinterpretations and – if they are handled purposefully – attention and achievement deficits among students (Hascher, 2005). But, the extent to which errors can be fruitful for learning depends on their individual nature and how they are taken up on and converted (Oser et al., 1999). Two important prerequisites for errors to "enter the stage" are a learning-oriented approach and a supportive classroom climate.

Fostering a Learning-Oriented Approach Towards Errors

Teachers can deal with errors in different ways. On the one hand, teachers can try to prevent and to avoid the occurrence of errors (for instance, by applying mistake-prophylactic behavior), ignore or abandon them (so-called "Bermuda triangle") (Oser et al., 1999). On the other hand, they can pick up occurring errors and use them constructively. Santagata (2005) refers to these two reactions to errors theoretically as a *behaviorist* or a *constructivist* way of dealing with mistakes. These offer two entirely different views of the function of errors in instruction: The behaviorist understanding refers to the obsolete understanding that errors should be avoided because their occurrence can reinforce wrong answers; the constructivist approach interprets errors as an unavoidable and necessary part of the learning process. If a teacher has a behaviorist understanding of learning, he/she will certainly avoid errors as a consequence. Thus, one prerequisite for learning from errors is the constructivist belief that errors can be converted into something fruitful, and that they can be deliberately provoked and purposefully handled.

Creating a Supportive Social Climate

Another prerequisite for learning from errors is a classroom climate which allows for error making and mistakes. In theory, this would be a classical learning situation and is to be distinguished from situations in which students have to demonstrate their competencies for evaluative purposes. *Learning situations* should implicate conditions for experiencing and enhancing competencies and knowledge, whereas *achievement situations* are supposed to assess students' competencies. Learning and achievement situations initiate different motivational and affective processes (Seidel & Prenzel, 2003). While learning situations offer the possibility to deal with learning subjects in a relaxed, stress-free, and pleasurable way, achievement situations can cover positive but also important negative aspects, such as test anxiety and negative attributional patterns of the students because of the risk of failing and its consequences. For this reason, errors and mistakes probably play a different role in the two kinds of instructional situations described. Errors can be experienced as challenging in learning situations, but may well be thought of as a personal failure in achievement situations (BLK, 1997). Yet, it seems to be typical for German instruction that learning and achievement situations are often blurred and it is difficult to distinguish between the two (Meyer et al., 2006). This is a problem, because it implies that students cannot differentiate whether error making is acceptable or not in certain instructional situations. In research about error making in instruction, situational aspects often play the main role rather than the constitution of the errors themselves (Heinze, 2006). This is certainly connected to the emotional aspect of error making and the fact that cognition and emotion are interwoven constructs. An established example for this linkage in cognition–emotion research is the domain of test anxiety (Pekrun, 1992). In the case of blending learning and achievement situations, students might be more cautious and reserved in their participation. Such a non-supportive climate for making errors can be indicated by a tense atmosphere or anxiety among students, or their guardedness in order to avoid humiliation and disregard. Students who dare to actively participate and clearly show an interest in the lesson's contents might mirror an instructional learning situation or at least a situation in which it is "worth taking the risk". As a consequence of a study by Laukenmann and von Rhöneck (2003) in German physics instruction about the impact of emotions on learning in instructional phases, the authors recommend that instructional phases should be handled purposefully, depending on whether they address learning or achievement situations. Spychiger et al. (1999) also drew the conclusion from an intervention study in Switzerland that it really is important to clarify whether instructional sequences are meant to be practicing parts or controlling parts of the lesson.

The perception of the classroom climate can differ from individual student to individual student within a class. Nevertheless, the teacher has the possibility to influence the climate in certain ways. An important factor is how errors and mistakes are made public (Oser & Spychiger, 2005). Thus, a positive classroom climate and teacher support might affect students' participation in instruction. Otherwise, for instance, if errors and mistakes are taken up on in the public part of the lesson and, at the same time, the classroom situation and teacher support is tense, an individual student can experience the situation as humiliating and painful.

Thus, a learning-oriented approach and an adequate social climate are prerequisites for handling errors in instruction (Spychiger, 2003). The extent to which students perceive a climate which fosters a learning-oriented culture towards mistakes depends on the classroom climate and the teacher's acceptance. In this chapter, we aim to compare the conditions present in Swiss and German instruction. So far, findings indicate that Swiss teachers and their instruction might provide better possibilities for learning from errors. Thus, we investigate to what extent a climate which allows for errors can be identified in Swiss and German physics instruction (ninth grade) from the observers' as well as the students' perspective.

Research Questions

Video studies provide detailed information about what actually goes on in the "natural setting" of a classroom. The design of the video study presented considers observational as well as questionnaire data. This offers the possibility to take the observers' perspective as well as the students' perspective into account. In this way, we use indicators from different methods to identify the climatic conditions necessary in order for students to learn from error making. The theoretical background indicates that a better instructional embedding and acceptance of errors provides learning possibilities in instruction. Thus, we are interested in the extent to which these aspects can be found in ninth grade physics instruction from two points of view:

1. To what extent can video observers identify classroom indicators of a climate which facilitates learning from errors? Can more positive indicators be identified in the Swiss physics lessons?
2. How do students perceive and rate their opportunities to learn from errors? Do Swiss students perceive a better "error and mistake culture" than German students?

Design and Methods

Design

The design of the study integrates multiple methods. Questionnaires/tests, and interview and video data were collected to investigate physics instruction with a specific focus on problem areas well known in German physics and Swiss instruction. Among the areas "instructional activities", "goal clarity and coherence", "embedding experiments", "process-oriented teaching", the question concerning a "learning-oriented culture of handling errors" was pursued.

The design (Fig. 12.1) of the study included three measuring points within one school year. The data was collected over the school years 2002/2003 (Germany) and 2003/2004 (Switzerland).[1] This chapter refers to the video data and the student questionnaire collected at the second measuring point.

Sample

The sample consists of a stratified random sample of 82 [50 German and 32 Swiss (German-speaking)] physics classes in which 82 double lessons in the two topics

---

[1]We would like to thank the Swiss research team of Prof. Peter Labudde, which conducted the Swiss part of this study.

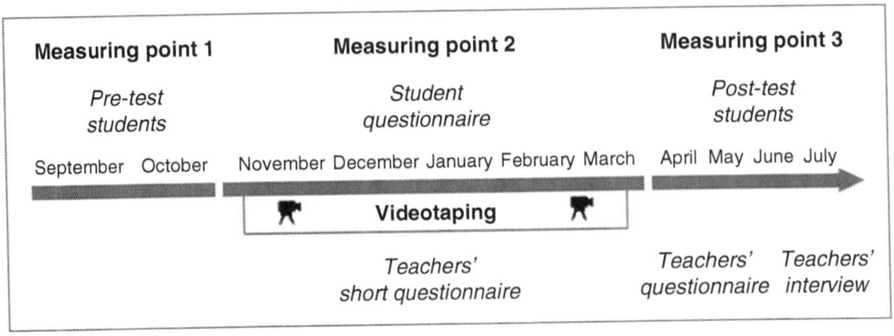

Fig. 12.1 Design of the Swiss-German video study in physics

"optics" and "mechanics" were videotaped. Conceivable provisions against biases were made; for instance, a stratified random sample was considered. Nevertheless, the representativeness of the study is limited due to, for instance, the fact that the sample is based upon two different school systems and a pre-selection of upper level school classes. All videos were collected according to standardized guidelines developed along the lines of the TIMSS 1995 Video Study (Stigler et al., 1999), but supplemented with certain aspects concerning physics instruction and the specific facilities in German and Swiss classrooms (Seidel, Dalehefte, & Meyer, 2005).

Instruments and Methods

The study presented here considers the observational category system "Blending of learning and achievement situations" (Schulmeiß, Seidel, & Meyer, 2005) and data from the student questionnaire concerning "Perceived mistake culture" (Rimmele et al., 2005) which considers errors and mistakes. The questionnaire was answered by the students directly after videotaping the lessons.

The Observational System "Blending of Learning and Achievement Situations"

The observational rating system "Blending of learning and achievement situations" referred to in this chapter is a high-inference rating system consisting of five items. These are based on the self-determined theory of motivation (Deci & Ryan, 1991) which accentuates the three fundamental psychological needs for competence, autonomy, and social relatedness. Within the framework of the IPN Video Study, the basic needs were carefully worded towards instructional conditions that are important for error making in the sense of blending learning and achievement situations (Schulmeiß et al., 2005). Table 12.1 lists the themes and items considered in the observational system.

Table 12.1 Observational system "Blending of learning and achievement situations" (Schulmeiß et al., 2005)

Theme	Item
Atmosphere	1. In the classroom, a tense atmosphere prevails
Error response	2. The class reacts contemptously when classmates make mistakes
Anxiety	3. Students who have not volunteered and are asked a question or asked to do something are anxious
Demonstration of competence	4. The students who say something in class try to appear to be competent
Humiliation	5. The students who say something in class try to avoid making mistakes to avoid humiliation

Observers came from Germany and were trained on the basis of another (but structurally similar) sample until a common understanding of the theoretical background and rating items was achieved. Each videotaped lesson was rated according to the items on a Likert scale ranging from 0 (does not apply) to 3 (applies). A high value indicates a rather unfavorable climate for error making. In order to test for inter-rater reliability, the generalizability coefficient was calculated. The minimum generalizability coefficient for the German sample ($N=100$) was .84 and the minimum inter-rater percentage agreement 84%. (cf. Schulmeiß et al., 2005). The coders for the Swiss sample were first trained using the German sample. The generalizability coefficient between the raters of the German and the Swiss sample ($N=74$) was a minimum of .64 except for the fourth item (cf. Table 12.1), which was .54 (inter-rater percentage: 60%). The minimum generalizability coefficient for the Swiss sample was .75 and the minimum inter-rater percentage 81% ($N=64$). Thus, with one exception, video analysis data shows satisfactory inter-rater agreement results. For further analyses, we refer to the mean value of the two rated lessons recorded per class ($N=82$). Significances referred to are based on regular SPSS t test procedures (one-tailed, $\alpha=.05$). The reported effect sizes (Cohen's d) were calculated with G*Power 3 (Faul, Erdfelder, Lang, & Buchner, 2007).

Perceiving a Culture of Mistake Making: Student Questionnaire

Seidel, Meyer and Dalehefte developed the student questionnaire "Perceived mistake culture" for the IPN Video Study (Rimmele et al., 2005). It refers to the general atmosphere in the class and student perceptions of teacher behavior relevant to mistake making. Table 12.2 gives an overview of the items.

The students rated items on a Likert scale ranging from 0 (= I do not agree) to 3 (= I agree). Some items were recoded so that a high value indicates a positive student perception. The scale characteristics are published in Rimmele et al. (2005). Both scales show a Cronbachs α of .57 which indicates that they should be optimized for further use. This is also a problem according to other existing scales, i.e. the L-UFS (Spychiger, Oser, Mahler, & Hascher, 1998) has been criticized because of the low variance due to the response tendencies of the students (Wuttke, Seifried, &

Table 12.2 Questionnaire items "Perceived mistake culture" (student ratings; Rimmele et al., 2005)

Perceived mistake culture – classroom	Perceived mistake culture – teacher
During the past two lessons…	
…It was embarrassing to ask questions (recoded)	…The teacher was responsive to our questions
…It was bad to say something incorrect (recoded)	…The students' contributions were intently observed by the teacher
…It was okay to make a mistake	…It was awkward to be asked to do something by the teacher (recoded)
…Only the good students participated (recoded)	…A lot of times I thought: hopefully I will not be called upon now (recoded)

Mindnich, 2008). We therefore refer to the two scales on an item level, since we conjecture a descriptive value of student ratings in the area of perceived mistake culture. Significances referred to are based on regular t test (one-tailed, $\alpha = 0{,}05$) procedures for two independent groups. The effect sizes were calculated with G*Power 3 (Faul et al., 2007).

Results

The following results show the findings of (1) the video analysis and (2) the student questionnaire. These two instruments mirror two different perspectives: the one of external observers and the students' internal view of the conditions necessary in order for them to learn from errors.

The Observers' Perspective

The results of the observed conditions of the learning climate show that, in general, the conditions in the classrooms were rated quite positively. The items could be rated from 0 (does not apply) to 3 (applies). A high value indicates quite a negative classroom climate. The maximum mean value across all items is 1.15 which shows that the indicators in general were rated rather low for both countries.

A negative classroom climate (negative error response climate or a tense atmosphere in the class) was hardly observed at all, either in the German or in the Swiss sample. Nevertheless, at first glance, Fig. 12.2 shows some unexpected results related to the more individual components of the classroom climate which were expected to indicate a negative classroom climate. It shows that Swiss students are more likely to try to appear competent [$M_{CH} = .85$; $SD_{CH} = .31$ vs. $M_G = .18$; $SD_G = .32$ ($t_{80} = -9.388$; $p = .000$; $d = 2.13$)] and to be more anxious [$M_{CH} = .81$; $SD_{CH} = .45$ vs. $M_G = .58$; $SD_G = .44$ ($t_{80} = -2.329$; $p = .011$; $d = .52$)]. In tendency (but not significantly), German rather than Swiss students show defensive behavior to avoid humiliation

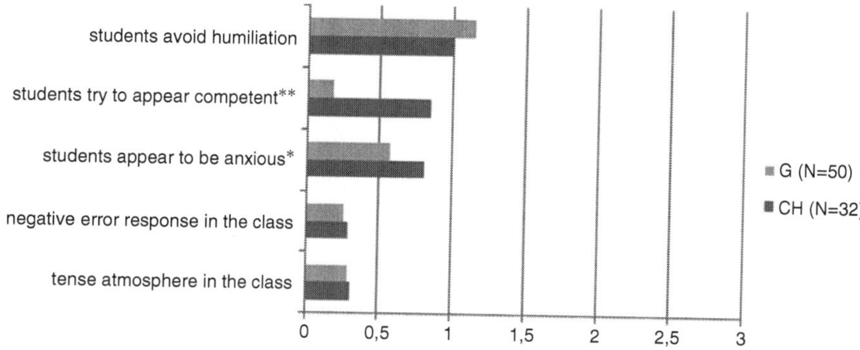

Fig. 12.2 Mean video ratings of classroom climate for mistakes; *G* Germany, *CH* Switzerland; $^{*}p<.05$, $^{**}p<.01$

($M_{CH}=1.00$; $SD_{CH}=.45$ vs. $M_G=1.15$; $SD_G=.49$). The mean values for "negative error response in the class" ($M_{CH}=.29$; $SD_{CH}=.34$ vs. $M_G=.27$; $SD_G=.31$) and "tense atmosphere in the class" ($M_{CH}=.31$; $SD_{CH}=.40$ vs. $M_G=.30$; $SD_G=.43$) are almost identical for both samples. This statement throws light on further questions which have to be investigated more intensively. The observers were additionally asked to give their subjective impression of single lessons. In positively rated lessons, they sum up that humor and a lively discussion in lessons are key characteristics that seem to be very important aspects in establishing a pleasant climate. The characteristics of the most positively rated lessons are, for instance, that the teacher often commends his/her students and animates them to play an active role in the lesson; and that the teacher supports his/her students, and lets them speak out and formulate their solutions themselves. One core problem in the negatively rated lessons seems to be connected to communication problems and a low amount of student participation.

The Students' Perspective

Our second question concerns how students perceive and rate their opportunities to learn from errors and the extent to which they report experiencing different conditions in the two countries. We distinguish between the two aspects "class" and "teacher". Figure 12.3 presents descriptive item data from the students' questionnaire "Perceived mistake culture in the class". Three of the items were recoded so that a high mean value indicates a positive classroom climate.

If we take a look at what students report in the questionnaire, we find that Swiss students compared to German students find it less embarrassing to ask questions [$M_{CH}=2.67$; $SD_{CH}=.70$ vs. $M_G=2.59$; $SD_G=.76$ ($t_{1278,26}=-2.189$; $p=.015$; $d=.11$)] and that they do not find it bad to say something incorrect in the class [$M_{CH}=2.64$; $SD_{CH}=.75$ vs. $M_G=2.47$; $SD_G=.88$ ($t_{1373,77}=-4.080$; $p=.000$; $d=.21$)]. They report that it was okay to make a mistake [$M_{CH}=2.37$; $SD_{CH}=.94$ vs. $M_G=2.17$; $SD_G=.98$

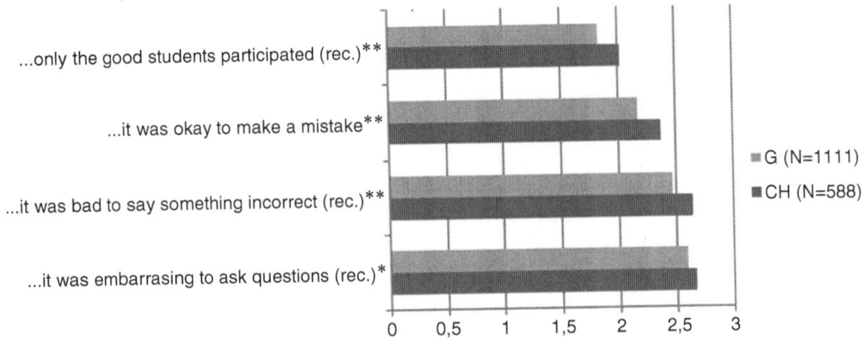

Fig. 12.3 Students ratings of the perceived mistake culture in the class (mean values); *G* Germany, *CH* Switzerland; $^{*}p<.05$, $^{**}p<.01$

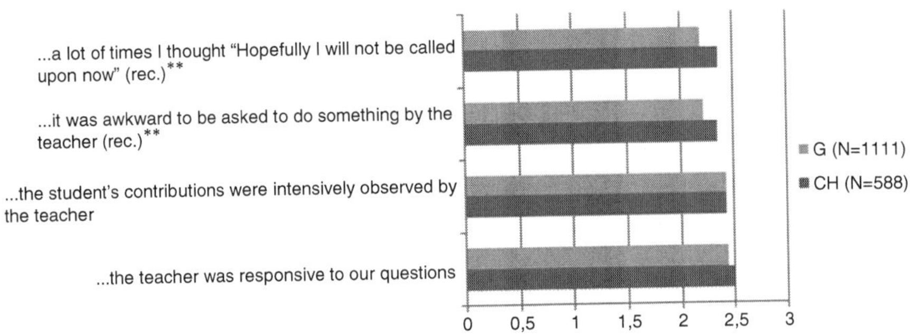

Fig. 12.4 Student ratings of the "Perceived mistake culture – Teacher" (mean values); *G* Germany, *CH* Switzerland; $^{*}p<.05$, $^{**}p<.01$

($t_{1688}=-4.107$; $p=.000$; $d=.21$)] and that not only the good students participated during the two videotaped lessons [$M_{CH}=2.02$; $SD_{CH}=.99$ vs. $M_G=1.83$; $SD_G=1.00$ ($t_{1669}=-3.65$; $p=.000$, $d=.19$)]. Thus, given the students' perception of the mistake culture in class, we find a more positive view in Swiss lessons than in the video ratings of the external observers.

Not only the climate in the class but also the teacher plays an important role in the perception of a culture which allows for errors and mistakes. This was analyzed to identify how far teachers establish positive learning conditions towards errors. Our assumptions that Swiss students perceive the conditions provided by the teacher more positively than German students are confirmed. Also, with regard to students' perception of how teachers' behavior establishes a climate for error making, there seems to be a better atmosphere in the Swiss lessons. Figure 12.4 shows the data from the students' questionnaire "Perceived mistake culture – Teacher". Some of the items were recoded so that a high value indicates a positive classroom climate.

The students' answers in the questionnaire "Perceived mistake culture – Teacher" show that Swiss students rather than German students report having a higher composure due to being asked something by the teacher [$M_{CH}=2.35$; $SD_{CH}=.91$ vs. $M_G=2.22$; $SD_G=.96$; ($t_{1694}=-2.792$; $p=.005$; $d=.14$)] and to be called upon [$M_{CH}=2.35$; $SD_{CH}=.91$ vs. $M_G=2.22$; $SD_G=.96$; ($t_{1317,31}=-3.405$; $p=.001$, $d=.17$)]. The items "…the students' contributions were intently acknowledged by the teacher" ($M_{CH}=2.43$; $SD_{CH}=.79$ vs. $M_G=2.43$; $SD_G=.78$) and "the teacher was responsive to our questions" ($M_{CH}=2.51$; $SD_{CH}=.78$ vs. $M_G=2.44$; $SD_G=.78$) show no significant differences in the two samples.

According to the students' ratings presented, we proceed on the assumption that Swiss students experience better conditions for experiencing and learning from mistakes. We have to take into consideration though that the reported effects are rather small.

Discussion

Generally, the classroom climate in both countries seems to be quite comfortable from an observer's perspective. At first glance, the findings indicate that the Swiss students are more anxious and more concerned about how they behave in front of the class. This was an unexpected result, but could be interpreted in the way that Swiss students rather take the risk and actively engage in classroom discourse, whereas the German students tend to behave more defensively in order to avoid humiliation. However, the question of whether this interpretation is correct remains open and has yet to be focused on. Interviews with students could be helpful here to identify cultural specific aspects which perhaps can explain students' behavior. Further case studies could also be helpful to identify relevant aspects. So far, the observations point to some quality indicators (humor, relaxed atmosphere) as well as to problems (communication) in the lessons.

The data from the students' questionnaire show that the Swiss students in general perceive a learning supportive culture towards errors, and this more strongly than their German colleagues. This holds true for both the classroom and the teacher aspects. Further analyses are necessary to find out what it really is that makes the culture for errors and mistakes in Swiss classrooms better. In our case, video analyses were a helpful tool to get a first impression about blending learning and achievement situation. However, to get a more complete understanding of the role of errors and mistakes, a more differentiated category system is needed.

Videos make the repeated observation of different situations in instruction possible. In addition, these observations can be combined with each other or with other data-collecting instruments, which might offer a more holistic view of errors and mistake making in instruction. However, instructional elements are woven constructs. Thus, learning conditions which incorporate a culture towards errors and mistakes should be connected to other conditions of instruction. A combination of different observational systems could be a fruitful way to learn more about errors in instruction, though to date little is known about the role that cumulative, interactive, compensatory, and contextual effects play in learning outcomes (Weinert, Schrader, & Helmke, 1989).

A question-developing instruction style can be conducted in different qualities (Seidel, 2011). Nevertheless, in Germany, the question-developing instruction style that has manifested itself over the years seems to provide less space for errors (BLK, 1997). The fact that errors hardly occur in German instruction also makes it necessary to think about possible reasons for this. If learning from errors is to be possible, then errors must occur. This means, at least from a German perspective, that instructional procedures have to be reconsidered. This reconsideration must aim at at least two levels of instruction. On a surface level, student-centered activities have to be incorporated into instruction in order to enhance the possibilities to make and experience errors. But, student activities are certainly not enough. Teachers and students have to change their attitudes towards errors and to detect the learning potential of making errors. Working with teachers and mentors has turned out to be a fruitful approach in Switzerland to establishing good climatic conditions for learning from errors (Spychiger, 2003). First attempts to foster learning from errors in German school development programs were conducted within SINUS (BLK, 1997; Stadler, 2009). Within this study, strategies to thematize and to make errors visible were introduced in order to force strategies to learn from them (Stadler, 2009).

So far, little is known about how teachers manage to establish instructional situations which allow for errors. Apart from a behaviorist-oriented comprehension of handling errors, there are additional – perhaps more practical, situational, and emotional – reasons for neglecting errors as a chance for learning. Teachers often experience mistakes as interruptions to the lesson flow rather than as learning opportunities (BLK, 1997; Oser et al., 1999). It is more comfortable to conduct recipe-like instruction than to cope with errors which may cause a new and unknown direction in the course of the lesson. These might be reasons to abandon errors. A further reason might be an uncertainty about how to handle errors in instruction. If students are supposed to learn from errors, it implies that a teacher needs some "diagnostic" competency towards the individuals in the class. In addition, the instructional situation is a hierarchical situation with a downgrade between teacher and student expertise, which may have a daunting effect. This public and hierarchic constellation might also play a role in why errors hardly occur in instruction. Teachers may avoid picking up on errors in order to avoid humiliating situations or situations which may question their authority. In enforcing instruction which includes learning from errors, it might be helpful to train teachers to acquire a certain security in how to identify and "pick up on" errors in an appropriate way (Spychiger, 2003). Also, in this case, video recordings can be useful to illustrate examples of instructional problem situations and to foster discussions among teachers about possible fruitful solutions.

In cultures in which error making plays a marginal role in instruction, a methodological problem also arises. How can errors be investigated if they do not occur? In this case, a look at how errors are handled in other cultures can be worthwhile and might generate hypotheses and ideas about how errors can be treated and turned into something fruitful for learning processes. Teaching patterns mirror different belief systems about teaching and learning among professionals in a culture (Stigler & Hiebert, 1999). A look at the instructional routines in other countries can offer ideas for practical use as well as for intervention studies. Nevertheless, the question of the extent to which teachers can learn to elaborate on and to establish a good learning climate from observing videos has not yet been clarified. Two projects which followed in the wake of the IPN Video Study in physics instruction, LUV and Observe, go into further detail about this (Seidel et al., 2009).

National patterns of instruction – whether good or bad – are continued as they are forwarded from one generation to the next. This "cultural nature of teaching" might be a very strong source for the convergence of instruction within countries (Bogard Givvin, Hiebert, Jacobs, Hollingsworth, & Gallimore, 2005). To change a culturally manifested instructional script is a difficult task to undertake. A first step towards establishing an instructional climate which supports error making and allows for mistakes might be to integrate instructional elements from other cultures which seem to have a more positive view of errors and treat errors in a more fruitful way.

Acknowledgements The authors of the chapter wish to express their gratitude to Peter Labudde, Birte Knierim and Bernhard Gerber from the Swiss project "Teaching and Learning cultures in physics instruction" and the co-researchers of the IPN-Video Study Maja Brückmann, Reinders Duit, Constanze Herweg, Mareike Kobarg, Lena Meyer, Rolf Rimmele, Ilka Schulmeiß, Katharina Schwindt, Maike Tesch, Marieke Pilz, Claudia Overath and other members of the staff for their support. The German project "Teaching and learning processes in physics instruction – a video study" was funded by the German Research Foundation (DFG) within the framework of the BIQUA Priority Program on the quality of schooling, and the Swiss project "Teaching and learning cultures in physics instruction– a video study" by the Swiss National Science Foundation (SNF).

References

Beaton, A., Martin, M., Mullis, I. V., Gonzalez, E., Smith, T. A., & Kelly, D. (1996). *Science achievement in the middle school years: IEA's third international mathematics and science study (TIMSS)*. Chestnut Hill, MA: Boston College.

BLK. (1997). *Gutachten zur Vorbereitung des Programms "Steigerung der Effizienz des mathematisch-naturwissenschaftlichen Unterrichts"*. Bonn, Germany: Bund-Länder-Kommission für Bildungsplanung und Forschungsförderung.

Bogard Givvin, K., Hiebert, J., Jacobs, J., Hollingsworth, H., & Gallimore, R. (2005). Are there national patterns of teaching? Evidence from the TIMSS 1999 video study. *Comparative Education Review, 49*, 311–343.

Dalehefte, I. M., Rimmele, R., Prenzel, M., Seidel, T., Labudde, P., & Herweg, C. (2009). Observing instruction "next-door". A video study about science teaching and learning in Germany and Switzerland. In T. Janík & T. Seidel (Eds.), *The power of video studies in investigating teaching and learning in the classroom* (pp. 83–102). Münster, Germany: Waxmann.

Deci, E., & Ryan, R. M. (1991). A motivational approach to self: Integration in personality. In R. Dienstbier (Ed.), *Nebraska symposium on motivation. Perspectives on motivation* (pp. S. 237–S. 288). Lincoln, NE: University of Nebraska Press.

Faul, F., Erdfelder, E., Lang, A.-G., & Büchner, A. (2007). G*Power 3: A flexible statistical power analysis program for the social, behavioral, and biomedical sciences. *Behavior Research Methods, 39*, 175–191.

Hascher, T. (2005). Emotionen im Schulalltag: Wirkungen und Regulationsformen [Emotions in everyday school-life: Effects and regulation forms]. *Zeitschrift für Pädagogik, 51*, 610–625.

Heinze, A. (2004). Umgang mit Fehlern im Geometrieunterricht der Sekundarstufe I – Methode und Ergebnisse einer Videostudie. *Journal für Mathematikdidaktik, 25*, 221–245.

Heinze, A. (2006). Umgang mit Fehlern im Mathematikunterricht – Empirische Ergebnisse zur Schülerwahrnehmung. In *Beiträge zum Mathematikunterricht* (pp. 251–254). Hildesheim, Germany: Franzbecker.

Klieme, E., & Reusser, K. (2003). Unterrichtsqualität und mathematisches Verständnis im internationalen Vergleich – Ein Forschungsprojekt und erste Schritte zur Realisierung [An international comparative study of instructional quality and the first steps in its realisation]. *Unterrichtswissenschaft, 31*, 194–205.

Labudde, P. (1999). Reaktionen auf TIMSS in der Schweiz. *Unterricht Physik, 10*, 46–48.

Labudde, P. (2002). *Lehr-Lern-Kultur im Physikunterricht: eine Videostudie* [Teaching and learning culture in physics instruction: A video study]. SNF Project Proposal. Bern, Switzerland: University of Bern/CH.

Labudde, P. (2003). Fächer übergreifender Unterricht in und mit Physik: eine zuwenig genutzte Chance. *Physik und Didaktik in Schule und Hochschule, 1*(2), 48–66.

Laukenmann, M., & von Rhöneck, C. (2003). The influence of emotional factors on learning in physics instruction. In P. Mayring & C. von Rhöneck (Eds.), *Learning emotions. The influence of affective factors on classroom learning* (pp. 67–80). Frankfurt am Main, Germany: Lang.

Meyer, L., Seidel, T., & Prenzel, M. (2006). Wenn Lernsituationen zu Leistungssituationen werden: Untersuchung zur Fehlerkultur in einer Videostudie. *Schweizerische Zeitschrift für Bildungswissenschaften, 28*, 21–41.

OECD. (2000). *Knowledge and skills for life. First results from the OECD Programme for International Student Assessment (PISA)*. Paris: OECD Publications.

OECD. (2004). *Learning for tomorrow's world – First results from PISA 2003*. Paris: OECD Publications.

Oser, F. (2007). Aus Fehlern lernen [Learning from errors]. In M. Göhlich, C. Wulf, & J. Zirfas (Eds.), *Pädagogische Theorien des Lernens* [Pedagogical theories of learning] (pp. 203–212). Weinheim, Germany: Beltz.

Oser, F., Hascher, T., & Spychiger, M. (1999). Lernen aus Fehlern. Zur Psychologie des "negativen" Wissens. In W. Althof (Ed.), *Fehlerwelten. Vom Fehlermachen und Lernen aus Fehlern* (pp. 11–41). Fribourg, Switzerland: Leske + Budrich.

Oser, F., & Spychiger, M. (2005). *Lernen ist schmerzhaft. Zur Theorie des Negativen Wissens und zur Praxis der Fehlerkultur*. Weinheim, Germany: Beltz.

Ostermeier, C., Prenzel, M., & Duit, R. (2010). Improving science and mathematics instruction – The SINUS project as an example for reform as teacher development. *International Journal of Science Education, 32*, 303–327.

Pekrun, R. (1992). Kognition und Emotion in Studienbezogenen Lern- und Leistungssituationen: Explorative Analysen. *Unterrichtswissenschaft, 20*, 308–324.

Prenzel, M., Euler, M., Duit, R., & Lehrke, M. (1999). Lehr-Lern-Prozesse im Physikunterricht: Eine Videostudie *Teaching and learning processes in physics instruction: A video study* DFG Project Proposal. Kiel, Germany: IPN.

Rimmele, R., Seidel, T., Knierim, B., Kobarg, M., Dalehefte, I. M., Schwindt, K., et al. (2005). Scale documentation – Student questionnaire. In T. Seidel, M. Prenzel, & M. Kobarg (Eds.), *How to run a video study* (Technical report of the IPN Video Study) (pp. 224–281). Münster, Germany: Waxmann.

Santagata, R. (2004). "Are you joking or are you sleeping". Cultural beliefs and practices in Italian and U.S. teachers' mistake-handling strategies. *Linguistics and Education, 15*, 141–164.

Santagata, R. (2005). Practice and beliefs in mistake-handling activities: A video study of Italian and US mathematics lessons. *Teaching and Teacher Education, 21*, 491–508.

Schulmeiß, I. (2004). *Vermischung von Lern- und Leistungssituationen und ihre Bedeutung für die Qualität der Lernmotivation – eine Videostudie im Physikunterricht*. Unpublished diploma thesis, IPN/Institut für Psychologie, Kiel.

Schulmeiß, I., Seidel, T., & Meyer, L. (2005). Coding manual – Blending of learning and achievement situations. In T. Seidel, M. Prenzel, & M. Kobarg (Eds.), *How to run a video study* (Technical report of the IPN Video Study) (pp. 165–171). Münster, Germany: Waxmann.

Seidel, T. (2011). Lehrerhandeln im Unterricht. In E. Terhart, H. Bennewitz, & M. Rothland (Eds.), *Handbuch der Forschung zum Lehrerberuf* (pp. 605–629). Münster, Germany: Waxmann.

Seidel, T., Dalehefte, I. M., Meyer, L. (2005). Standardized guidelines – How to collect videotapes. In T. Seidel, M. Prenzel, & M. Kobarg (Eds.), *How to run a video study* (Technical report of the IPN Video Study) (pp. 29–53). Münster, Germany: Waxmann.

Seidel, T., & Prenzel, M. (2003). Mit Fehlern umgehen – Zum Lernen motivieren. *Praxis der Naturwissenschaften – Physik in der Schule, 52*, 30–34.

Seidel, T., Prenzel, M., Rimmele, R., Herweg, C., Kobarg, M., Schwindt, K., et al. (2007). Science teaching and learning in German physics classrooms. Findings from the IPN Video Study. In M. Prenzel (Ed.), *Studies on the educational quality of schools* (pp. 79–99). Münster, Germany: Waxmann.

Seidel, T., Prenzel, M., Schwindt, K., Stürmer, K., Blomberg, G., & Kobarg, M. (2009). LUV and observe: Two projects using video to diagnose teachers' competence. In T. Janík & T. Seidel (Eds.), *The power of video studies in investigating teaching and learning in the classroom* (pp. 243–258). Münster, Germany: Waxmann.

Spychiger, M., Oser, F., Mahler, F., & Hascher, T. (1998). Fehlerkultur aus der Sicht von Schülerinnen und Schülern. Der Fehlerfragebogen S-UFS: Entwicklung und erste Ergebnisse. Schriftenreihe zum Projekt "Lernen Menschen aus Fehlern?", Nr. 4. Departement Erziehungswissenschaften der Universität Freiburg (CH).

Spychiger, M. (2003). Fehler als Fenster auf den Lernprozess. Zur Entwicklung einer Fehlerkultur in der Praxisausbildung. *Journal für Lehrerinnen- und Lehrerbildung, 3*, 31–38.

Spychiger, M., Oser, F., Hascher, T., & Mahler, F. (1999). Entwicklung einer Fehlerkultur in der Schule. In W. Althof (Ed.), *Fehlerwelten* (pp. 43–69). Bonn, Germany: Leske + Budrich.

Stadler, M. (2009). Aus Fehlern lernen. In M. Prenzel, A. Friedrichs, & M. Stadler (Eds.), *Von SINUS lernen – Wie Unterrichtsentwicklung gelingt* (pp. 27–30). Seelze-Velber, Germany: Kallmeyer Klett Verlag.

Stigler, J. W., Gonzales, P., Kawanaka, T., Knoll, S., & Serrano, A. (1999). *The TIMSS videotape classroom study: Methods and findings from an exploratory research project on eight-grade mathematics instruction in Germany, Japan and the United States*. Washington, DC: National Center for Educational Statistics.

Stigler, J., & Hiebert, J. (1999). *The teaching gap: Best ideas from the world's teachers for improving education in the classroom*. New York: Free Press.

Weinert, F., Schrader, F.-W., & Helmke, A. (1989). Quality of instruction and achievement outcomes. *International Journal of Educational Research, 13*, 895–914.

Wuttke, E., Seifried, J., & Mindnich, A. (2008). Umgang mit Fehlern und Ungewissheit im Unterricht – Entwicklung eines Beobachtungsinstruments und erste empirische Befunde. In M. Gläser-Zikuda & J. Seifried (Eds.), *Lehrerexpertise. Analyse und Bedeutung unterrichtlichen Handelns* (pp. 91–111). Münster, Germany: Waxmann.

Chapter 13
Learning from Errors: The Role of After-Event Reviews

Shmuel Ellis

After-Event-Reviews: Definition and Goals

An after-event review (AER) is a learning from experience procedure that gives learners an opportunity to systematically analyze the various actions that they selected to perform a particular task, to determine which of them was wrong or not necessary, which should be corrected, and which should be reinforced. In a typical AER, learners with the help of a facilitator (instructor) try to understand the reasons for the outcome of their actions (task performance). The facilitator brings learners to think about the event or task and systematically reflect on questions such as: What was supposed to happen and what actually happened and why, what worked, what did not and why, and what should be done differently next time. In sum, AERs enable individuals and groups to reflect on their performance and to understand why interim objectives were not accomplished, to know what lessons can be drawn from their past experience, and to evaluate how these lessons can be quickly internalized to improve performance.

The after-event review (AER) is an organizational learning mechanism that has been traditionally discussed under different names (such as incident reviews, problem investigation, post-project reviews) in the organizational learning literature (Busby, 1999; Carroll, 1995; Carroll, Rudolph, & Hatakenaka, 2003; Darling & Parry, 2001; Gulliver, 1987; Ron, Lipshitz, & Popper, 2006). After-event reviews are also called "after-action reviews (AARs)" by practitioners, especially in the military. In the present chapter, I deliberately use the term AER because I think that AER and AAR can have different meanings. First, reviews do not have to be performed only at the end of target activities. Rather, they can be performed

S. Ellis, Ph.D. (✉)
Faculty of Management, The Leon Recanati Graduate School of Business Administration, Tel Aviv University, Tel Aviv, Israel
e-mail: sellis@post.tau.ac.il

J. Bauer and C. Harteis (eds.), *Human Fallibility: The Ambiguity of Errors for Work and Learning*, Professional and Practice-based Learning 6,
DOI 10.1007/978-90-481-3941-5_13,

after each identifiable event in organizational life, thus becoming a live learning process in which lessons can be learned and applied. Second, whereas AAR means focusing on single actions, AER means examining sets of inter-related actions aiming to respond to an external event, to achieve a goal or to complete a particular task. In other words, whereas the AER's unit of analysis is an event or project, the unit of analysis of the AAR should be one or more actions that are or are not part of an overall event. For example, a navigation task is comprised of a sequence of actions that are supposed to bring navigators to their desired target points. An AER will address the question of why the overall mission was not accomplished or, in operational terms, why the navigators failed to complete all their assignments. An AAR, in contrast, will relate to the analysis of particular actions or decisions that ultimately led to a deficient deviation from the expected outcome (Frese & Zapf, 1994; Senders & Moray, 1991). It should be noted that errors (failed actions) do not necessarily lead to task or event failure. One may err in relatively many actions but still succeed in accomplishing the mission. And vice versa – one may make only a few errors, but fail in the overall task or event. Nevertheless, in the present chapter, it is assumed that more (and more serious) errors are made in failed events and fewer (and no fatal) errors are made in successful events.

The military is known as the main user of after-event reviews, which are usually carried out after operations or training activities with small or large groups comprised of all ranks, from low-ranking soldiers to commanders, to gather and analyze information that might contribute to future performance improvement. As noted in military documents , the AER (or AAR in military jargon) is perhaps one of the ultimate performance improvement tools, because it encourages all stakeholders to share and learn for the sake of continuous improvement. Baird and his associates (Baird, Henderson, & Watts, 1997; Baird, Holland, & Deacon, 1999) studied the US Army Center for Lessons Learned (CALL) and summarized the essence of an effective review: it focuses on a few critical issues; it is done immediately after the action; it includes all those who took part in the action; it follows a structural process; and leads back to actions as soon as possible. Ron et al. (2006), in an in-depth analysis of post-flight reviews in a fighter aircraft squadron of the Israeli Air Force, demonstrated not only the effectiveness of after-event reviews as a learning and training mechanism per se (learning from failures, learning from others) but also highlighted their other functions such as social control (disciplining and capability fixing, socialization, communicating commanders' intent), and psychological response (resilience building, bonding recognition and reward, social comparison and involvement).

In spite of its extensive use in the military as well as service or industrial organizations, no systematic research has been done to demonstrate if and why AERs are effective tools for learning. The aforementioned articles of Ron et al. (2006), Carroll (1995), Carroll et al. (2003), and Busby (1999) are more descriptive studies that do not provide causal evidence pertaining to the impact of AER on performance improvement in organizations. Furthermore, since these studies were more oriented toward understanding the importance of AERs as organizational learning mechanisms, they did not provide in-depth analysis of the cognitive and motivational effects of AERs on performance improvement at the individual level. This is the gap that the present chapter aims to bridge.

During the last 5 years, several studies have shown the positive effect of the AER on individual learning from experience and have demonstrated its potential contribution to organizational learning (Anseel, Lievens, & Schollaert, 2009; Ellis & Davidi, 2005; Ellis, Ganzach, Castle, & Sekely, 2010; Ellis, Mendel, & Aloni-Zohar, 2009; Ellis, Mendel, & Nir, 2006). In the present chapter, I will try to summarize and integrate the theory and findings pertaining to how AERs contribute to learning from errors. I will first discuss the cognitive aspects of their contribution to learning from experience and then highlight the importance of motivational factors in learning from experience through AERs.

How Do AERs Help to Promote Learning from Experience?

Cognitive Aspects

Anderson, Krull, and Weiner (1996) suggested a four-stage model of the process of explaining events. In the first stage, learners must notice the event that has the characteristics that attract their attention. Unnoticeable errors or failures will not attract attention and will not stimulate the explanation process (Postman & Brown, 1952). In the second stage, individuals must interpret the experienced event in terms of success or failure. The higher the ambiguity of the event's data, the more open it is to the subjective interpretation of the learner (Trope & Liberman, 1996).

In the third stage, problem formulation, learners try to find the best explanation for the experienced event. This process of chaining backward from the to-be-explained event to its causes relies on perceptual principles of causal attribution such as temporal order, temporal and spatial continuity, and similarity (Hilton, Mathes, & Trabasso, 1992; Kelley, 1973).

Problem resolution is the fourth stage, in which learners test their hypothesized explanatory model against available evidence in order to determine their confidence in it (Anderson et al., 1996; Kruglanski, 1989). It should be noted that the selected causal model is always a tentative explanation of the event. When learners are not fully satisfied with their explanatory model, or when new evidence emerges, they can reformulate the problem and test it again. The intensity and ending of the process are regulated by motivational factors (Kruglanski, 1989).

Modern cognitive social psychologists use various terms like *schemata*, *scripts*, *cognitive maps*, or *mental models* to describe the explanatory models. All these terms reflect various kinds of knowledge structures. Social cognitive research has demonstrated the influence that knowledge structures have on the way people process information and on the way they interact with their social and physical environment (see Fiske & Taylor, 1991). Knowledge structures formulate the way that people perceive, comprehend, and remember new information. These knowledge structures provide perspectives that help individuals define their world and are used as guides for action (Day, Arthur, & Gettman, 2001).

If knowledge structures guide our responses to various social stimuli, then one can define *learning* from experience as the process of formulating and updating knowledge structures. That is, learning from experience is the process of noticing and incorporating new variables that are relevant to explaining and predicting various social phenomena or, in other words, the process of hypothesis generation and validation (Ellis & Davidi, 2005). In terms of experience-based learning, learning is the process of drawing lessons from experience via continuous improvement of one's knowledge structures. Errors exemplify deviations from the right solution of a problem, requiring a change in one's mental model that is supposed to lead to a solution. Errors are usually detected by comparing actual with expected outcomes (Miller et al., 1960). Unexpected outcomes, therefore, might evoke systematic thinking.

Within this theoretical framework, the role of AERs can be described as intensifying cognitive elaboration of experiential data, under the assumption that this process leads to the right and appropriate cognitive structures that will ultimately promote the necessary behavioral changes. Furthermore, one may argue that AERs are a kind of a guided self-reflection technique that helps learners to increase their awareness of their personal experiences and therefore their ability to learn from them (Anseel et al., 2009; Gray, 2007). In terms of dual-process models (e.g., Chaiken & Trope, 1999; Evans, 2008), the role of AERs is to switch the learners' mode of information processing from automatic to conscious. In the automatic mode, people run well-learned scripts and respond to external cues only in terms of their well-established existing mental models. In contrast, in the conscious mode, their cognitive activity is characterized by more awareness, attention, information gathering, and reflection (Chanowitz & Langer, 1980; Louis & Sutton, 1991).

AERs affect individuals' information elaboration processes and the changes in their mental models in four ways: by intensifying self-explanation, by advancing data verification, by providing process feedback, and by enhancing self-efficacy. In what follows, I will elaborate in more depth on these four functions of AERs.

Intensifying Self-explanations

Richness of mental models is positively correlated with successful performance (Carley, 1997; Evans, 1988). During AERs individuals are asked to analyze their actions in a particular event and to suggest explanations for their relative success or failure in general and for specific erroneous actions in particular. Previous studies in which individuals were asked to generate explanations for their actions (Chi, de Leeuw, Chiu, & Lavancher, 1994) succeeded in promoting the skill acquisition of these individuals. Others, such as Nathan, Mertz, and Ryan (1994), found the number of self-explanations to be correlated with problem-solving successes in various content domains. As an *active process* of gathering, analyzing, and integrating data, self-explanation has been found not only to direct learners to reflect on their past behavior but also to facilitate the construction of "if-then" rules that help to improve subsequent performance, and encourage the integration of newly learned materials with existing knowledge (Chi et al., 1994).

Ellis and Davidi (2005) demonstrated the important relationships between AERs, mental models, and performance in an experimental opportunity they created for soldiers from two companies of the Israel Defense Forces (IDF), taking a ground navigation course to reflect on failed and successful navigation exercises. One of the companies was supposed to analyze failed events while the other was expected to reflect on successful events. Since the army rejected the possibility of having experimental conditions of "AER focused only on success" or "no AER", one group learned by drawing lessons from failed navigations whereas the second group learned from failed as well as from successful navigations. Thus, soldiers in one company were not encouraged to analyze successful experiences during the event reviews conducted after each navigation exercise, whereas soldiers of the second company were debriefed systematically on successful as well as on failed experiences.

The results showed a significant learning effect across experimental conditions. Despite the fact that the level of difficulty of the navigation assignments increased steadily from day to day, subjects' performance improved across trials. Second, it was found that the learners' performance improvement was even greater in the learning from the failed and successful navigation group. In order to understand the relationships between learning from experience by AERs and the kind of self-explanations, a sample of soldiers went through in-depth interviews in which they were asked to describe one of their failed and one of their successful navigation events in as much detail as possible, and to list all the reasons for their failure or success. These were conducted three times during the navigation training week: before the first AER, after the AER in the middle of the training week, and after the last AER. Ellis and Davidi (2005) described the learners' mental models of their successes and failures as causal maps (see Fig. 13.1).

The nodes in these maps represent causes or outcomes that were enacted by learners with respect to the failed or successful navigation exercise or with respect to a particular action in this event. The arrows reflect the soldiers' beliefs about the causal relationships among a particular group of causes and outcomes. A particular cause may have a direct or indirect causal link with other causes and outcomes. The following examples reflect direct effects: "I selected the wrong route" *because* "I did not have enough time to learn the navigation route yesterday" (i.e., "learning time"→"wrong action"), "I wasted valuable time" *because* "before I had gone one mile I took the wrong direction" (i.e., "wrong action"→"time loss"). Adding a third direct effect exemplifies the creation of an indirect effect: "I didn't reach all the target points" *because* "I wasted valuable time" (i.e., "time loss"→"failed event"), therefore "wrong action"→"time loss"→"failed event". This is an indirect or a mediated effect.

It was found that AERs had a significant impact on learners' mental models. They increased mental model richness in terms of both number of nodes and number of ties. More specifically, the number of nodes and ties was greater after each

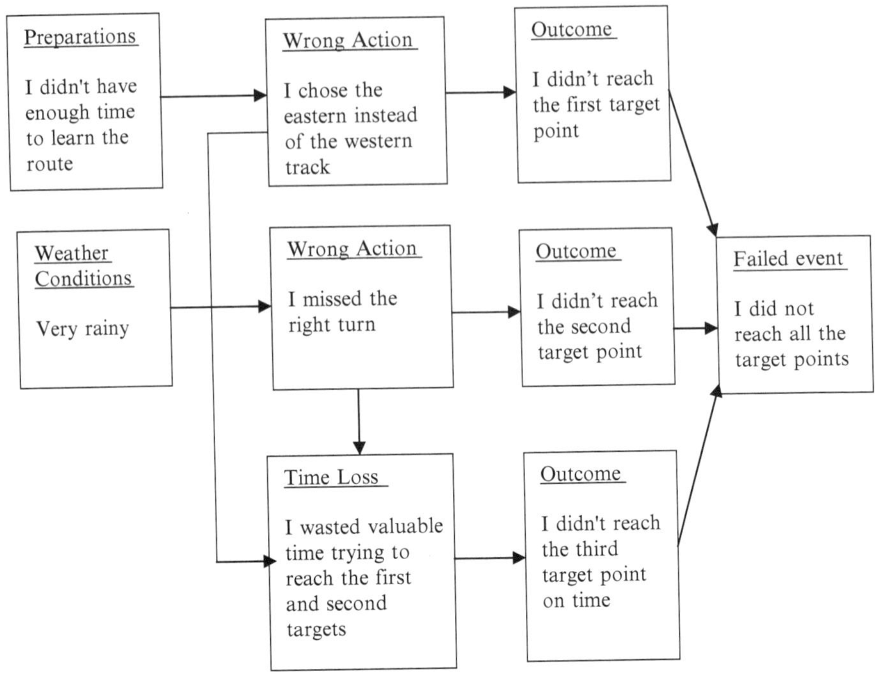

Fig. 13.1 Cognitive cause map

additional AER. Furthermore, even the structure of the mental models became increasingly complex in terms of the number of indirect as opposed to direct cause-effect relationships. The complexity of the cause maps reflect, on the one hand, learners' deep understanding of the causal structure of the events' outcomes, and on the other hand, it exemplifies the willingness of the learners to get closer to the root cause of the outcomes in order to reach this level of understanding.

Interestingly, Ellis and Davidi (2005) found that when individuals are required to explain failures or failed actions (as opposed to successful events or actions), they generate multiple explanations, most of which are contextual or ad hoc explanations such as "bad weather conditions" as opposed to essential causes (such as "route planning" or "prior learning") that do not help to improve learning and performance. However, the AERs act to change the proportion between the essential/contextual explanations. In other words, AERs contribute to the improvement of learners' mental models and thus to improving the odds of the right behavioral change.

Data Verification and Interpretation

Insofar as learning from past events is open to errors and biases, the lessons drawn may also turn out to be irrelevant, invalid, or even misleading. Several cognitive biases have been found to be potential sources of danger to optimal learning. One such bias is the confirmation bias (Feldman, 1989), that is, the tendency of individuals to overlook information that is not compatible with their a priori hypotheses. The hindsight bias (Fischhoff, 1982), implying that knowledge of outcomes strongly affects how people view their past experience, poses another threat to the validity of lessons drawn from the past.

AERs can provide indirect solutions to improve the reliability of the data elaborated by learners. First of all, when AERs are conducted in groups, learners are confronted with different perceptions of the same data. It is the facilitator's role to direct learners via questions or remarks to doubt their old perceptions or to question evidence they already hold. Although there is no guarantee that learners will yield to other people's views, it can be argued that they will, at least, have to relate to them and even to re-elaborate this information before they reject it. In sum, one may say that AERs enable learners to cross-validate the information they hold before changing or correcting their mental models.

Ellis et al. (2006) conducted an experiment in which they manipulated two independent variables: type of event – AER after successful as opposed to failed event, and kind of AER – focus on positive aspects of task performance or correct actions, focus on negative aspects of task performance or erroneous actions, focus on negative as well as positive aspects, and a control group. Participants played a computer game and their performance was evaluated twice: before and after the AER. The findings exemplified the huge impact that AERs (across type) have on learning from experience.

In order to understand how AERs contribute to effective learning and ultimately to performance improvement, Ellis et al. (2006) asked the participants in their study to list all the causes for their failure or success, and then classified them into specific ("I sold the beer at the right price," "I had a large amount of money at the beginning of the game") and general causes (causes that could be generalized across situations such as "lack of information", "fear of failure").

The rationale behind this classification was that a general cause of an outcome is clearly less informative than a specific cause, and knowledge of the specific factors leading to specific actions is obviously more useful for guiding behavior in subsequent task performance. Abramson, Seligman, and Teasdale (1978), for example, found that general attributions, which do not point to a distinct feature of a person or a situation, are associated with maladaptive thoughts and depression, whereas specific attributions are associated with no depression. Mikulincer and Nizan (1988) showed that attribution of failure to global (general) causes diminished performance. Finally, recent findings from the field of organizational learning show the utility of specific knowledge: when asked to attribute the performance of their organization, most managers in key positions belonging to high-performing firms gave specific suggestions for improvement, whereas only general suggestions were given by managers in the low-performing firms (Gronhaug & Falkenberg, 1998). In learning from experience terms, updated mental models on the basis of specific causes which are probably more reliable might be better predictors of performance improvement.

Indeed, according to their expectations, Ellis et al. (2006) found that, following AERs, learners tended to attribute more specific causes to their relative achievement in task performance. Furthermore, the specific–general classification moderated the effect of AERs on performance, i.e., learners who saw internal reasons as the attributes causing their failures or successes demonstrated greater performance improvements. In other words, following the AER, learners refined their causal attributions and directed them toward more specific and accurate causes that leave less room for subjective interpretations.

Last but not least is the accountability issue. When learners expect to succeed and fail, they tend to put the blame on the task, but when they expect to fail and succeed, they take the credit for themselves (McGill, 1989). In such biased information processing, errors may be dismissed and attributed to contextual causes like isolated events (Bies, 1989). As noted above, Ellis and Davidi (2005) differentiated between essential causes and ad hoc causes of successes or failures. Whereas the essential causes relate to major issues such as learners' prior knowledge or task preparations such as "route planning", "prior experience" and "studying the route", ad hoc causes pertain to contextual issues such as "ground conditions" and "distractions" that enable learners to bypass direct and genuine coping with their failed actions. This is probably why the relative number of ad hoc causes was greater before the AER than after the AER. However, it seems that the AER acts to help the learner to confront the real causes of his or her errors and not to attribute them to non-relevant situational factors. Ron et al. (2006), in their study of after-flight reviews in the Israeli Air Force, quoted pilots as saying that the most important effect of self-debriefing is proving that they made the error and that it was their responsibility. Once they have done that, performance improvement is the next natural step. Taking responsibility is essential, then, to increasing internal attributions and ultimately for doing better the next time around.

Wong and Weiner (1981) argued that, because individuals generally have better control over their own actions than over their physical or social environment, those who behave adaptively probably give causal explanations attributing relatively more internal causes to their performance (success or failure) than external. These people take more responsibility for their actions and can face the next challenge more adequately.

Ellis et al. (2006) argued that AERs constitute an excellent opportunity for individuals not only to improve the reliability of their mental models but also to learn to take responsibility for their successes as well for their failures. Therefore, they predicted that AERs will contribute more to performance improvement when participants attribute their performance achievements to *internal as opposed to external* causes. As expected, the findings showed that performance improved from the first trial to the second trial when more internal reasons were elicited following the AER. This moderating effect clearly leads to the conclusion that causal attributions comprising mostly internal causes are essential to performing successfully. When the AER channels the learners' information search to internal causes, it probably enables them to obtain a better (and more objective) understanding of their own errors and increases their sense of control and accountability for their own behavior, which can result in higher achievement motivation (Weiner, 1985, 2000).

Providing Process Feedback

An important by-product of the AER process is feedback, defined as information with which a learner can confirm, add to, overwrite, tune, or restructure information in memory, whether that information is domain knowledge, meta-cognitive knowledge, beliefs about self and task, or cognitive tactics and strategies (Alexander, Schallert & Hare, 1991). In the present context, it is imperative to distinguish between performance outcome and task process feedback. Without outcome feedback, AERs or simple reflection are not very effective because they are not focused and goal directed (Anseel et al., 2009; Strange & Mumford, 2005). The outcome feedback has first of all a motivational value. It triggers learners to start asking the "why" questions and to find explanations for their failed or successful performance. Second, it gives them an initial sense of the performance gap they have to bridge or how extensive their task behavior analysis should be. The main advantage of feedback that is received in AERs is that it concentrates not only on performance outcomes but also and especially on the process of task performance, that is, the particular actions and decisions that allegedly affected task performance. Various types of cognitive feedback focusing on different aspects of task performance have been suggested as mechanisms of learning improvements. For example, Balzer, Doherty, and O'Connor (1989) suggested the concepts of task validity, cognitive validity, and functional validity feedback. Thus, task validity feedback, for instance, might bring the learner's attention to the relationship between the presence and use of a compass and the probability of successful navigating performance. Cognitive validity feedback might suggest to the learner the use of the compass to plan his/her navigation route. Finally, functional validity feedback might help learners to understand the gap between their estimates of their achievements and their actual performance. It should be noted, however, that, in contrast to feedback, AER is a learning-from-experience procedure aiming to help individuals and groups to gather and analyze data that will ultimately improve their performance. It is a kind of guided self-explanation in which learners are encouraged to find the answers to the "why" questions by themselves under the guidance of a facilitator. Traditional feedback, by contrast, is generally provided by an external authority and conveys already elaborated information to the learner. In a review of 19 published studies, Webb (1989) showed that giving elaborate explanations yielded more and stronger correlations with individual achievements than receiving elaborate explanations.

Enhancing Self-efficacy

Since learners in AERs are encouraged to elaborate their behavior by themselves, and, because failing to interpret experience accurately as success or failure may hinder learning from this experience (Hogarth, Gibbs, McKenzie, & Marquis, 1991), it is imperative for learners to be able to count on their own knowledge in the AER sessions. Several studies that have highlighted the role of the self as a source of knowledge (Ellis & Kruglanski, 1992; Ellis et al., 2009) argued that when individuals do not have an external source of knowledge (epistemic authority) on which to depend for data interpretation, they rely on their own authority (self-ascribed epistemic authority, SAEA). They argued that individuals' readiness to rely on themselves in choosing whether to utilize particular evidence for improving, validating, or using their mental models depends on their assessment of how much they know (i.e., the validity of their knowledge structures), relative to others, in the particular domain.

Ellis and Kruglanski (1992) found that people with high SAEA, that is, those feeling more competent to assess their behavioral experience as a success or a failure, benefited from experiential information more than did individuals with low SAEA. In contrast, participants who perceived an external source of information as having a level of epistemic authority higher than their own were more likely to benefit from the information delivered by this source than were individuals who placed more trust in their own epistemic authority.

According to Ellis and Kruglanski (1992), the concept of self-ascribed epistemic authority bears a strong resemblance to the concept of self-efficacy used in Bandura's theory of social learning (1997). In Bandura's theory, self-efficacy refers to individuals' expectations of successfully performing behaviors necessary to attain desired outcomes. In this sense, both self-ascribed epistemic authority and self-efficacy refer to a person's own perceived competence in a domain. However, whereas the notion of self-efficacy refers to perceived behavioral capabilities, the notion of self-ascribed epistemic authority refers to one's cognitive expertise – that is, to one's perceived knowledge in a domain and one's ability to adequately conceptualize pertinent topics and issues. In practice, however, the two constructs are expected to have the same predictions with regard to cognitive tasks, because of the high correlation between knowing what to do and how to do it.

In a recent study, Ellis et al. (2010) demonstrated that AERs can boost self-efficacy and ultimately improve task performance. They argued that AERs help learners to make sense of their past behavior by creating valid cognitive models of the reasons for their failed or successful performance (Ellis & Davidi, 2005). When learners can trust these models, they feel greater mastery of their own behaviors and, as a result, their self-efficacy is increased. In other words, AERs boost self-efficacy by fostering empowering appraisals of performance. For example, self-explanation facilitates appraisal of performance by enabling learners to better explain the outcomes of their actions, create rules to improve performance, and assist in the acquisition of skills. The data verification function assists in elaborating the reasons for these outcomes and overcomes mental biases in interpreting information, while the feedback function provides detailed information on overall success or failure along with specific information about task performance. Additionally, as already noted, AERs can assist learners in identifying more internal and specific causes of behavior, leading to a greater sense of control and accountability, and a more accurate model of their performance (Ellis et al., 2006). Thus, by clarifying the reasons for outcomes, providing ways to improve and overcome challenges and cultivate self-knowledge which may boost self-efficacy, AERs can lead to more empowering appraisal of performance and raise self-efficacy.

Finally, in their study, Ellis et al. (2010) demonstrated not only the direct effects of AERs on self-efficacy and that of self-efficacy on performance improvement but they also showed that measures of self-efficacy at different time points function as moderator or mediator of the effect of AERs on performance improvements. In this study, the researchers used two repeated measures of self-efficacy (before task performance and AER, and after task performance and AER). It was found that the initial self-efficacy (AER before task performance and AER) moderated the AER's influence on performance improvement – the stronger the self-efficacy, the stronger the effect of the AER on performance improvement. Those who perceived their ability in the relevant domain as high might have learned more from their experience and ultimately improved their performance. As expected, when learners are required to understand what they have done right or wrong and to work out the reasons for their behavior (Ellis et al., 2006), those who can count on their own judgment are more likely to do better than those who cannot.

The second measure of self-efficacy (that was measured after task performance and AER) mediated the relationships between the AER and performance improvement. That is, when self-efficacy was held constant, the AER effect disappeared. This reflects the important *cognitive role* that self-efficacy has in the AER process, namely to help in data interpretation. At the end of the review process, learners are supposed to know not only what to do next time they undergo a similar experience but also to understand what they have done wrong or right and especially why they did it. In other words, they are supposed to have richer and more valid cognitive models of the reasons for their failed or successful performance (Ellis & Davidi, 2005; Ellis et al., 2006). This kind of knowledge facilitates task performance.

Motivational Aspects

The motivational aspect of learning from experience deals with questions such as: When do learners stop seeking explanations for their behavior? When do they tire of looking for more relevant evidence? And when do they doubt their own knowledge and start or continue generating alternative options for changing their relevant mental models? In more theoretical terms, the motivation to learn from experience pertains to the intensity and duration of the knowledge acquisition processes, or, in other words, to the braking or starting mechanisms of the knowledge acquisition sequence (Kruglanski, 1989, 1996). More specifically, Kruglanski suggested closure seeking (vs. avoidance) as the braking mechanism of the epistemic processes. This need reflects the desire for a clear and unambiguous answer to a question and prompts intensive activities aimed at the attainment of closure. The desire for closure is assumed to be positively related to the perceived benefits of closure (e.g., meeting an important deadline, removing the necessity for further information processing) and to the perceived costs of lack of closure (e.g., additional time and effort needed to attain closure). The desire to avoid closure is opposite to the need for closure and pertains to situations in which judgmental non-commitment is desired. The need to avoid closure is assumed to be positively related to the perceived costs of closure and the perceived benefits of a lack of closure. Individuals experiencing high fear of invalidity because of the expected high cost of a mistaken judgment will prefer to refrain from making high-commitment decisions. Consistent evidence has already been gathered by Kruglanski and his associates demonstrating the effect of closure needs on knowledge formation (for a review, see Kruglanski, 1996).

Failed experience indicates that errors have been made. These errors trigger learners to figure out how to correct them in order to improve future performance. In Kruglanski's terms, failures or errors evoke a high fear of invalidity in individuals with experience of previous closure that proved to be inadequate (Freund, Kruglanski & Schpitzajzen, 1985). Individuals who feel that the knowledge structure on which they based a failing performance was flawed want to improve their knowledge in order to fix their erroneous actions and to improve their performance (Weiner, 1985). More specifically, if learners genuinely wish to improve their performance, they increase their epistemic activity in order to revise their mental models (Hastie, 1984; Wong & Weiner, 1981), halting it as soon as they have to utilize the revised knowledge. In other words, the sooner the next experience, the higher the need to attain cognitive closure. Schunk (1987), in his theory of failure-driven learning, argued that failed expectations trigger tweaking, a cognitive process that ultimately adapts an explanation pattern to an unexpected situation.

The motivational value of coping with failures or facing erroneous actions is even more salient when it is contrasted with learning from successful events or actions. Experiencing a successful event does not create an urgent need for information gathering or for generating new ideas in order to change the relevant mental model. Since successes generally confirm prior expectancies (Weiner, 1985, 2000) and increase confidence in old routines (Weick, 1984), they generally reduce the cost of remaining in closure and tend to discourage any cognitive activity designed to invoke immediate change. According to Sitkin (1992), successful outcomes tend to restrict search, reduce attention, and increase complacency and risk aversion. Successful events or correct actions provide a stable basis for future activity (Weick, 1984), and encourage people to develop expectations that these outcomes will be repeated (Sitkin, 1992; Weick, Sutcliffe & Obstfeld, 1999).

Ellis et al. (2006) manipulated the variable of success or failure in order to examine the effectiveness of AERs under different motivational conditions. At the end of the first trial of playing a strategic business computerized game, called "the beer war game", participants were either congratulated on their success or were consoled by the experiment for their failure. After an AER session, participants were asked to try the same task again in order to examine their progress. Participants received one of three kinds of AERs: (1) an AER in which learners were asked to focus only on the specific actions that supported or explained their successful decisions or moves; (2) an AER in which the experimenter channeled the participants' attention toward their erroneous actions that probably hindered their progress in the game; (3) an AER that was a combination of the previous two kinds, focusing on both the positive and negative aspects of their task performance; and (4) a control group that did not receive an AER.

The findings clearly showed that performance improvement under the two motivational conditions, failed and successful events, was contingent upon the particular type of AER. When learning took place after failure, all types of AERs improved performance, demonstrating the strong motivational influence of learning from failures. It seems that learners are inclined after failures to intensify their learning process and are probably willing to use any new information in order to improve their knowledge and, accordingly, their performance. In contrast, after a successful event, only AERs that treated the erroneous actions of the previous experience improved subsequent performance. This demonstrates that an AER that directs successful learners to reflect on their errors can call into question the appropriateness of their knowledge and boost their motivation to test it, update it, and ultimately use it for improving their performance. In epistemic motivation terms (Kruglanski, 1989), AERs that focus on errors evoke a high fear of invalidity and make learners feel less confident in their current knowledge. Although fear of invalidity usually results in a heightened need to avoid closure, when the learners' goal is to accomplish immediate performance improvement, they probably gather and elaborate as much relevant information as fast as they can before attaining new closure and using it in subsequent behavior. Thus, directing learners to detect and elaborate errors when they experience relative success may be even more important than doing so after relative or complete failure.

An alternative explanation to why AERs focusing on errors after a successful event are more effective than any kind of AER that are conducted after failed events has to do with the notion of "psychological safety" (Edmondson, 1999). It seems that, after successful events, learners feel more secure in discussing their errors and more willing to draw lessons from these data. In other words, they are more willing to accept feedback when they feel valued (Tyler & Lind, 1992).

Conclusions and Implications

AER is a learning-from-experience procedure that gives learners an opportunity to systematically analyze the various actions that they selected to perform or not to perform a particular task or to respond to a particular event. This procedure enables learners to determine which of their actions was wrong or not necessary, which was missing, which should be corrected, and which should be reinforced. In contrast to the traditional literature pertaining to the role of reflection in learning from experience, the AER is a *guided* (as opposed to *free*) reflection procedure. The underlying assumption of this procedure is that the facilitator can both motivate and direct the learners' systematic analysis of their performance in order to understand why they functioned as they did in a given task and how to change their behavior in order to improve performance.

As shown above, the best trigger for learning from experience is the outcome feedback, i.e. the failure. After failure, any kind of AER (focused on error, successful actions or both) is effective, because individuals, following failure, are highly motivated to correct their decisions and actions, to improve their performance outcomes, and to attain closure. Interestingly, however, learning from errors was even more effective after success, because of the psychological safety it inspires on the learner. This result has two implications. First, in AERs conducted after failure (the most common reason for conducting AERs), the facilitator faces a tough challenge – to create a safe psychological learning environment even though the performance failure is being reviewed. No behavioral techniques have been developed and examined to deliberately enhance psychological safety. This is one of the first challenges that researchers should meet in order to help organizations to improve employees' performance. Organizations should do their best to distinguish between AERs and "investigations". The goal of AERs is purely to learn the lessons from past behavior. Under this definition, individuals will not deny their responsibilities and will feel accountable for their behavior. Therefore, they will not attribute their erroneous actions to non-relevant external causes, and will draw the right lessons from the AER. Second, after successes, the facilitator must find the way to trigger the motivation to learn without hurting the existing feeling of psychological safety. When the reviewed event is defined as a success, the errors detected are probably not major ones (otherwise the event would have been defined as a failure). These errors, based on Ellis et al. (2006), do not decrease the psychological safety. One of the issues that researchers must address is how to promote the psychological safety of learners after a failed event or what to do when, during the AER, one of the errors, that was initially defined as minor and easy to correct, is found to be major and difficult to cope with. Will it affect the initial psychological safety? If yes, how does one preserve the psychological safety of the learners'?

The above issues might be related to a different issue that has never been investigated in this context – affect or mood. Does mood (after success or failure) mediate the effect of AERs on performance? Is mood associated with the cognitive and motivational processes that determine the impact of AERs on performance? These important questions are still open for research at the individual as well as at the group level.

A major issue concerning psychological safety is related to how the process feedback is provided. Process feedback is given indirectly: the facilitator, by asking questions, directs the learners to find the causes for their errors by themselves and to revise their mental models accordingly. On the one hand, this strengthens learners' self-efficacy and improves their ability to learn from experience, but, on the other hand, it creates a non-authoritative relationship between the facilitator and learners which might lead to increased psychological safety or to low need for closure. Further research is still needed to determine the different role of the two kinds of feedback on performance improvement.

The main role of the AER facilitator, beyond the motivating function, is to guide the learners in a systematic analysis of their performance in order to understand why they functioned as they did in a given task, where and why they made mistakes, how to correct these errors, and how to change their behavior in order to prevent such errors in future events and to improve performance. The studies that have been done up to now indicate that: (1) the richer the learners' mental models, the better they learn from their experience and improve performance; (2) mental models comprised of essential causes lead to better performance improvement than mental models including contextual or ad hoc causes; (3) learners who attribute their erroneous actions to themselves demonstrate better performance improvement than learners who attribute the consequences of their behavior to external causes; and (4) learners who attribute their erroneous actions to specific causes demonstrate better performance improvement than learners who attribute the consequences of their behavior to general causes.

One main practical implication emerges from these findings. As opposed to unguided reflection, in guided reflection sessions such as AERs, facilitators can and must control the learning process by systematic questioning and by indirectly preventing learners from attributing their failed performance-related actions to contextual or ad hoc causes instead of to essential causes. Facilitators must exploit their role in the AER session to change the direction of search of the learners from the contextual to the essential and to alter their attributional tendencies from external to internal. A successful reflection session is not one in which learners generate superficial causes for their behavior but one that digs deeply into the tough issues trying to get as close as possible to the root causes of the erroneous actions. Furthermore, as noted above, in order to create revised mental models based on reliable data, facilitators should create an organizational climate that values transparency and issue orientation (Ron et al., 2006) in which they confront learners with different perceptions of the same data, cast doubts on the causes the learners suggest for their performance, and push them to try harder in finding the right answers. This is the only way to get rich and valid mental models comprised of relevant reliable causes for the failed event.

References

Abramson, L. Y., Seligman, M. E. P., & Teasdale, J. (1978). Learned helplessness in humans: Critique and reformulation. *Journal of Abnormal Psychology, 87*, 49–74.

Alexander, P. A., Schallert, D. L., & Hare, V. C. (1991). Coming to terms: How researchers in learning and literacy talk about knowledge. *Review of Educational Research, 61*, 315–343.

Anderson, C. A., Krull, D. S., & Weiner, B. (1996). Explanations: Processes and consequences. In E. D. Higgins & A. W. Kruglanski (Eds.), *Social psychology: Handbook of basic principles* (pp. 271–296). New York: Guilford Press.

Anseel, F., Lievens, F., & Schollaert, E. (2009). Reflection as a strategy to enhance task performance after feedback. *Organizational behavior and human decision making processes, 10*, 23–35.

Baird, L., Henderson, J. C., & Watts, S. (1997). Learning from action: An analysis of the center of the army lessons learned (CALL). *Human Resource Management, 36*, 385–395.

Baird, L., Holland, P., & Deacon, S. (1999). Learning from action: Imbedding more learning into the performance fast enough to make a difference. *Organizational Dynamics, 27*, 19–32.

Balzer, W. K., Doherty, M. E., & O'Connor, R. (1989). Effects of cognitive feedback on performance. *Psychological Bulletin, 106*, 410–433.

Bandura, A. (1977). Self-efficacy: Toward a unifying theory of behavioral change. *Psychological Review, 84*, 191–215.

Bandura, A. (1997). *Self-efficacy: The exercise of control*. Stanford, NY: W.H. Freeman and Company.

Bies, R. J. (1989). Managing conflict before it happens: The role of accounts. In M. A. Rahim (Ed.), *Managing conflict: An interdisciplinary approach* (pp. 83–91). New York: Praeger.

Busby, J. S. (1999). The effectiveness of collective retrospection as a mechanism of organizational learning. *The Journal of Applied Behavioral Science, 35*, 109–129.

Carley, K. M. (1997). Extracting team mental models through textual analysis. *Journal of Organizational Behavior, 18*, 533–558.

Carroll, J. S. (1995). Incident reviews in high hazard industries: Sense making and learning under ambiguity and accountability. *Industrial and Environmental Crisis Quarterly, 9*, 175–197.

Carroll, J. S., Rudolph, J. W., & Hatakenaka, S. (2003). Learning from organizational experience. In M. Easterby-Smith & M. A. Lyles (Eds.), *The Blackwell handbook of organizational learning and knowledge management* (pp. 575–600). Oxford, UK: Blackwell.

Chaiken, S., & Trope, Y. (Eds.). (1999). *Dual-process theories in social psychology*. New York: Guilford.

Chanowitz, B., & Langer, E. J. (1980). Premature cognitive commitment. *Journal of Personality and Social Psychology, 41*, 1051–1063.

Chi, M. T. H., de Leeuw, N., Chiu, M. H., & Lavancher, C. (1994). Eliciting self-explanations improves understanding. *Cognitive Science, 18*, 439–477.

Darling, M. J., & Parry, C. S. (2001). After action reviews: Linking reflection and planning in a learning practice. *Reflections, 3*, 64–72.

Day, E. A., Arthur, W., & Gettman, D. (2001). Knowledge structures and the acquisition of a complex skill. *Journal of Applied Psychology, 86*, 1022–1033.

Edmondson, A. (1999). Psychological safety and learning behavior in work teams. *Administrative Science Quarterly, 44*, 350–383.

Ellis, S., & Davidi, I. (2005). After event reviews: Drawing lessons from failed and successful events. *Journal of Applied Psychology, 90*, 857–871.

Ellis, S., Ganzach, Y., Castle, E., & Sekely, G. (2010). Can filmed AERs of relevant others improve trainees' performance? The mediating and moderating role of self-efficacy. *Journal of Applied Psychology, 95*(1), 122–131.

Ellis, S., & Kruglanski, A. W. (1992). Self as epistemic authority: Effects on experiential and instructional learning. *Social Cognition, 10*, 155–177.

Ellis, S., Mendel, R., & Aloni-Zohar, M. (2009). The effects of accuracy of performance evaluation on learning from experience: The moderating role of after-event reviews. *Journal of Applied Social Psychology, 39*(3), 541–563.

Ellis, S., Mendel, R., & Nir, M. (2006). Learning from successful vs. failed events: The moderating role of kind of after-event-review. *Journal of Applied Psychology, 91*(3), 669–680.

Evans, J. S. B. T. (1988). The knowledge elicitation problem: A psychological perspective. *Behavior and Information Technology, 7*, 111–130.

Evans, J. S. B. T. (2008). Dual-processing accounts of reasoning, judgment, and social cognition. *Annual Review of Psychology, 59*, 255–278.

Feldman, J. (1989). On the difficulty of learning from experience. In H. P. Sims & D. A. Gioia (Eds.), *The thinking organization* (pp. 263–292). San Francisco: Jossey-Bass.

Fischhoff, B. (1982). For those condemned to study the past: Heuristics and biases in hindsight. In D. Kahanman, P. Slovic, & A. Tversky (Eds.), *Judgment under uncertainty: Heuristics and biases*. Cambridge, UK: Cambridge University Press.

Fiske, S. T., & Taylor, S. E. (1991). *Social cognition*. Reading, MA: Addison Wesley.

Frese, M., & Zapf, D. (1994). Action as the core of work psychology: A German approach. In H. C. Triandis, M. D. Dunnett, & L. M. Hough (Eds.), *Handbook of industrial and organisational psychology* (2nd ed., Vol. 4, pp. 271–340). Palo Alto, CA: Consulting Psychologists Press.

Freund, T., Kruglanski, A. W., & Schpitzajzen, A. (1985). The freezing and unfreezing of impressional primacy: Effects of need for structure and fear of invalidity. *Personality and Social Psychology Bulletin, 11*, 479–489.

Gray, D. E. (2007). Facilitating management learning: Developing critical reflection through reflection tools. *Management Learning, 38*, 495–517.

Gronhaug, K., & Falkenberg, J. S. (1998). Success attributions within and across organizations. In C. Eden & J. C. Spender (Eds.), *Managerial and organizational cognition: Theory, methods, and research* (pp. 93–107). London: Sage.

Gulliver, F. R. (1987). Post-project appraisals pay. *Harvard Business Review, 67*(2), 128–132.

Hastie, R. (1984). Causes and effects of causal attribution. *Journal of Personality and Social Psychology, 46*, 44–56.

Hilton, D. J., Mathes, R. H., & Trabasso, T. (1992). The study of causal explanation in natural language: Analyzing reports of the challenger disaster in the *New York Times*. In M. L. McLaughin, M. J. Cody, & S. J. Read (Eds.), *Explaining one's self to others* (pp. 41–60). Hillsdale, NJ: Erlbaum.

Hogarth, R. M., Gibbs, B. J., McKenzie, C. R. M., & Marquis, M. A. (1991). Learning from feedback: Exactingness and incentives. *Journal of Experimental Psychology: Learning, Memory, and Cognition, 17*, 734–752.

Kelley, H. H. (1973). Attribution in social interaction. In E. E. Jones, D. E. Kanouse, H. H. Kelley, R. E. Nisbett, S. Valins, & B. Weiner (Eds.), *Attribution: Perceiving the causes of behavior* (pp. 1–26). Morristown, NJ: General Learning Press.

Kruglanski, A. W. (1989). *Lay epistemics and human knowledge: Cognitive and motivational bases*. New York: Guilford Press.

Kruglanski, A. W. (1996). Motivated social cognition: Principles of the interface. In E. T. Higgins & A. W. Kruglanski (Eds.), *Social psychology: Handbook of basic principles* (pp. 493–520). New York: Guilford Press.

Louis, M. R., & Sutton, R. I. (1991). Switching cognitive gears: From habits of mind to active thinking. *Human Relations, 44*, 55–76.

McGill, A. L. (1989). Context effects in judgments of causation. *Journal of Personality and Social Psychology, 57*, 189–200.

Mikulincer, M., & Nizan, B. (1988). Causal attribution, cognitive interference, and the generalization of learned helplessness. *Journal of Personality and Social Psychology, 55*, 470–478.

Miller, G. A., Galanter, E., & Pribram, K. H. (1960). Plans and the structure of behavior. New York: Holt, Rinehart & Winston.

Nathan, M. J., Mertz, K., & Ryan, B. (1994, April). *Learning through self-explanations of mathematical examples: Effects of cognitive load.* Paper presented at the annual meeting of the American Educational Research Association, New York, NY.

Postman, L., & Brown, D. R. (1952). The perceptual consequences of success and failure. *Journal of Abnormal and Social Psychology, 47*, 213–221.

Ron, N., Lipshitz, R., & Popper, M. (2006). *Post-flight reviews in an F-16 fighter squadron: An application of a multi-facet model of organisational learning.* Unpublished manuscript, University of Haifa, Haifa, Israel.

Schunk, D. H. (1987). Peer models and children's behavioral change. *Review of Educational Research, 57*, 149–174.

Senders, J. W., & Moray, N. P. (1991). *Human error: Cause, prediction, and reduction.* Hillsdale, NJ: Lawrence Erlbaum Associates.

Sitkin, S. B. (1992). Learning through failure: The strategy of small losses. *Research in Organizational Behavior, 14*, 231–266.

Strange, J. M., & Mumford, M. D. (2005). The origins of vision: Effects of reflection models, and analysis. *The Leadership Quarterly, 16*, 121–148.

Trope, Y., & Liberman, A. (1996). Social hypothesis testing: Cognitive and motivational mechanisms. In E. T. Higgins & A. W. Kruglanski (Eds.), *Social psychology: Handbook of basic principles* (pp. 493–520). New York: Guilford.

Tyler, T. R., & Lind, E. A. (1992). A relational model of authority in groups. In L. Berkowitz (Ed.), *Advances in experimental social psychology* (Vol. 25, pp. 115–191). New York: Academic.

Webb, N. M. (1989). Peer interaction and learning in small groups. *International Journal of Education Research, 13*, 21–39.

Weick, K. E. (1984). Small wins: Redefining the scale of social problems. *American Psychologist, 39*, 40–49.

Weick, K. E., Sutcliffe, K. M., & Obstfeld, D. (1999). Organizing for high reliability: Processes of collective mindfulness. In B. Staw & R. Sutton (Eds.), *Research in organizational behavior*. Greenwich, CT: JAI Press.

Weiner, B. (1985). An attributional theory of achievement motivation and emotion. *Psychological Review, 92*, 548–573.

Weiner, B. (2000). Intrapersonal and interpersonal theories of motivation from an attributional perspective. *Educational Psychology Review, 12*, 1–14.

Wong, P. T. P., & Weiner, B. (1981). When people ask "why" questions, and the heuristics of attributional search. *Journal of Personality and Social Psychology, 40*, 650–663.

Chapter 14
Incident Reporting Systems in Hospitals: How Does Learning Occur Using this Organisational Instrument?

Yvonne Pfeiffer and Theo Wehner

Incident Reporting Systems: Aims and Theoretical Foundation

Aims Linked to Implementing Incident Reporting Systems in Healthcare

In healthcare, errors can have fatal consequences for both patients' lives and for clinicians, who often suffer from guilt and blame after having been involved in an adverse event (Wu, 2000). Hospitals therefore aim at developing organisational structures to support safety in patient care. Fostering the reporting of incidents, errors and near misses is a part of this development, because these events offer insights into the processes of patient care. Incident reporting systems are widely considered an important instrument for patient safety in healthcare, not only by healthcare institutions (Kohn, Corrigan, & Donaldson, 1999) and hospital risk managers but also by physicians and nurses (Sexton, Thomas, & Helmreich, 2000). Thus, incident reporting is expected to help to identify "accidents waiting to happen" (Perrow, 1984, p. 14): incidents represent "free lessons" (Reason, 1990) in accident-prone work practices without a real accident or severe adverse event having to occur. Healthcare managers and clinicians who implement incident reporting systems aim to reveal latent conditions of the organisation that provoke threats to patient safety (Reason) by analysing reported incidents and defining subsequent corrective actions designed to address these threats (for the operation of an IRS, see Box 14.1).

Y. Pfeiffer, Ph.D. (✉) • T. Wehner, Ph.D.
Center for Organisational and Occupational Sciences, ETH Zurich, Kreuzplatz 5, 8032 Zurich, Switzerland
e-mail: ypfeiffer@ethz.ch; twehner@ethz.ch

J. Bauer and C. Harteis (eds.), *Human Fallibility: The Ambiguity of Errors for Work and Learning*, Professional and Practice-based Learning 6,
DOI 10.1007/978-90-481-3941-5_14,

Box 14.1 Design of Incident Reporting Systems in Healthcare

The basic idea of incident reporting systems (also known as adverse event reporting systems) is to collect collaborators' reports about safety-relevant events and share them within an organisation or other community dealing with high-risk environments. Staff are expected to report the events they perceive as potentially critical for patient safety. These reports are collected and analysed in a central system, and appropriate measures are defined and implemented.

The processes constituting incident reporting systems in healthcare largely divide into five steps (see also Fig. 14.1): The first is the collection of data, which means that members of staff report critical incidents by filling out a reporting form. Secondly, the collected incidents are analysed by an analysis team which is composed of either experts and/or designated staff members. In a third step, this team infers measures from the analysis. The measures are then implemented and relevant organisational members become involved. Finally, in order to check whether the measures had the intended effect,

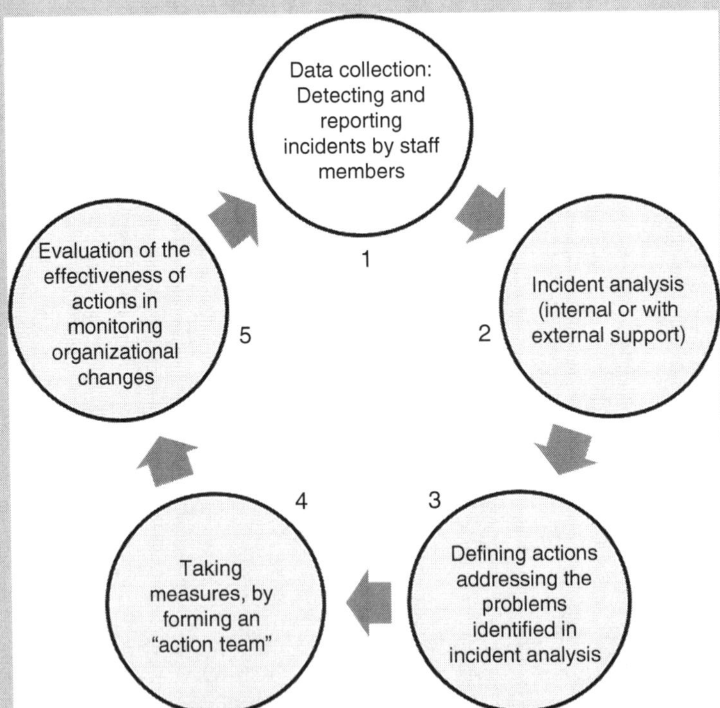

Fig. 14.1 Steps in an incident reporting system

(continued)

Box 14.1 (continued)

evaluation is needed. This step is largely neglected by the designers and users of incident reporting systems in the healthcare sector.

This description represents a prototype procedure in incident reporting systems. In fact, these systems vary considerably. In the text, we give some examples of the broad variability of designs of incident reporting systems in healthcare.

Furthermore, the thematic scope of incident reporting systems diverges: some systems only treat special kinds of errors in healthcare, such as MEDMARX in the US, which centres on adverse drug events. Other systems have a broader scope that encompasses all kinds of incidents regarded as critical for patient safety. Hospitals differ in the kind of incidents they require to be reported: some permit incidents that have already affected the patient and others decline to report incidents that had a negative impact on the patient.

In addition, the procedure of analysing incidents is conducted in very different ways. Sometimes, the reported events are not analysed at all and the incident reporting system serves only for data collection. Some systems rely on external expert boards to comment on their incidents via the Internet. Others designate internal staff to analyse incidents and communicate their results. In hospital-wide systems, staff groups at unit level are often responsible for operating the reporting system. These groups are mostly coordinated at hospital level by a hospital risk manager. Surprisingly, in contrast to other industries, where incident investigation is a field of expertise, incident analysis is mostly in the hands of practitioners who may be more or less skilled.

Incident reporting systems represent a patient safety activity that has been transferred to medicine from other high-risk industries such as aviation, nuclear power and petrochemical processing (Benn et al., 2009; Tamuz & Harrison, 2006). Historically, the need for analysing incidents which could have led or did lead to undesirable outcomes arose from the desire to identify at an early stage organisational failures that might possibly end in catastrophes, such as a plane crash or nuclear accident. Following Barach and Small (2000), incident reporting systems in non-medical industries share the emphasis on a systems approach to error analysis. As medicine is still characterised by a strong tendency to individual-oriented blame in the occurrence of an adverse event, it is unsurprising that the idea of bringing out the systems approach by implementing incident reporting in hospitals has found rapidly increasing appreciation in healthcare. However, the medical sector differs from other high-risk industries in many aspects, such as work organisation, professional cultures (Reason, 2004) and error friendliness. In 2002, Leape stated that "evidence of the effect of voluntary reporting systems is largely anecdotal" in healthcare (p. 1634). Incident reporting systems may consequently be of limited applicability as long as they are not adapted to the conditions of work in healthcare. In this chapter, therefore, we propose that the mere transfer of incident reporting to a completely different work setting without any profound adaptations will not necessarily lead to effective organisational learning. We therefore analyse the point at which learning is promoted or impeded by the layout of today's incident reporting systems, how organisational learning from incidents can take place when using current incident reporting systems, and what potential barriers hinder organisational learning from such incidents.

The Idea of Incident Reporting Systems: Theoretical Foundations

From a psychological perspective, the development of incident reporting systems in healthcare has not been theoretically driven. Researchers often cite Flanagan's (1954) critical incident technique as a starting point in the evolution of incident collection and analysis. His work concerned the identification of competence-relevant aspects of pilots' tasks in aviation. So the original idea did not refer to using this technique for organisational learning in medicine. In fact, theories describing the specific challenges of work in high-risk organisations have made a crucial contribution to constituting the existence of incident reporting systems in theoretical terms. Both high reliability theory (HRT; Weick, Sutcliffe, & Obstfeld, 1999) and normal accident theory (NAT; Perrow, 1984) draw upon high-risk organisations from two different viewpoints: while NAT accentuates the potential for catastrophic failures in tightly coupled and highly interactive systems from an organisational sociological perspective, HRT optimistically sheds light on organisational characteristics that promote reliability in high-risk organisations. After years of being regarded as controversial viewpoints, NAT and HRT have been linked because they highlight complementary aspects of high-risk organisations (Rijpma, 1997).

Tamuz and Harrison (2006) investigated the positions of these two theories with respect to incident reporting systems and conclude that although NAT and HRT do not explicitly promote such systems as a safety measure, they are consistent with them. From an HRT perspective, incident reporting allows decision makers to gather information from the front-end about safety threats, but they warn that this reporting is undermined when hospitals blame individuals for making mistakes. Accordingly, from a NAT point of view, incident reporting systems can provide the feedback that organisations need to learn from their experience. From this viewpoint, reward systems defined by appropriate policies could misguide reporting, for example by fostering fear of litigation. NAT additionally attaches importance to inter-organisational learning, which means that organisations can also exploit and learn from near misses on a system-wide level. This conforms to the establishment of nationwide incident reporting systems such as MedMARX in the U.S., or CIRRNET in Switzerland.

Organisational Learning from Incident Reporting Systems

The implicit model of knowledge that prevails in medicine is "the application of a body of knowledge derived from medical science and perfected by a physician's own personal experience" (Carroll & Edmondson, 2002, p. 52). Learning which results from the accumulation of experience is inseparably linked to the individual and often remains implicit (Sturmberg & Martin, 2008). In response to this fact, a development towards systematic organisational learning, supporting for example the transformation of tacit into explicit knowledge, is claimed for healthcare. This discussion often calls for the establishment of incident reporting systems (see, for example, Kohn et al., 1999) without any further specification of the organisational processes that are expected to advance learning from these systems.

There exists a large body of literature on organisational learning in psychology. Surprisingly, the literature on incident reporting systems makes little use of it. The rationale for such systems seems to stem mainly from organisational practice, where the need for systematic assessment of minor incidents pointing to organisational structures that may potentially facilitate accidents was experienced as already noted. For the design of incident reporting systems in hospitals, evidence of research on organisational learning has not played an important role. This might explain why the mechanisms designed to promote learning from incidents remained largely unspecified. There seems to be an emphasis on developing appropriate software tools for reporting and communicating analysis results, while the design of organisational processes and structures for implementing incident reporting seems to be rather neglected. Only recently has an analysis and comparison of incident reporting systems stressed the importance of valid feedback cycles for the effective use of these systems in healthcare (Benn et al., 2009).

Research on investigating the reporting behaviour of clinicians describes a major underreporting of incidents in healthcare (Schuerer et al., 2006; Stanhope, Crowley-Murphy, Vincent, O'Connor, & Taylor-Adams, 1999). Numerous studies have analysed which characteristics could raise the acceptance of incident reporting systems as a tool for improving patient safety (for an overview, see Pfeiffer, Manser, & Wehner, 2010). They mention factors such as confidentiality, timely feedback, a non-punitive environment and a simple reporting process (Bocion, Sennhauser, & Frey, 2006; Kingston, Evans, Smith, & Berry, 2004; Leape, 2002; Vincent, Stanhope, & Crowley-Murphy, 1999). These features refer to the design of existing incident reporting processes and their effect on the motivation to participate. However, it has hitherto not been investigated *how* incident reporting systems affect patient safety from a learning perspective. They are implemented with the aim of promoting organisational learning, but which processes actually turn the mere use of incident reporting systems into effective organisational learning?

In order to link up organisational practice in incident reporting systems and psychological theories on learning from incidents, we analyse the current use of incident reporting systems in healthcare by applying the four questions Engeström (2001) proposes for describing learning processes: Who and where are the subjects of learning? Why do they learn? What do they learn? And how do they learn? On the basis of this examination, we finally point out potential opportunities for improving the design of incident reporting systems in healthcare from a learning point of view.

Learning During and Through the Incident Reporting Process: Current State

Engeström (2001) argues that cultural–historical activity theory can shed light on organisational learning processes. He differentiates five principles of activity theory: firstly, the prime unit of the analysis is a collective, artefact-mediated and object-oriented activity system. With regard to healthcare, this means that analysing learning mechanisms should account for the role played in medical work by the collectivity and the artefacts. Secondly, activity systems are multi-voiced, which means that their members have multiple and differing viewpoints on issues. This is especially true for healthcare, where professions with completely different origins and traditions work closely together (physicians, nurses, managers, and allied healthcare staff). The third principle in activity theory is historicity, which means that healthcare work needs to be analysed with respect to the history of the organisation or unit in question and also in broader terms with respect to the history of the medical profession. This could play a specifically important role for the analysis of incidents. Fourth, contradictions in the sense of structural tensions between activity systems are regarded as sources of change and development. From this perspective, conflicts and disturbances between physicians and nurses can be seen as contradictions potentially leading to change or innovation. As a fifth principle of activity systems, Engeström stresses the possibility of expansive transformations. This means that the actual activity executed in certain units or organisations becomes re-conceptualized in order to open up a much wider horizon of possibilities in interaction with other activity systems. According to this viewpoint, expansive learning means a "collective journey through the zone of proximal development of the activity" linking to Vygotsky's idea (Engeström, p. 137).

Who and Where Are the Subjects of Learning in Incident Reporting Systems?

The group of staff involved in the reporting system varies with the kind of system under investigation: While some systems are designed for certain disciplines, such as the PaSOS anaesthetists' reporting system in Germany (Rall, Dieckmann, & Stricker, 2006), other systems are implemented on a hospital-wide level and involve all groups of staff. Local systems are sometimes pooled at national level, such as CIRRNET in Switzerland, which integrates anaesthesia incidents from a number of affiliated Swiss hospitals. There are also thematically focused incident reporting systems such as MedMARX in the U.S., which focuses on hospital medication errors.

According to the focus and scope of incident reporting systems, their reporting members vary. The more locally such systems are implemented, the more they focus on organisational learning from incidents. When local systems are pooled at higher (national or discipline) level, the locus of the group involved shifts. Although measures derived from analyses on this meta-level refer to everyday professional work in healthcare, they may also point to opportunities and needs for action, for example by regulatory bodies, professional associations for example by regulatory bodies, or professional associations.

Incident reporting systems as a hospital-focused tool endeavour to enhance individual and organisational learning from incidents. Asking for the subjects of learning also points to the duality of organisational learning (Lipshitz, 2000): on the one hand, an organisation provides opportunities for individuals to learn and accrue new knowledge, and on the other hand, the structure, procedures, artefacts, and culture of an organisation are manifest representations of learning processes or knowledge bodies. This means that organisations are both representations of learning results and knowledge as well as being environments for the acquisition of new knowledge for their members. This duality also refers to the fact that learning in organisations is mainly understood as learning by individuals in organisational settings. Argyris and Schön (1996) highlighted the importance of individual learning leading to organisational learning: “Organisational learning occurs when individuals within an organisation experience a problematic situation and inquire into it on the organisational behalf” (Argyris & Schön, p. 16). In current designs of incident reporting systems, only a few employees participate in the cause analysis and the search for the solution to a problem. In some systems, the workforce is involved in defining how to take corrective action. However, as only a few members of a unit operate the incident reporting system, most staff are excluded from the processes constituting learning and knowledge – the inquiry processes in the sense of Argyris and Schön. Wang and Ahmed (2003) underline the fact that “collective learning … may even occur independently of each individual. However, collective learning cannot take place if the employees of an organisation are prevented from learning” (p. 9). Thus, it is critical for the success of an incident reporting system that its processes are permeable to all groups of staff. This opens up design alternatives for these systems (see section “Future Opportunities for Designing Incident Reporting Systems in Healthcare”).

Why Do Clinicians Learn in Incident Reporting Systems: What Makes Them Make the Effort?

In a survey of 1,082 physicians, Garbutt et al. (2008) found that – in contrast to current assumptions – physicians are willing to report medical errors and near misses and thus to share their knowledge with their institution. However, the physicians found that current reporting systems were inadequate and therefore preferred informal discussions with colleagues. These findings conform to a large body of studies that have been conducted to analyse the barriers to incident reporting. In a review of this research, Pfeiffer et al. (2010) argue that most of the barriers that were analysed refer to characteristics of the incident reporting systems and propose to include motivational concepts in the analysis of barriers. First empirical evidence from a survey study we conducted in Swiss hospitals shows that an important motivator for using incident reporting systems is the belief that they are an instrument for avoiding the repetition of errors or assuring learning from them.

Engeström (2001) draws upon situated learning theory (Lave & Wenger, 1991) to explain why employees engage in organisational learning processes. Situated learning theory supposes that individuals are motivated to learn in collective practices when they can participate in them. Participation allows active involvement in defining and solving problems, and thus experiencing the creation of something useful. Thus, the motivation to make the laborious effort required for expansive learning, which involves revealing contradictory working demands among different activity systems searching jointly for a solution, must be triggered by the context (Engeström). This involves the motivation to look at the unconscious patterns of assumptions underlying activities in collective systems.

So, for organisational practice, it is important that the motivation to report and work effectively and openly on problems as they arise is not corroded by mechanisms inherent to the incident reporting systems, but is rather supported and enhanced by them. From the viewpoint of situated learning (Lave & Wenger, 1991), this can be achieved by allowing the employees to participate. Two aspects of participation in incident reporting systems can be distinguished: taking part in reporting and implementing changes on the one hand and being part of the whole process on the other hand, which also means contributing to incident investigations. As healthcare usually involves a large workload, not all staff members can be implicated in all activities deriving from incident reports. The reported incidents may point to several areas of required action – depending on the reporting rate. The incident reporting system manager can consequently assign specific staff groups to the analysis and implementation of a specific thematic area. These groups could then bring together all activity systems that are affected by the problem, and could also consult or call upon other organisational members or experts in their team. In participating actively in incident reporting processes, the co-workers simultaneously promote the dissemination or implementation of the analysis results.

In finding out why people engage in organisational learning processes, we also shed light on deutero-learning as a kind of unconscious learning (Bateson, 1972) driven by the contextual factors of organisational practices. Deutero-learning has been misconceived or ambiguously understood in the literature of organisational learning, as Lipshitz (2000) and Visser (2007) point out. They suggest that we accept Bateson's original view, according to which deutero-learning refers to the behavioural adaptation to patterns of conditioning at the level of relationships in organisational contexts. Deutero-learning means that people unconsciously learn the "message" that is inherent to the context of a situation. Rowe and Boyce (2009) illustrate the influence of deutero-learning on managing change in public health. This kind of learning is not necessarily positive, as is underlined by the concept of a double bind, i.e. the experience of two contradictory messages in a certain situation (Bateson, 1972; Engeström, 2001). In this pathological form, deutero-learning does not lead to individual or organisational improvement. Visser differentiates between the concepts of deutero-, meta-, and planned learning. Deutero-learning is continuous and largely unconscious, and thus tends to escape explicit steering and organising. Meta-learning is conceptualised as steerable inquiry processes at individual and group levels, which can take the form of single- or double-loop learning (Argyris & Schön, 1996). Planned learning comprises the development and implementation of organisational systems which aim to establish regular meta-learning. This understanding conforms to our perspective on incident reporting systems. Thus, a functioning incident reporting system would be an organisational instrument allowing meta-learning and implemented by a planned learning approach.

We argue that from the perspective of deutero-learning, incident reporting systems have effects on the climate and interpersonal actions: a physician who is used to working in an "error-hostile" organisation and fears blame as a reaction to an error may interpret the implementation of an incident reporting system as a sign of emerging error-friendliness in the organisation. This is new to medicine, which has a long tradition of postulating that errors simply should not be committed. Errors tend to be regarded as a personal deficiency in a physician's knowledge or aptitude. This culture of blame (Runciman, Merry, & Tito, 2003) is supported by current legislation, where admitting an error can incur enormous costs for the hospital and potentially for the physician involved. The idea of analysing errors and incidents by looking for system causes represented a novelty for the traditional organisational culture in healthcare. Hospital employees thus learn from the mere existence of an incident reporting system that their leaders recognise that errors happen and can be a source of learning.

An aspect of incident reporting systems might imply two contradictory messages and therefore lead to pathological deutero-learning: incident reporting systems are said to promote systemic thinking and to help abolish an individual-centred view of error causation in healthcare. However, the current design of incident reporting systems lacks any means to impede individual blame in analysing incidents. So incident analysis reports often transmit the message that healthcare staff have to take more care. This reasoning follows the logic of individual blame and neglects the intended systemic focus of incident reporting systems. Thus, on the level of deutero-learning, hospital staff may learn that the individual will still be blamed for an incident. In order to avoid such misuse and misconceptions, organisational practice and research have to create design options that assure adequate analysis procedures and results (for example, by implying expertise in investigation and action taking by promoting the training of hospital staff; see section "Future Opportunities for Designing Incident Reporting Systems in Healthcare").

On the other hand, if incident reporting systems really do apply a systemic focus in all their processes, they can enable positive deutero-learning. As Rowe and Boyce (2009) point out, learning can occur at local organisational level when a shared value acts as a driving force towards collaborative learning efforts. Staff who become involved in problem-solving activities may form communities of practice and thus engage in active learning.

Box 14.2 Reportable Incidents in Healthcare

Wald and Shojania (2001) differentiate between three basic categories of events that can be reported as incidents: no-harm events, near misses and adverse events. For example, anaphylaxis after penicillin represents an adverse event, but if the medication order is stopped before it is administered – for example because a nurse became aware of the allergy documented in the patient's history – the event would be called a near miss. When patient injury is only avoided by chance, this constitutes a no-harm event. In contrast to disease complications, incidents are events in which a patient is (almost) unintentionally harmed by medical treatment. In the WHO guidelines (2005) on incident reporting systems, an incident is defined as: "any deviation from usual medical care that causes an injury to the patient or poses a risk of harm; including errors, preventable adverse events, and hazards" (p. 9). Near misses or no-harm events occur more frequently than adverse events (Wald & Shojania) and are less likely to provoke guilt or other psychological barriers to reporting. Therefore, learning from them is expected to be easier than from severe adverse events which potentially imply litigation.

What Do They Learn?

In asking what can be learnt from incidents, three aspects of the incident reporting systems can have a particularly important impact: the act of reporting, the analysing procedures and the actions following the incident analysis. In the following, we therefore describe the various influences on the content of learning from incident reporting as they appear during these steps.

First, the reporting staff members need to detect a reportable incident (see Box 14.2). Hospitals differ in the types of incidents they include in their systems. Some only target incidents involving no patient harm, while others also allow reporting of adverse events implying patient harm. In many countries (apart from the US), incident data are not protected from use by the prosecution in case a hospital or physician is being sued. Some hospitals therefore seek to assure that their incident reports cannot be used in litigation by only admitting no-harm incidents.

Thus, the question emerges as to how individuals in organisations and in the course of their everyday work perceive an event and label it as an incident or a near miss. Because disease complications are a regular part of everyday work in healthcare, physicians and nurses have many potential scenarios in mind of what may happen during a patient care process. So it may be difficult to identify a near miss in the flow of patient care work. To put it in terms of Gestalt Psychology (see also Wehner & Stadler, 1994) for medical activities, it may be difficult to discern the "figure" of a near miss regarding patient safety against a background of a large number of potential disease complications that clinicians have in mind (and are prepared for) during the care process. Therefore, the triggers for detecting incidents to be reported depend not only on the definition of an incident by the system, but also on clinicians' perceptions of what they conceive of as events relevant to patient safety. As the focus lies particularly on the near misses to be reported, the "reportability" of an incident cannot be inferred from the severity of its consequences.

The base of reported incidents does not reflect a proportion of all types of incidents and near misses occurring in the organisation but a biased choice of incidents which employees were willing and did not fear to report. The types of incidents reported do not, therefore, allow us to infer a valid diagnosis of the prevailing problems of a unit or hospital (Billings, 1998; Wald & Shojania, 2001). Studies of under-reporting stress the influence of incident characteristics on the willingness of a clinician to report the incident. For example, the severity of outcome was found to be relevant to reporting behaviour (Jayasuriya & Anandaciva, 1995; Lawton & Parker, 2002; Wild & Bradley, 2005). Evans et al. (2006) showed that staff may see near misses as not important enough to be reported.

Among other studies, Stanhope et al. (1999) found that incident reporting systems do not reveal the real number of incidents that occur; the number of incidents reported is likely to be an underestimate of their true rate. As the reliability of incident reporting systems is very restricted, instruments such as retrospective chart reviews or safety audits remain important means to estimate the prevalence of safety problems (Vincent et al., 2008). From her study on adverse drug events, Edmondson (1996) concludes that the reporting rate may be higher in units with a positive safety culture, because employees dare to report events without fearing negative consequences. The importance of psychological safety (Baer & Frese, 2003; Edmondson, 2004) is also stressed, because an adequate analysis involving employee participation requires clinicians to speak up openly about errors. Edmondson emphasises the critical role of leadership for establishing a culture engendering a positive attitude towards learning from failure.

Another influence on what can be learnt stems from the short, narrative and often anonymous way in which incidents are reported. An incident report necessarily reflects subjective views and abstracts from the original context. Thus, the context of the incident gets lost in the act of reporting because the reporting person pays attention to specific aspects of the incident and neglects others. According to Bateson (1972), data are not events or objects, but always represent descriptions or memories of events or objects. Therefore, subjective transformation of the data takes place during reporting and interpretation of an event. So, we have to take into account that insights into an organisation based on incident reports are incomplete.

Secondly, to examine how investigation procedures influence what is learnt from incident reporting systems, we integrate evidence from other high-risk industries: Carroll (1995) identified four cognitive and cultural factors that impede fruitful learning from incident reviews in nuclear power plants. They represent pitfalls that can be transferred to healthcare and influence the outcomes of incident analysis.

- Root cause seduction is the tendency to think in linear cause–effect loops and to avoid ambiguous interpretations. In doing so, the incident analysis tends to become narrowly focused on single reasons, which is detrimental to a systemic perspective.

- The second cognitive effect is called the sharp-end focus and means that incident investigators tend to begin their analyses by considering staff at the sharp end and attributing their behaviour to personal factors rather than situational circumstances. Carroll (1995) traces this effect back to the fundamental attribution error which makes observers attribute events to people rather than to circumstances (Tetlock, 1985). Thus, the results of incident analyses biased by the sharp-end focus give the impression that staff should have been able to foresee and therefore avoid the incident. This is in line with the simple call to pay more attention to something, which is often the conclusion of incident analysis in healthcare.
- As a third effect, Carroll (1995) brings up the solution-driven search in problem analysis. He argues that it is against their culture for engineers to talk about problems without knowing a solution – we assume that this may also apply to health professionals. Solution-driven search occurs when people do not want to lose their perception of control and therefore refuse to admit that they do not know what to do in a certain context. Carroll argues that learning from best practices represents a product of a solution-driven search, as best practices are short problem-and-solution descriptions. He criticizes a lack of organisational context to permit the receiving organisation to achieve a deep understanding of how the best practice may fit into their particular organisation and its problems.
- The fourth factor influencing the outcome of incident analysis is account acceptability. It refers to the tendency of refusing to name groups or organisational units outright that are held responsible for the occurrence of an incident, because incident investigators tend to avoid blaming their own unit, profession or group.

Learning from incidents seems to be very attractive because it offers a way of repairing or correcting procedures, according to the saying that "adversity is the school of wisdom". In addition to this incremental learning style, learning from incidents also can trigger or even enable processes of gaining new insights into underlying patterns of assumptions which define "how things are done around here". This refers to the concept of theories of action brought up by Argyris and Schön (1996), which differentiates between espoused theories and theories-in-use present in an organisation. Espoused theories are the overtly communicated standards and guideline in an organisation – they are at the surface of what is communicated in an organisation. Theories-in-use are the underlying assumptions guiding actions without necessarily being verbalized. They act as principles and may be contradictory to what is highlighted as policies or guidelines. Argyris and Schön highlight that organisational learning that allows discovering and thus potentially changing theories-in-use helps to overcome defensive action patterns. In our view, one challenge to current practice and research in healthcare with respect to incident reporting systems is to find ways of supporting this kind of learning, which is also called double-loop learning (see also section "Future Opportunities for Designing Incident Reporting Systems in Healthcare").

How Do They Learn?

Argyris and Schön (1996) differentiate between single-loop and double-loop learning. When an organisation learns on a single-loop level, the possibilities of transfer are very restricted: staff will be able to use the new knowledge only if the same situation reappears in the organisation. In contrast, double-loop learning "emphasises continuous experimentation and feedback in an ongoing examination of the way organisations go about defining and solving problems" (Lipshitz, 2000, p. 459). Following Argyris and Schön, inquiries that individuals conduct in collaborative groups for solving problems are at the core of organisational learning. Lipshitz stresses that stable solutions are not to be expected from organisational learning because it usually involves the generation of new problems.

In large hospitals, the central risk or quality manager is normally in charge of designing and implementing incident reporting procedures. In each hospital unit, a group of co-workers is often designated to analyse the reported incidents and define the actions to be taken. In some hospital-wide incident reporting systems, the incident reports are also open to other units, while in other ones they are restricted to be read and analysed only within the unit and are only disseminated further when this is regarded as necessary. Likewise, reporting procedures vary considerably across hospitals. In some systems, the employees of *all* units report to a single confidential risk manager who then passes the reported incident to the appropriate unit or person. In other systems, the reporting process is organised at unit level, and employees report to the group of collaborators responsible for the unit's incident reporting.

When performed thoroughly, the activities of the staff group involved in analysing incidents and taking measures represent problem-solving processes because they are often faced with quite ill-defined problems. So the kind of learning challenge imposed by the report has to be investigated in the first step of an incident analysis. When no instant solution to the problem is readily available, the learning challenge requires an organisational learning effort. If multiple activity systems are involved, this effort can be conceptualised by the expansive learning concept of Engeström (2001). Of course, the intensity of problem solving involved in the group activity varies according to the type of incident reported and to the procedures defined in the reporting system. Incident reporting systems consequently provide a problem-solving platform for hospitals or healthcare units.

The framework for analysing risk and safety in clinical medicine proposed by Vincent, Taylor-Adams, and Stanhope (1998; see also Taylor-Adams, Vincent, & Stanhope, 1999) presents an approach designed to support organisational practice. In order to apply human factors methods to the investigation and analysis of adverse clinical events, Vincent et al. transferred Reason's (1990) accident causation model to healthcare. They argue that a large and complex chain of events may lead to an adverse outcome, and that the spectrum of potential contributory factors is very diverse: organisation and management decisions, work environments such as shift patterns, team factors, and individual factors such as task motivation and attitude or patient characteristics are all contributing factors that represent latent conditions. According to Vincent (2003), the analysis of clinical events needs to include a definition of the care management problems which are the healthcare equivalent to Reason's unsafe acts. After the care management problems have been identified, they are linked with potential contributory factors. In order to discover information about the factors contributing to an incident, the investigating team relies on written records and systematic interviews with the staff involved, asking what exactly happened, as well as why and how. Vincent also advises that the patient and his or her family should be involved. The contributory factors that appear as organisational problems in this analysis should be the target of any measures to be taken. This procedure is also known as the London Protocol. Vincent suggests that, if substantial changes in incident analysis occur, the results of other such analyses should additionally be taken into account and possibly other kinds of information sources, too, such as audits and outcome data. He stresses that it is essential that there should be people who feel responsible for the implementation of the required actions and monitor the consequences.

The design of current incident reporting systems includes no further specifications as to how the measures should be defined and implemented – the framework proposed by Vincent et al. (1998) represents a heuristic for analysing contributory factors rather than a support for defining actions. Accordingly, the need for evaluating the corrective action derived from incident investigation is widely neglected in current practice. Although relevant evidence exists from other high-risk industries, healthcare practice lacks a methodological foundation for procedures that may be applied to adverse events, which has an important impact on the appropriateness of the consequent actions taken. For other high-risk industries, Carroll, Rudolph, and Hatakenaka (2002) found that actions often failed to match the results of incident investigations. So, even if the incident reviews addressed the underlying assumptions about work practices relevant to the problem, the proposed action often remained corrective and thus superficial with respect to the actual problem. We assume that this is an important finding which should be mapped by current incident analysis tools in healthcare.

Once an incident is investigated, it is essential for learning that feedback is disseminated throughout the organisation. Benn et al. (2009) state that lessons learnt from incident reporting systems are promulgated neither within nor between hospitals. Their study has shown several requirements for incident reporting systems to assure effective feedback systems in healthcare: they include the role of leadership, the credibility and content of information, effective dissemination channels, the capacity for rapid action and the need for feedback at all levels of the organisation. They particularly highlight that the feedback loop cycle has to be closed by ensuring that reporting, analysis and actions all take place in good time.

As regards the effectiveness of nationally or internationally assembled incident reporting systems and the impact of learning changes: solutions that are disseminated throughout the participating organisations need to be addressed to problems emerging in highly standardised contexts, otherwise their applicability may be restricted (Perrow, 1984). As to the contextual situatedness of incident occurrence and analysis, we think that only those learning results which do not imply change of latent principles of action (theories-in-use, as mentioned above) can be transferred to *all* organisations. This does not reduce the importance of national or international incident reporting systems, but we consider their scope to be restricted to specific solutions to standardised problems. Furthermore, incident reporting systems can become important when we look at the occurrence of very rare adverse events, which may happen only once and are then disseminated throughout the whole medical system. Incident reporting systems may also have an influence on policy making at national level, because the relevance of problems such as fatigue can be illustrated by using specific cases emerging from incident reports.

Future Opportunities for Designing Incident Reporting Systems in Healthcare

Despite widespread enthusiasm about its advantages, clinicians and healthcare managers also question the effectiveness of learning by using incident reporting systems in healthcare (Leape, 2002; Wald & Shojania, 2001). This is understandable, because the transfer of incident reporting systems to healthcare did not include a specification as to how to proceed in applying them in medicine.

Coming back to the question of whether learning occurs at individual or organisational level, we argue that incident reporting systems are only effective if staff become involved in incident investigation and action taking. Individual learning then takes place through participation in the process. This is probably the most important impact that incident reporting systems can have at hospital level. However, due to limited healthcare resources, not all members of a unit or hospital can take part in all incident investigation processes. We propose that one member of every staff group that is affected by a problem should be part of the analysis process to assure that all information is integrated and that the learning results are subsequently disseminated. At the level of organisational learning, new procedures, techniques or management insights may emerge from incident reporting systems which then affect all employees. For learning at hospital level, the structures of incident reporting systems should ensure that the results of incident investigations are translated into appropriate action taking and that their effectiveness is evaluated, because the results of learning processes are never stable.

To sum up, we assume that participation is the decisive factor for simultaneously achieving individual and organisational learning in incident reporting systems. In line with activity theory, participation promotes the integration of historical aspects of problems in incident investigation. From this perspective, a reported incident or summary of incidents would constitute the starting point of a situated learning process (Lave & Wenger, 1991). In future, incident reporting systems need to engage in local and problem-oriented collaborative learning processes. Lipshitz and Popper (2000) claim that organisational learning mechanisms need to be implemented structurally as well as culturally. From their perspective, incident reporting systems largely represent non-integrated learning mechanisms in which the operators and clients of a learning procedure are not identical. We propose that current incident reporting systems for internal hospital use should move from being non-integrated organisational learning mechanisms to integrating all staff members concerned by a specific issue.

Furthermore, as learning from incidents starts with detecting an incident, adverse event or near miss, the implementation of incident reporting systems needs to be supported by clinician training. We therefore recommend that, when implementing incident reporting systems, a short training in error causation and incident reporting systems should be offered to all members of staff.

Not all incidents reported in a hospital can be analysed thoroughly due to resource constraints. This means that incident reports have to be screened and sorted. Itoh, Omata, and Andersen (2009) presented a taxonomy for sorting incident reports in a hospital. This sorting job is challenging because it has to be done *before* an in-depth investigation takes place. We argue that members of clinical staff should already participate in deciding which incidents or groups of similar incidents are to be used for organisational learning, in order to ensure that the incident investigation process tackles problems that are regarded as relevant at the "sharp end". Sorting reported incidents before analysing them does not necessarily mean that only problems which are most frequently mentioned are chosen. March (1991) argues that, with the aid of appropriate techniques, a single incident can help staff to identify relevant problems and engage in a fruitful learning process.

In order to target the use of incident reporting systems on one thematic field, it may be useful to introduce new reporting strategies: for example, to ask clinicians to pay attention to a certain aspect of care delivery during a certain period of time. During this time, incidents are collected that relate to a single safety issue. This would help to focus on the detection of reportable incidents and at the same time produce a rich information base as a starting point for analysis. As the context of incident occurrence would be narrowed down by the invitation to focus on a single issue, the analysis of the incidents would more easily point to underlying problems because the context information stemming from several incidents would be much richer.

To assure that healthcare staff act competently in using incident reporting systems, we assume it to be highly relevant that training in incident investigation procedures is promoted in healthcare. Only if incident investigation is really performed with a systemic focus and does not result in blaming individuals, can incident reporting systems contribute to changing the healthcare culture. This can be assured if trained investigators take part in the analysis and subsequent actions. As it is probably impractical to train all clinicians to participate in incident reporting and investigation, it would be advisable to train just some members of a unit so that they can later act as moderators in incident analysis. According to Lipshitz and Popper (2000), this would mean training the operators of the hospital's incident reporting system in incident analysis. To sum up, promotion of training also helps to avoid counterproductive forms of deutero-learning (see section "Why Do Clinicians Learn in Incident Reporting Systems: What Makes Them Make the Effort?").

Some systems have already integrated external support in incident investigation by giving expert hints via the Internet after reporting (Rall et al., 2006). This kind of external management ensures that similar incidents occurring in different hospitals may be traced back to a single problem source. The institutions providing the external support can also be involved in building up communication channels to medical industry in order to address issues emerging from technological or medication design. However, these external experts can play an advising role with respect to organisational learning within the hospital, but they cannot replace actual collaborative efforts on site.

We assume that one important aspect of future incident reporting systems implemented in healthcare is their ability to promote expansive learning and thus to support the collaboration between different groups such as nurses and physicians, or different hospital units. Engeström (2001) highlights the necessity for learning across organisational boundaries that includes different interacting activity systems, and transforms organisational practices into questioning and verbalising familiar routines and habitual procedures. The resulting new organisational practices "are literally learned as they are being created" (Engeström, p. 138). Developing new organisational practices or knowledge in a situational context represents an opportunity for designing incident reporting systems in healthcare. Thus, the success of these systems in hospitals also depends on the ability to grasp and work on contradictions emerging between professions and other groups and to create positive interdisciplinary cooperation.

We propose that both forms of learning, single-loop *and* double-loop, should play a role in incident reporting systems. Current systems of this kind are operated in a way that mainly allows incremental, single-loop forms of learning which are tightly associated to the reported event and do not aim at broader generalisation. The four-stage model of organisational learning (Carroll & Rudolph, 2006; Carroll et al., 2002) integrates Argyris' and Schön's (1996) theory: The first stage starts at a local learning level where only bounded know-how is available and problems are largely denied. Learning in the second stage moves to a controlled level characterised by rule compliance and activities designed to fix the problem symptoms. In our view, current incident reporting systems mainly operate on these two levels. According to Carroll et al., organisations in the third stage develop towards more proactive approaches and double-loop processes incorporating open learning. Finally, organisations can achieve the stage of deep learning, which means that learning is accomplished from a systemic perspective and assumptions are challenged. From our perspective, allowing deep learning is the aim towards which incident reporting in healthcare needs to develop. According to this model, organisations do not move logically from stage to stage, their activities may rather correspond to all levels. As regards learning from incidents, this means that an organisation able to react in a controlling manner and able to react in a deep learning manner can choose which reaction is appropriate to a specific incident. We suggest that this variety of potential reactions and handlings of learning from incidents is vital for a well-functioning incident reporting system in healthcare.

Organisational learning activities that focus on exploiting or repairing the status quo must be balanced with other activities that explore new alternatives beyond existing paradigms (March, 1991). Katz-Navon, Naveh, and Stern (2009) argue that explorative, active learning reduces the resources which can be allocated on enhancing safety. Their results from a healthcare study suggest that both insufficient and excessive prioritisation of safety may in fact be detrimental to safety for organisations with a highly active learning climate.

To assure comprehensive organisational learning in healthcare, Carroll and Edmondson (2002) propose to "combine values, skills and structures" (p. 52). They especially highlight the importance of reflection in using learning technologies and the role of leadership in healthcare (see also Lipshitz & Popper, 2000). Incident reporting processes may constitute a collective sense-making process and we therefore propose that a shift needs to take place from a controlling to a collaborative learning orientation (Carroll & Rudolph, 2006) aiming at rethinking organisational practices rather than enhancing control over them.

Acknowledgement Many of our insights into incident reporting systems in hospitals stem from our research in this field. We would therefore like to thank PD Dr. Tanja Manser, Matthias Briner, and Oliver Kessler, Dr. Marcus Rall as well as our partners in the hospitals for working with us in our studies on clinical risk management and barriers to incident reporting.

References

Argyris, C., & Schön, D. (1996). *Organisational learning II: Theory method and practice*. Reading, PA: Addison-Wesley.

Baer, M., & Frese, M. (2003). Innovation is not enough: Climates for initiative and psychological safety, process innovations, and firm performance. *Journal of Organizational Behavior, 24*, 45–68.

Barach, P., & Small, S. D. (2000). Reporting and preventing medical mishaps: Lessons from non-medical near miss reporting systems. *British Medical Journal, 320*, 759–763.

Bateson, G. (1972). *Steps to an ecology of mind. Collected essays in anthropology, psychiatry, evolution, and epistemology*. Chicago: University of Chicago Press.

Benn, J., Koutantji, M., Wallace, L., Spurgeon, P., Rejman, M., Healey, A., et al. (2009). Feedback from incident reporting: Information and action to improve patient safety. *Quality and Safety in Health Care, 18*, 11–21.

Billings, C. (1998). Incident reporting systems in medicine and experience with the aviation safety reporting system. In R. I. Cook, D. D. Woods, & C. Miller (Eds.), *A tale of two stories: Contrasting views of patient safety. Report from a workshop on assembling the scientific basis for progress on patient safety*. McLean, VA: National Patient Safety Foundation at the AMA.

Bocion, C., Sennhauser, F. H., & Frey, B. (2006). Critical incident monitoring in schweizerischen Intensivstationen. Verbreitung, Einstellung und Faktoren, welche die Meldehäufigkeit beeinflussen. *Schweizerische Ärztezeitung, 87*, 886–894.

Carroll, J. S. (1995). Incident reviews in high-hazard industries: Sense making and learning under ambiguity and accountability. *Organization Environment, 9*, 175–197.

Carroll, J. S., & Edmondson, A. C. (2002). Leading organizational learning in health care. *Quality and Safety in Health Care, 11*, 51–56.

Carroll, J. S., & Rudolph, J. W. (2006). Design of high reliability organizations in health care. *Quality and Safety in Health Care, 15*(suppl_1), i4–i9.

Carroll, J. S., Rudolph, J. W., & Hatakenaka, S. (2002). *Organizational learning from experience in high-hazard industries: Problem investigations as off-line reflective practice* (MIT Sloan Working Paper No. 4359-02). Retrieved from SSRN: http://ssrn.com/abstract=305718 or doi:10.2139/ssrn.305718

Edmondson, A. C. (1996). Learning from mistakes is easier said than done: Group and organizational influences on the detection and correction of human error. *Journal of Applied Behavioral Science, 32*, 5–32.

Edmondson, A. C. (2004). Learning from failure in health care: Frequent opportunities, pervasive barriers. *Quality and Safety in Health Care, 13*(suppl_2), ii3–ii9.

Engeström, Y. (2001). Expansive learning at work: Toward an activity theoretical reconceptualization. *Journal of Education and Work, 14*, 133–156.

Evans, S. M., Berry, J. G., Esterman, A. J., Selim, P., O'Shaughnessy, J., & De Wit, M. (2006). Attitudes and barriers to incident reporting: A collaborative hospital study. *Quality and Safety in Health Care, 15*, 39–43.

Flanagan, J. C. (1954). The critical incident technique. *Psychological Bulletin, 51*(4), 327–358.

Garbutt, J., Waterman, A. D., Kapp, J. M., Dunagan, W. C., Levinson, W., Fraser, V., et al. (2008). Lost opportunities: How physicians communicate about medical errors. *Health affairs, 27*, 246–255.

Itoh, K., Omata, N., & Andersen, H. B. (2009). A human error taxonomy for analysing healthcare incident reports: Assessing reporting culture and its effects on safety performance. *Journal of Risk Research, 12*, 485–511.

Jayasuriya, J. P., & Anandaciva, S. (1995). Compliance with an incident report scheme in anaesthesia. *Anaesthesia, 50*, 846–849.

Katz-Navon, T., Naveh, E., & Stern, Z. (2009). Active learning: When is more better? The case of resident physicians' medical errors. *Journal of Applied Psychology, 94*, 1200–1209.

Kingston, M. J., Evans, S. M., Smith, B. J., & Berry, J. G. (2004). Attitudes of doctors and nurses towards incident reporting: A qualitative analysis. *The Medical Journal of Australia, 181*, 36–39.

Kohn, L. T., Corrigan, J. M., & Donaldson, M. S. (Eds.). (1999). *To err is human: Building a safer health system*. Washington, DC: National Academy Press.

Lave, J., & Wenger, E. (1991). *Situated learning: Legitimate peripheral participation*. Cambridge, UK: Cambridge University Press.

Lawton, R., & Parker, D. (2002). Barriers to incident reporting in a healthcare system. *Quality and Safety in Health Care, 11*, 15–18.

Leape, L. L. (2002). Reporting of adverse events. *New England Journal of Medicine, 347*, 1633–1638.

Lipshitz, R. (2000). Chic, mystique, and misconception: Argyris and Schon and the rhetoric of organisational learning. *Journal of Applied Behavioral Science, 36*, 456–473.

Lipshitz, R., & Popper, M. (2000). Organizational learning in a hospital. *Journal of Applied Behavioral Science, 36*, 345–361.

March, J. G. (1991). Exploration and exploitation in organizational learning. *Organization Science, 2*, 71–87.

Perrow, C. (1984). *Normal accidents: Living with high-risk technologies*. New York: Basic Books.

Pfeiffer, Y., Manser, T., & Wehner, T. (2010). Conceptualising barriers to incident reporting: A psychological framework. *Quality and Safety in Health Care, 19*(6), 1–10.

Rall, M., Dieckmann, P., & Stricker, E. (2006). Patient safety optimization system (PaSOS) – The new country wide incident reporting system of DGAI/BDA (registers for safety-relevant events). *Anasthesiologie & Intensivmedizin, 47*, S20–S24.

Reason, J. (1990). *Human error*. New York/Cambridge, UK: Cambridge University Press.

Reason, J. (2004). Beyond the organizational accident: The need for "error wisdom" on the frontline. *Quality and Safety in Health Care, 13*(suppl_2), ii28–ii33.

Rijpma, J. A. (1997). Complexity, tight-coupling and reliability: Connecting normal accidents theory and high reliability theory. *Journal of Contingencies and Crisis Management, 5*, 15–23.

Rowe, P. A., & Boyce, R. A. (2009). Deutero-learning: Implications for managing public health change. *The Learning Organization, 16*, 298–310.

Runciman, W. B., Merry, A. F., & Tito, F. (2003). Error, blame, and the law in healthcare – An antipodean perspective. *Annals of Internal Medicine, 138*, 974–980.

Schuerer, D. J. E., Nast, P. A., Harris, C. B., Krauss, M. J., Jones, R. M., Boyle, W. A., et al. (2006). A new safety event reporting system improves physician reporting in the surgical intensive care unit. *Journal of the American College of Surgeons, 202*, 881–887.

Sexton, J. B., Thomas, E. J., & Helmreich, R. L. (2000). Error, stress and teamwork in medicine and aviation: Cross sectional surveys. *British Medical Journal, 320*, 745–749.

Stanhope, N., Crowley-Murphy, M., Vincent, C., O'Connor, A. M., & Taylor-Adams, S. E. (1999). An evaluation of adverse incident reporting. *Journal of Evaluation in Clinical Practice, 5*, 5–12.

Sturmberg, J. P., & Martin, C. M. (2008). Knowing – In medicine. *Journal of Evaluation in Clinical Practice, 14*, 767–770.

Tamuz, M., & Harrison, M. I. (2006). Improving patient safety in hospitals: Contributions of high-reliability theory and normal accident theory. *Health Services Research, 41*, 1654–1676.

Taylor-Adams, S., Vincent, C., & Stanhope, N. (1999). Applying human factors methods to the investigation and analysis of clinical adverse events. *Safety Science, 31*, 143–159.

Tetlock, P. E. (1985). Accountability: A social check on the fundamental attribution error. *Social Psychology Quarterly, 48*, 227–236.

Vincent, C. (2003). Understanding and responding to adverse events. *The New England journal of medicine, 348*, 1051–1056.

Vincent, C., Aylin, P., Franklin, B. D., Holmes, A., Iskander, S., Jacklin, A., & Moorthy, K. (2008). Is health care getting safer? *British Medical Journal, 337*, a2426.

Vincent, C., Stanhope, N., & Crowley-Murphy, M. (1999). Reasons for not reporting adverse incidents: An empirical study. *Journal of Evaluation in Clinical Practice, 5*, 13–21.

Vincent, C., Taylor-Adams, S., & Stanhope, N. (1998). Framework for analysing risk and safety in clinical medicine. *British Medical Journal, 316*, 1154–1157.

Visser, M. (2007). Deutero-learning in organisations: A review and a reformulation. *Academy of Management Review, 32*, 659–667.

Wald, H., & Shojania, K. G. (2001). *Incident Reporting' and 'root cause analysis'*. Rockville, MD: Agency for Healthcare Research and Quality.

Wang, C. L., & Ahmed, P. K. (2003). Organisational learning: A critical review. *The Learning Organisation, 10*, 8–17.

Wehner, T., & Stadler, M. (1994). The cognitive organization of human errors: A Gestalt theory perspective. *Applied Psychology: An International Review, 43*, 565–584.

Weick, K. E., Sutcliffe, K. M., & Obstfeld, D. (1999). Organizing for high reliability: Processes of collective mindfulness. *Research in Organizational Behavior, 21*, 81–123.

WHO. (2005). *WHO draft guidelines for adverse event reporting and learning systems*. Geneva, Switzerland: WHO.

Wild, D., & Bradley, E. H. (2005). The gap between nurses and residents in a community hospital's error-reporting system. *Joint Commission Journal on Quality and Patient Safety, 31*(1), 13–20.

Wu, A. W. (2000). Medical error: The second victim. *British Medical Journal, 320*, 726–727.